Satyagraha and nonresistance

With much appreciation
& loving regards

William W Brown

19 2014

Occasional Papers, no. 27
Institute of Mennonite Studies

Occasional Papers are occasional publications of the Institute of Mennonite Studies at Associated Mennonite Biblical Seminary, Elkhart, Indiana. IMS was founded in 1958 to promote and create opportunities for research, conversation, and publication on topics and issues vital to Mennonite congregations and the Anabaptist faith tradition.

In the Occasional Papers series, IMS—sometimes in collaboration with other Mennonite publishers—publishes essays in the fields of Bible, history, theology, ethics, and pastoral ministry. The intent of the series is to foster discussion and to seek counsel, particularly from within the Mennonite theological community. Many essays are in finished form; some may be in a more germinal stage, released for purposes of testing and inviting critical response.

In accepting papers for publication, IMS gives priority to authors (faculty, students, alumni) from Mennonite seminaries, colleges, and universities..

Satyagraha and nonresistance

A comparative study of
Gandhian and Mennonite nonviolence

Weyburn W. Groff

Foreword by John Paul Lederach

Occasional Papers, no. 27

Institute of Mennonite Studies
Elkhart, Indiana

Co-published with Herald Press
Scottdale, Pennsylvania
Waterloo, Ontario

Co-published with Herald Press
616 Walnut Avenue, Scottdale, Pennsylvania15683
490 Dutton Drive, Unit C8, Waterloo, Ontario N2L 6H7
www.heraldpress.com

Library of Congress Cataloging-in-Publication Data

Groff, Weyburn W.
  Satyagraha and nonresistance : a comparative study of Gandhian
and Mennonite nonviolence / Weyburn W. Groff.
    p. cm. — (Occasional papers ; no. 27)
  Originally presented as the author's thesis (doctoral)—1963.
  Includes bibliographical references (p.   ).
  ISBN 0-936273-43-7
  1. Evil, Non-resistance to. 2. Mennonites—Doctrines. 3. Passive
resistance. 4. Gandhi, Mahatma, 1869-1948. 5. Pacifism—Religious
aspects--Comparative studies. I. Title.
  BX8128.P4G76 2009
  261.8'73—dc22
                        2009038609

Book design by Mary E. Klassen

Cover image: "The Pahar," drawing by Margaret Groff, May 1985,
prismacolor on paper, 9 x 12 inches. Used by permission. All rights
reserved.

Dedication for the 2009 edition

THIS BOOK IS LOVINGLY DEDICATED to Thelma Miller Groff, my wife of sixty-five years, whose companionship and encouragement have been immeasurably significant throughout the years, with my numerous travels, absences for research, and protracted times of university study. It is also dedicated to our children, Raechel White, Margaret Groff and Hans Reinhardt, Cheryl Groff and Ronald Hess, and Edwin Groff, whose vocational interests and values—with respect to the global family of peoples and nations, through the arts, education, and humanitarian services—embrace the cause of justice and peace. And it is dedicated to our grandsons, Alex Hess, Conrad Hess, and Peter Reinhardt, purposefully studying and exploring in order to understand and contribute to the world of their time.

Contents

Foreword

PERHAPS THE MOST IMPORTANT WORDS of Weyburn Groff's *Nonviolence: A Comparative Study of Mohandas K. Gandhi and the Mennonite Church on the Subject of Nonviolence* are found in his concluding sentence: "It is the opinion of this investigator that in the development of a systematized agape-love ethic, a major consideration must be the discovery of the meaning of agape-love in responsible citizenship." For readers familiar with ongoing peace position debates among Mennonite theologians and ethicists over the past half-century (some might prefer to call these exchanges "discernment"), the significance of the sentence may be apparent. For those less familiar, perhaps the best starting place for introducing this manuscript is a visit to the context in which it was written.

Weyburn Groff wrote this text, originally submitted in 1963 as a doctoral dissertation, out of his experience in India. He took up an approach that paralleled in some ways but also departed from that of his better-known Mennonite theologian contemporaries, in exploring the tensions between the Anabaptist notion of nonresistance and Gandhian views of nonviolence. Nonresistance, based on Jesus' injunction "Do not resist an evildoer," tended to pull back from movements—such as Gandhi's—that pursued social and political change through active nonviolence, resistance, and non-cooperation with evil systems. At the heart of Mennonite debates were questions of whether, how, and to what degree the faithful should support or be influenced by forms of pacifism that did not rise from or fully cohere with a Christian source and ethos. For most Mennonite theologians of the day, the search for proper belief and morality set nonresistance and nonviolence against each other.

Groff's definition of the problem in this text presents us with his intriguing personal communication with the most widely read Mennonite defender of nonresistance at the time, Guy F. Hershberger, who commended Groff's research as "a most significant undertaking." It was. And it has been a long time in coming to a wider readership. Three things stand out in this manuscript, both for their historical significance relative to better-known Mennonite treatises of the time (the late 1950s and early 1960s—predating the greater part of the work of John Howard Yoder) and for their contribution to current theological exchange.

First, most Mennonite theologians addressing peace issues in this period wrote from a North American or European context. This manuscript represents engagement of the issues from Asia and focused on India, with a far more direct entry into the thinking and life of Gandhi. One wonders whether the North American Mennonite peace ethos coming out of the 1950s was influenced as much by notions of separateness in the American context as by the prophetic call to proactively engage the requirements of agape-love in its fullest expression. Groff enters this debate more fully, in part because the context from which he wrote was so distinctly different.

Second, this text includes correspondence and citations from some prominent Mennonites. Groff's research and exchanges suggest that two realities had begun to put pressure on the narrower sectarian ethos of nonresistance, which feared and kept distant from other forms of pacifism and nonviolence; these were the dawn of the nuclear age and the arrival of Martin Luther King Jr. The threat of nuclear war, promising mass destruction of humanity and creation, called out for a more engaged response than could be provided by a nonresistance applying narrowly to interpersonal relationships. Deeper reflection started to emerge about the legitimacy of system change as part of Christian witness.

Similarly, in the American context, where people struggled to confront personal, community, and systemic racism, Gandhi's nonviolence influenced Martin Luther King Jr., who helped birth an imaginative ethos of Christian-based public engagement. The civil rights movement began to open greater space for collaboration between those who had been proponents of nonresistance and those forging nonviolent responses to systemic evil. Perhaps King's example in the American context catalyzed a creative ambiguity that yielded an engaged Anabaptism and inspired a new generation of peacebuilders. I, for one, consider myself a child of King's inspiration.

In the late 1950s and early 1960s, Groff identified a range of areas for potential mutual engagement by proponents of nonresistance and of nonviolence. In his view, agape-love from which nonresistance emerges could include forms of public protest, noncooperation with evil systems, negotiation, and third-party intervention. These possibilities went beyond what most Mennonite theologians and ethicists at the time would have advocated, but Groff's insights now seem prescient, as we have observed the rise over the past decades of Christian Peacemaker Teams, conciliation services, and restorative justice efforts.

Third, Groff highlights the significant differences around source, worldview, motivations, and techniques between Mennonite nonresistance and Gandhian satyagraha—but he also begins to explore what faithful allegiance to Christ's kingdom requires of a responsible citizen. And here we return to his concluding sentence. Agape-love when fully expressed cannot help but find ways to make itself visible and to engage the world it lives in, from interpersonal and local to national and global levels. Inevitably in the modern world, this engagement takes account of the rights and responsibilities citizenship brings to those in the believers church.

With this wider context in mind, Groff's comparative study of Gandhi and Mennonites is both a historical document and a contemporary challenge well worth turning to in our continued discernment, for nuclear issues remain at the top of our global challenges, our neighbors are global no matter where we live, and the world continues to need prophetic and pastoral expressions of agape-love.

—John Paul Lederach
June 2009

Abstract

THE PURPOSE OF THE INVESTIGATION is to study the philosophy of Mohandas K. Gandhi and the Mennonite Church on the subject of nonviolence and to explain and illustrate the application of their respective doctrines in social and political conflict situations.

In this study, satyagraha and nonresistance are considered against the background of pacifism, a term generally employed to cover many varieties of peacemaking. Neither of the two schools of thought represented in this study find the generic term adequate. However, if conflict and violence—which often accompanies conflict—are to be mitigated, it will require mutual understanding and cooperative experiment on the part of distinctive peace-minded movements.

Chapter 2 is a survey of the literature of pacifism. Chapter 3 is a study of Gandhian satyagraha, and chapter 4 is a study of Mennonite nonresistance. The structure common to chapters 3 and 4 consists of (1) historical survey, (2) metaphysical presuppositions, (3) ethical principles, and (4) an exposition. The summary chapter 5 follows the same pattern. The expositions of satyagraha and nonresistance, respectively, include an expanded definition, an analysis of moral dynamics, and a description of modes of application.

In comparison, it becomes clear that satyagraha and nonresistance overlap in a limited measure only. Nonresistance is primarily applicable in the prevention of conflict by constructive action, which reduces tension and removes the causes of tension. It is applicable further in reducing tension and witnessing against violence by abstention. It cultivates the mental and spiritual resources that enable persons to suffer injustice and abuse. Beyond these measures, nonresistance, as defined by the Mennonite Church, provides no technique for the conduct of conflict.

Satyagraha is also concerned with prevention of conflict by removing some of the social and economic causes through the program of Sarvodaya (welfare of all), and in addition it proposes techniques for the conduct of conflict.

A conclusion of this comparison is that of identification of the respective roles of nonresistance and satyagraha in the field of pacifism. The limitation of nonresistance derives from its metaphysical presuppositions and the requirements of agape-love. Satyagraha, having a broader definition of nonviolence and a more flexible metaphysics, has greater scope for coercive action.

Recognizing these distinctive factors, it is inferred that proponents of nonresistance will find some forms of coercive action employed in satyagraha to be compatible with the agape-love ethic of the New Testament. Inherent in satyagraha action and in such action performed under the motivation of agape-love is a self-informing principle which tests the rightness of the cause and of the action employed.

Preface to the 2009 edition

IN A WORLD TORN BY CONFLICTS of many kinds, and with fear and mistrust escalating, many concerned people of various philosophical and religious persuasions seek to address the causes of violence. Because violence begets further violence, we need to find solutions in the form of constructive nonviolent alternatives.

The study should be read as an effort to contribute to dialogue on nonviolence and nonresistance. It examines the thought and practice of the Mennonite Church, a relatively small segment of the Christian church with a nonresistant history, and the Gandhian movement, which exercised the effective nonviolent resistance of satyagraha. It invites the reader to enter the dialogue about and active pursuit of nonviolent conflict resolution.

This study can also be read as a personal saga. In 1961, when I was working on a doctorate at New York University, the subject of this dissertation gradually came into focus. My research included examination of documents of the Mennonite Church and writings of individuals of the period of Mahatma Gandhi's activity. My study took me to North American libraries and archives and to the Gandhi Memorial Library in New Delhi. Nearby, along the Yamuna River, was the site of Mahatma Gandhi's memorial samadhi, where he had been cremated.

This study was in part an outgrowth of my experiences and reflections during and after World War II. I had graduated from high school in Ontario in 1939. Several of my friends had entered military service as part of the Allied offensive against the Nazi-led rampages in Europe. Some of these friends were killed, and I was challenged to consider my duty.

In 1941 I went to Goshen (Indiana) College, to prepare for service in India as a missionary under the auspices of Mennonite Board of Missions and Charities. At home and in church I had been nurtured as a conscientious objector to war. College strengthened this conviction through historical and theological study but also by giving me a broader awareness of the realities of war, including the staggering loss of life in World War II, the devastation in Europe, the horrors of Hiroshima and Nagasaki.

After college, my wife, Thelma Miller Groff, and I were appointed to go to India. Just before we left home, the newspapers announced in March 1946 that Great Britain would grant India its independence, after many years of struggle. At the center of that struggle had been the physically diminutive but morally powerful figure of Mohandas Karamchand Gandhi. Gandhi would not be an official in the new government, yet his thought and conviction inspired and guided many; he had been accorded the honorific title Mahatma, "Great Soul" in Sanskrit.

We boarded ship in San Francisco and crossed the Pacific, with a stop in the Philippines, where war with Japan had started in 1941. Near the island of Luzon, our ship stopped briefly and anchored in a quiet sea brightened by a clear tropical sun. A brief memorial service conducted on deck honored soldiers who had lost their lives there. A mother had sent some flower petals and prayers to scatter in remembrance of her son and others who had died there. We sang "Lead me gently home, Father."

Then we stopped in the Manilla harbor. On board ship, Anna Nixon told us that she and other civilians had been en route to India and were anchored in that harbor when the war broke out. Now we were looking across the rusting hulks of vessels of various sizes. She pointed across this devastation to the buildings where she and others had been interned as prisoners of war for three and a half years. She had been nurtured in the pacifist tradition of the Quakers, and her convictions had been sorely tested but remained intact.

Months later, in January 1948, in our home in a quiet village in the heart of peasant India, we heard on the radio the announcement that Mahatma Gandhi had been assassinated. His murder was the act not of a foreign zealot but of a fellow citizen and coreligionist. Prime Minister Jawaharlal Nehru in simple and eloquent words expressed the sentiment of many: "The light has gone out of our lives."

By 1951 we were stationed at Union Biblical Seminary in Yeotmal (now Yavatmal),[1] Maharashtra. Gandhi's Sevagram Ashram was about forty miles away, near Wardha, and we often took students and guests of the seminary there. Gandhi had done much of his writ-

---

[1] Place names in the text of the dissertation retain the spellings or designations current in 1963: Bombay (now Mumbai); Madras (now Chennai); etc.

ing at the ashram, and he had conducted interviews and developed training institutions for teachers in order to provide instruction to village people in weaving, agriculture, and health and natural medicines. He sought to use available materials to yield a better quality of simple living for India's impoverished people. We were inspired by what we learned there.

Independence brought with it some apprehensiveness. It generated a breaking forth of national pride and cultural and religious fervor that called into question the legitimacy of foreign institutions represented by the Christian churches, many of which were financed and administered by non-Indians. From many quarters the question arose, would we be asked to leave? Gandhi's coming to the grounds of the Landour Language School in Mussoorie, established to teach Hindi to Christian missionaries, was a gracious gesture. His hopes and efforts in the New India were clearly directed toward freedom for all faiths. Prime Minister Nehru made similar affirmations.

Gandhi opposed the partition of India and Pakistan. When bloody conflicts broke out between religious factions in Calcutta (now Kolkata) and elsewhere, he was in the middle of the chaos, seeking to bring sanity and reconciliation. His idealism was tested and ultimately cost him his life. He was assassinated on January 30, 1948, on the grounds of Birla temple in New Delhi as he was on his way to a prayer meeting.

It was during these times that we began our life in India. Complex challenges called for imagination and creative energy. If that was true fifty years ago, it is no less true now, globally, in the twenty-first century. Openness to nonviolent options now seems crucial. I hope this study, completed in 1963, may bring to twenty-first-century readers some insight into the many efforts being made to find nonviolent ways to resolve conflicts and bring peace with justice.

For Mennonite readers whose energies may have been circumscribed by a too narrow definition of Christian discipleship, I offer this counsel: Our faithfulness is worked out not in isolation from the world but in the context of multiple faiths, when we act as citizens in particular times and places. We need to make common cause with all people who seek peace and justice. For other

Christians and people of other faiths: I hope that reading this work may give you inspiration for this task.

Many people in our world long for the day when greater creativity in the pursuit of peace will prevail, and with it, more sane ways of resolving the inevitable conflicts of the human community. Together let us keep alive our hope in God and our commitment to the welfare of all the peoples of the world.

—Weyburn Groff

Preface to the 1963 dissertation

SCIENTIFIC INVESTIGATION and experimentation have given humanity command of a vast amount of knowledge and power, which have removed many fears and hardships. Yet the fear engendered by the prospect of a nuclear war is doubtlessly unprecedented. The contentment and the hope that should accompany the intellectual and technological achievements of humankind are threatened by the inability to assure the constructive use of the knowledge and power we possess. If the weapons of destruction, which the nations of the world have at their command, are to be applied unrestrainedly in international conflict, civilization is doomed to annihilation. Must this state of affairs be accepted as inevitable? Or are there other dimensions of knowledge and power that may be marshaled to restrain destruction and turn the potential of humankind into political and social reconstruction? If alternatives to war are to be found, it will require creative thought and experimentation in every field of inquiry, with due respect for philosophical and religious categories, and their consideration for moral and ethical values. It would be unrealistic to suggest that in all this process there would be no conflict. However, it should be possible to find ways and means to conduct conflict on a plane consistent with human achievement in other areas.

It is the view of the present investigator that individuals and movements that consider warfare a problem of morality need to be creative and courageous in discovering alternative measures for controlling evil and assuring justice. Such measures would be designed to prevent conflict and tension, and to resolve conflict nonviolently when it arises. Furthermore, it is believed that a contribution can be made in this endeavor by the proponents of Gandhian satyagraha and the Historic Peace Churches, of which the Mennonite Church, holding the doctrine of nonresistance, is one. As a preliminary step in a common cause, it is necessary to examine the respective philosophical and ethical foundations, as well as typical modes of application of social and political concern. It is this purpose which is herewith pursued.

To some representatives of the Mennonite Church, the non-violent techniques of satyagraha offer a solution to the apparent political irrelevance of traditional nonresistance. It is possible that a greater measure of social and political responsibility may be borne by the proponents of nonresistance if coercive techniques employed in love can be evolved. On the other hand, many pacifists of the Gandhian tradition expect the Christian church to take more of a lead in the way of love in a world of violence. That the church as a whole, since Constantine, has given approval to the method of violence as it is exhibited in warfare, is attributed to a betrayal of Christian morality in the interest of political expedience. Thus it would seem that there is a twofold challenge to find ways and means in which love in its purest form may find expression in social and political reconstruction.

It is with sincere gratitude that I recognize the unstinted and stimulating guidance of the members of my sponsoring committee, Professor Lee A. Belford, Professor Frederick L. Redefer, and Professor Ethel J. Alpenfels. Each, at successive stages, offered criticism and encouragement which have been received with appreciation.

Others who have been consulted and who have shared generously of their time and knowledge are Shri Dharam Vir and Shri Prabodh Chowksi of the Gandhi Memorial Library, New Delhi; Dr. Melvin Gingerich; Dr. Guy F. Hershberger; and Dr. John H. Yoder of the Mennonite Research Foundation, Goshen, Indiana. To each of these, and others who have stimulated thought and inquiry, I am thankful.

Acknowledgement is due for the privilege of time and travel for this study to the principal and colleagues of Union Biblical Seminary, Yeotmal, India, and to the Mennonite Board of Missions and Charities, Elkhart, Indiana.

Quotations from various sources have been acknowledged and are used with the permission of the publishers concerned.

Hardly adequate is a word of appreciation for my wife, Thelma Miller Groff, whose encouragement and willingness to manage our family of four almost singlehandedly for over two years have been important factors in making this study possible.

—Weyburn Groff

Acknowledgements for the 2009 edition

I AM GRATEFUL to John Rempel, Mary H. Schertz, Barbara Nelson Gingerich, and the Executive Committee of the Institute of Mennonite Studies, whose interest and skills have brought this study to a broader readership. I am also grateful to Hatoko Inoue, volunteer at Associated Mennonite Biblical Seminary, who devoted many hours to scanning the 1963 text of this dissertation and carefully preparing it for formatting; and to James Nelson Gingerich, who spent many volunteer hours formatting it for publication.

Chapter 1

The problem and its scope

I. The problem

THE PURPOSE OF THIS INVESTIGATION is to study the philosophy of Mohandas K. Gandhi, and that of the Mennonite Church on the subject of nonviolence, and to explain and illustrate the application of their respective doctrines in social and political conflict situations.

Sub-problems

This investigation has involved an analysis of the basic writings of Mohandas K. Gandhi pertaining to his concept of nonviolence (which became defined as satyagraha) for the purpose of discovering the origin and fundamental characteristics of his concept. Similarly, the official documents and authorized writings of the Mennonite Church have been examined with a view to discovering the origins and fundamental characteristics of the doctrine of nonresistance. This has included a comparison of the modes of application of each in social and political conflict situations. Finally, an attempt is made to discover lines of demarcation between the two views and the areas of common thought and technique.

II. Definition of terms

Pacifism

As generally employed, the term *pacifism* is used to cover many varieties of peacemaking, which may or may not be Christian in their orientation. Some modern pacifists oppose all wars and some do not. Some who do oppose all wars find their authority in the will of God and in the word of scripture, while others find it largely in human reason.[1]

Nonviolence

Nonviolence is a policy adopted by an opposition group which refrains from the use of force as a matter of principle or expediency. In its dynamic condition, it is defined as conscious suffering. It does

---

[1] G. F. Hershberger, "Pacifism," *The Mennonite Encyclopedia* (Scottdale, PA: The Mennonite Publishing House, 1955–59), 4:104.

1

not mean meek submission to the will of the evildoer but the pitting of one's whole soul against the will of the tyrant.[2]

Satyagraha

The word *satyagraha* means insistence on truth. The concept has come to be applied to all the organized and concerted activities coordinated in a pattern under the control of a pledge of nonviolence. In most cases, these mass actions have been extra-legal and extra-constitutional; they have outgrown parliamentary procedure and become revolutionary. Thus satyagraha becomes a form of direct action insofar as the people take the law into their own hands. In contrast to war or violent revolution, however, satyagraha is non-violent direct action.[3]

Nonresistance

The term *nonresistance* in Anabaptist-Mennonite history has come to denote the faith and life of those who believe that the will of God requires the renunciation of warfare and other compulsive means for the furtherance of personal or social ends.[4]

Mennonite Church

The designation *Mennonite Church* is now used by a denomination descending from the Anabaptists of the Reformation period, which originated in Holland where the movement became reconstituted under the leadership of Menno Simons (1496–1561). The name *Mennonite* was given to his followers.[5] The Mennonite Church as referred to in this study consists of the body that is identified by this name in the United States of America.

III. Delimitations

In this investigation, the following delimitations have been observed.

---

[2] The first sentence of this definition is that of Edward C. Smith in the *New Dictionary of American Politics* (New York: Barnes and Noble, 1949), 266. The remainder of the definition is from Mohandas K. Gandhi, quoted from *Young India,* August 11, 1920 by Jag Prakash Chander, *Teachings of Mahatma Gandhi* (Lahore: The Indian Printing Works, 1945), 412.

[3] Krishnalal Shridharani, *War without Violence* (New York: Harcourt Brace and Company, 1939), 4.

[4] Guy F. Hershberger, "Nonresistance," *The Mennonite Encyclopedia,* 3:897.

[5] Harold S. Bender, "The Mennonite Church," *The Mennonite Encyclopedia,* 3:586–87.

1. Twentieth-century sources
Twentieth-century sources have been used; this was the period of Gandhi's activity, and because of the two world wars, was also a period during which there has been an intensified production of nonresistant apologetic literature on the part of the Mennonite Church.

2. Gandhian literature
Because of Gandhi's importance as the leader of the Indian independence movement and as a religious and social reformer, every effort has been made to collect and preserve every word that he ever wrote. Hence, there is an extensive Gandhian literature.

Though his books are few, many of his editorials, speeches, and essays have been collected and compiled in book form. The basic writings consulted have been those listed under "Satyagraha" in *Mahatma Gandhi* (*A Descriptive Bibliography*), compiled by Jagdish S. Sharma.[6]

Another source of interpretive material has been the quarterly journal *Gandhi Marg,* published since 1957 at Rajghat, New Delhi, India, under the auspices of the Gandhi Smarak Nidhi (Gandhi Peace Foundation). It represents contemporary international scholarship related to Mohandas K. Gandhi.

3. Mennonite literature
Material pertinent to the doctrine of nonresistance has been used as found in:
  a. Official confessions and pronouncements of the Mennonite Church or its authorized agencies.
  b. Books and pamphlets on the subject of nonresistance published under the auspices of the denomination or its authorized agencies. The standard work is *War, Peace, and Nonresistance,* by Guy F. Hershberger.[7]

---

[6] Jagdish S. Sharma, *Mahatma Gandhi (A Descriptive Bibliography)*, (Delhi: S. Chand and Company, 1955), 565. This bibliography was described by the librarian of the India Consulate library in New York as the latest, most authoritative work. It was submitted originally as a dissertation in partial fulfillment of the requirements for the degree of Doctor of Philosophy at the University of Michigan, in June 1954.
[7] Guy F. Hershberger, *War, Peace, and Nonresistance,* 2nd ed (Scottdale, PA: Herald Press, 1953). This book is described in the foreword by Harold S. Bender, chairman of the Peace Problems Committee of the denomination, as follows: "'The

    c. Pertinent articles in the *Mennonite Quarterly Review*, a scholarly research publication of the Mennonite Historical Society, Goshen College, Goshen, Indiana.

    d. Unpublished dissertations.

    e. Other documents listed in a bibliography of peace literature prepared under the auspices of the Mennonite Central Committee.[8]

4. Related literature

As a basic guide to the literature in the field of pacifism, "A Select Bibliography of Notable Books for Pacifists"[9] has been used. This bibliography of fifty-one titles was published under the auspices of the Fellowship of Reconciliation.[10] The selection was made from a larger bibliography of more than five hundred titles on the subject of pacifism. All titles were recommended by a panel of twenty-one scholars in the field. Those titles that were recommended by a minimum of eight persons were included in the "select" bibliography. In addition to these, other works have been consulted as required by problems that emerged in the course of the study.

IV. The significance of the study

This study is related to that category of social behavior identified as pacifism. As popularly employed, the term has a wide range of meanings in philosophy, in motivation, and in practice. It is thought of by some with the respect due to serious conviction, while others regard it as nothing but irrelevant idealism. In view of the magnitude of the tensions among peoples and ideologies of the world, and of the potential for destruction stored in national arsenals, pacifism seems to some to offer the only possible alternative to annihilation, while to others it seems the most certain route thereto.

---

longfelt need for a comprehensive and authoritative work on nonresistance in Christian faith and history is ably met by the volume which now appears under the title, *War, Peace, and Nonresistance*" (vii).

[8] Mennonite Central Committee, "Christian Peace Literature" (Akron, PA: 1962).

[9] William Robert Miller, "A Select Bibliography of Notable Books for Pacifists," *Fellowship* 28 (March 1960), 21.

[10] The Fellowship of Reconciliation is a religious organization based on the belief that love, such as that seen preeminently in Jesus, must serve as the true guide of personal conduct under all circumstances. The office of the fellowship is in Nyack, New York.

It is not the purpose of this investigation to attempt to justify pacifism in general, or in any particular form, or for any particular purpose, whether political, social, or religious. The purpose of this investigation is to identify two schools of pacifism, neither of which finds the generic term adequate; both, while similar in many respects, differ in essential features.

One reason for bringing these two schools together in this study is illustrated in the Montgomery integration movement led by Martin Luther King. Here is a synthesis of Christian motivation and Gandhian technique that may serve as a pilot demonstration for more widespread application in conflict situations.[11] A first step in this operational synthesis and cooperation is mutual understanding. This in turn can lead to interchange of thought and technique and ultimately to the projection of ways and means by which there may be effective nonviolent efforts in the pursuit of justice and peace. The universal anxiety that derives from the threat of nuclear warfare, while serving to some degree as a deterrent, does not elicit the full moral and ameliorative potential of the peoples of the world.

The moral responsibility related to the scientific knowledge that makes possible the weapons for nuclear warfare was brought to the attention of scientists in the annual meeting, December 1960, of the American Association for the Advancement of Science, by the eminent British author and scientist Sir Charles P. Snow. In his address entitled "The Moral Un-Neutrality of Science," he stressed especially the responsibility to inform the public of the alternatives presented by the knowledge of atomic fission.

> It throws upon scientists a direct and personal responsibility. It is not enough to say that scientists have a responsibility as citizens. They have a much greater one than that, and one different in kind. For scientists have a moral imperative to say what they know. It is going to make them unpopular in their own nation-states. It may do worse than make them unpopular. . . . We are faced with an either-or, and we haven't much time. The *either* is acceptance of a restriction of nuclear armaments. This is going to begin, just as a token. . . .

---

[11] Martin Luther King, *Stride toward Freedom* (New York: Harper and Brothers, 1958), 85: "Christ furnished the spirit and motivation, while Gandhi furnished the method."

This course involves certain risks. They are quite obvious, and no honest man is going to blink them. That is *either*. The *or* is not a risk but a certainty. It is this. There is no agreement on tests. The nuclear arms race between the U.S. and the U.S.S.R. not only continues but accelerates. Other countries join in. Within, at the most, six years, China and several other states have a stock of nuclear bombs. Within, at the most, ten years, some of these bombs are going off. I am saying this as responsibly as I can. *That* is the certainty on the one side. Therefore we have a finite risk. On the other side we have a certainty of disaster. Between a risk and a certainty, a sane man does not hesitate. It is the plain duty of scientists to explain this either-or. It is a duty which seems to me to come from the moral nature of the scientific activity itself.[12]

The moral responsibility thus defined should be borne not only by the scientists but by all concerned with the use of the knowledge they have discovered and disseminated. Thus it devolves upon scholars in the realms of social, political, and religious thought to search for the moral equivalent of nuclear power. The investigation herewith designed assumes that a large measure of responsibility resides in the Christian churches to discover basic presuppositions and to release constructive dynamics in the cause of justice and peace for the world.

In a book entitled *Christian Attitudes toward War and Peace,* published in 1960, Professor Roland H. Bainton of Yale Divinity School said,

At the present juncture there is more need for peace than there is for pacifism. If peace is preserved it will be through the efforts not of pacifists, but peace-minded non-pacifists, who do not renounce war absolutely, but who oppose war in our time on grounds of the humanitarian and pragmatic. The question then comes to be, what are the lineaments of a peace program of which those with differing presuppositions can make common cause? This will depend of course upon the ethic espoused by the national state and by the world community. The highest ethic which one can expect from

---

[12] Charles P. Snow, "The Moral Un-Neutrality of Science," *Science* 133, no. 3448 (January 27, 1961).

the state is the ethic of natural law. For the Church one has a right to assume the ethic of the gospel, however interpreted. The two in large measure will coincide, but they may also clash; natural law recognizes the principle that force may be repelled by force, whereas the gospel, if not entirely excluding this principle, certainly indicates a spirit of concession and even of renunciation.[13]

Professor Bainton, while thus drawing attention to the differing points of view as represented among pacifists and among Christians, points to the urgent necessity for a common front in the cause of peace. A beginning in this understanding was launched in 1948 by the first worldwide Assembly of the World Council of Churches, held at Amsterdam. The council received unanimously, and commended to the churches throughout the world, the following statement:

> We are one in proclaiming to all mankind: War is contrary to the will of God. War as a method of settling disputes is incompatible with the teaching and example of our Lord Jesus Christ. The part which war plays in our present international life is a sin against God and a degradation of man. We recognize that the problem of war raises especially acute issues for Christians today. Warfare has greatly changed. . . . The immense use of air forces and the discovery of atomic and other new weapons render widespread and indiscriminate destruction inherent in the whole conduct of modern war in a sense never experienced in past conflicts. In these circumstances the tradition of a just war, requiring a just cause and the use of just means is now challenged.[14]

Along with this statement went the plea to theologians to consider the theological problems involved in giving direction in the complexity of international conflict. It elicited an expression from the Historic Peace Churches in the form of a statement under the heading, "Peace is the Will of God." This was the first document to

---

[13] Roland H. Bainton, *Christian Attitudes toward War and Peace* (New York: Abingdon Press, 1960), 253.
[14] The Amsterdam Assembly Series, *Man's Disorder and God's Design,* Report of Section 4, "The Church and the International Disorder" (New York: Harper and Brothers, 1948), 218.

appear in response to the appeal of the council and is dated October 1953. It is identified in the preface as follows:

> The statement which is herewith presented to the World Council of Churches has been prepared in response to this "special call." It seeks to declare the shared testimony held since their foundation by the so-called Historic Peace Churches, the Church of the Brethren, the Society of Friends, and the Mennonites. Representatives of these three churches and of the International Fellowship of Reconciliation have collaborated in the preparation.[15]

The thesis set forth in the document referred to is: that on the basis of the New Testament ethic, war is contrary to the will of God and that, therefore, the Christian churches and their individual members should have no part in it. Briefly stated, the evidence for this is defined as follows:

> It is the heart of our position that once having been laid hold of by God through Christ, the Christian owes Him unqualified obedience. He may not calculate in advance what this may mean for himself or for society and obey only so far as seems practicable. The Christian is thus placed in a position of inevitable and endless tension. Though he lives in the world and participates in the activities that belong to human life, he must recurrently face situations where loyalty to Christ, to the new "aeon" in which he already stands, means refusal to the world, "in which" he is, but "of which" he is not. Perhaps nowhere does this conflict of loyalties become more articulate or more acute than in the question of war. But here as elsewhere in life the Christian has but one weapon, to overcome "evil with good." His whole life must be one of unflinching fidelity to the way of redemptive love, even though it be the way of the cross.[16]

The document also includes an examination of what are described as pseudo-Christian or secular attitudes and assumptions

---

[15] The Continuation Committee of the Historic Peace Churches in Europe, *Peace Is the Will of God: A Testimony to the World Council of Churches,* A Statement Prepared by the Historic Peace Churches and the International Fellowship of Reconciliation (Geneva: Brethren Service Commission, 1953), 3.
[16] Ibid., 16.

which "gradually and at times unconsciously have been accorded axiomatic status," and gives an elaboration of the above brief definition. It is intended to evoke response from other theologians and thus to clarify and promulgate the New Testament ethic and its application in contemporary society. The first response from the nonpacifist sector came from the combined thought of Bishop Angus Dun and Professor Reinhold Niebuhr. They identified some of the issues around which there was marked difference of thought. This draft appears in a document entitled *The Christian and War*, published by the Historic Peace Churches and the Fellowship of Reconciliation in October 1958. A subtitle describes it as *A Theological Discussion of Justice, Peace and Love*. The authors point out what they consider to be the basic error of the Christian pacifist position, namely, "nonpacifist Christians reject the position of absolute pacifism because it distorts the Christian concept of love and tries to apply an individual ethic to a collective situation,"[17] and "this partial view leads the pacifist to exalt peace over the claims of justice, when a choice between the two must be made. . . . Justice is an instrument of love in a sinful society. To abandon it, whenever violence is involved, is irresponsible."[18]

The authors (Dun and Niebuhr) take particular issue with the statement that the Christian "may not calculate in advance what this may mean for himself or for society." This is judged as irresponsibility in comparison with the criterion that "the calculation of consequences is part of a responsible moral decision."[19] Consequently the position represented by Niebuhr and Dun is well summarized in the title of their statement: "God Wills Both Justice and Peace."[20]

Thus, in the dialogue going on in the context of the World Council of Churches, the Christian pacifist is being forced to think apologetically, on the one hand testing theoretical presuppositions, and on the other subjecting hypotheses to pragmatic demands. The result should be continued honest search for alternatives to

---

[17] The Continuation Committee of the Historic Peace Churches in Europe, *The Christian and War: A Theological Discussion of Justice, Peace and Love* (Amsterdam: Historic Peace Churches and Fellowship of Reconciliation, 1958), 24.
[18] Ibid., 24.
[19] Ibid.
[20] Reinhold Niebuhr and Angus Dun, "God Wills Both Justice and Peace," *Christinaity and Crisis* 15 (June 13, 1955), 78.

violence which have the ultimate sanction of the New Testament ethic and are relevant to contemporary society as it is. In essence, the challenge is directed to pacifists to produce some method by which their idealism may be translated into a real and functional force, as an alternative to the violent means commonly employed to obtain justice and peace.

Likewise, the nonpacifists in the ecumenical dialogue, championing the cause of ecclesiastical unity, cannot close their eyes to the incongruity of their position: the justification of the use of violence between Christian and Christian.

Christian pacifism as it has been identified by the Mennonite Church has tended traditionally to remain aloof from conflict situations in regard to race, economic situations, and international conflict. Professor Guy F. Hershberger has written the recognized work representing this point of view in his book *War, Peace, and Nonresistance.* He presents in a scholarly way the origin, history, and application of the New Testament ethic defined in the Mennonite tradition as "nonresistance." This is characterized by absolute renunciation of coercion in any form for the purpose of getting justice.

But the Martin Luther King movement for racial equality in the South has prompted some new thinking on the part of Mennonite scholars. While recognizing that "nonresistance" and "nonviolent resistance" are essentially two discrete doctrines, the movement as led by Martin Luther King has demonstrated the possibility of limited synthesis in application. This was a movement carried out by a people to obtain a measure of justice for themselves. It has challenged sympathetic Mennonite scholars with the thought that Christian love would lead some into direct participation in such a movement rather than defending aloofness, particularly if they were not to benefit personally. In other words, Christian love which is held to be the highest ethic, and the basis for noninvolvement in conflict, should be allowed to lead the Christian into involvement in conflict situations. This would seem to be a more positive expression than that usually defended by the absolute nonresistant.

Thus there are those who would meet Professor Bainton's challenge:

> The indictment continues that the pacifist by his abstention, whatever his motive, actually makes himself irrelevant.

Justice requires action. In every circumstance something has to be done. What can be done may be far from ideal but under the circumstances it is the best alternative. To hold out for the absolute means to forfeit the relative good. To this the reply may be that to elect the relative may be to forfeit the absolute. There are circumstances in which the highest relevance is irrelevance.[21]

It is this relevance that the proposed investigation will pursue in the subject of nonviolence as identified with Mohandas K. Gandhi, as compared with the doctrine of nonresistance held by the Mennonite Church. That an investigation of this type is significant in the field of pacifism is borne out to some extent by a recognized scholar in Mennonite nonresistance, Guy F. Hershberger, who says, in a personal communication of February 16, 1961:

> In my opinion yours is a most significant undertaking, particularly in this nuclear age when most thoughtful people, whether pacifists or non-pacifists, are searching for some way which promises something better than the present chaotic and dangerous state of world affairs.
>
> Those of the Christian tradition, both pacifists and non-pacifists, need to explore more fully than has yet been done the compatibility with and relevance of Gandhi's contribution to Christianity. Anabaptist-Mennonitism needs to do the same with respect to the relevance of Gandhi for the nonresistant tradition. And Indians, both Christian and non-Christian, with a deep loyalty to Gandhi as a national hero will do well to submit this reverence to the searchlight of the Christian faith and the Christian ethic.
>
> To be sure, numerous writings on Christian pacifism have touched on these issues as incidental to some other central theme. In your project it is proposed to make this the heart of the study. This is a basic study much in need of being done, and in it you have my support and encouragement.[22]

---

[21] Roland H. Bainton, *Christian Attitudes toward War and Peace* (New York: Abingdon Press, 1960), 250.

[22] Guy F. Hershberger, Professor of History and Sociology at Goshen College, Goshen, IN. Quoted, with his permission, from a personal letter dated February 16, 1961.

In the preface to *War without Violence,* by Krishnalal Shridharani, Oswald Garrison Villard comments,

> To my mind Gandhi has merely been putting into practice the teachings of Jesus, whose non-resistance was also the most dangerous of resistances. "Resist not evil" was his command, but by that was never meant that there should be no spiritual resistance or no resistance whatever. If that were the meaning then all religion and all ethics would collapse. What Jesus meant was the refusal to match force with force, violence with violence. It was a counsel not to resist evil by stooping to evil.[23]

Villard is not alone in recognizing the challenge Gandhi presented to Christendom. Charles Freer Andrews, a long-time colleague of Gandhi in the freedom movement in India, and his biographer, in the preface to an autobiographical account of Gandhi's work, comments on the significance of Gandhi's religious idealism:

> Here then might be found just that "moral equivalent for war" which the American philosopher William James required. Mahatma Gandhi has shown us by practical experiment how the principle works. For the thoughtful Christian it has a remarkable likeness to the precepts of the Sermon on the Mount. Mr. Gandhi has never failed to acknowledge his debt of gratitude in his own religious life for that sublime teaching.[24]

A similar impression is recorded by Dr. E. Stanley Jones, also a long-time friend and admirer of Gandhi, who writes, after Gandhi's assassination: "Mahatma Gandhi is God's appeal to this age—an age drifting again to its doom. If the atomic bomb was militarism's trump card thrown down on the table of human events, then Mahatma Gandhi is God's trump card which He throws down on the table of events now—a table trembling with destiny."[25]

---

[23] Krishnalal Shridharani, *War without Violence* (New York: Harcourt, Brace and Company, 1939), xiii.

[24] Charles Freer Andrews, ed., *Mahatma Gandhi at Work* (New York: The Macmillan Company, 1931), 9.

[25] E. Stanley Jones, *Mahatma Gandhi: An Interpretation* (New York: Abingdon-Cokesbury, 1948), 159–60.

Jones was convinced that Gandhi in his self-sacrificing non-violent approach to social and political problems demonstrated the power of the spirit—thus pointing to the only one in history who was his mentor; referring to Christ, he says: "Gandhi, the Hindu, points us to Him! I don't care what he says about it; by his life and death he points us to Him; and in doing so precipitates a fresh crisis in humanity."[26]

That Gandhi himself felt that he had something to contribute to a clearer representation of Christ is perhaps no more clearly illustrated than in the following statement in an address to a Christian missionary conference in Madras on February 14, 1916: "I know I am now treading upon thin ice; but I do not apologize in closing this part of my subject by saying that the frightful outrage that is just now going on in Europe perhaps shows that the message of Jesus of Nazareth, the Son of Peace, has been little understood in Europe, and that light may have to be thrown upon it from the East."[27]

Professor Reinhold Niebuhr in his book *Moral Man and Immoral Society* presents a thorough discussion of the Gandhian doctrine of nonviolence, and finds a great deal of confusion in the minds of many people, and perhaps even in the thought of Gandhi himself, regarding the relationship between Gandhian nonviolence and biblical nonresistance. Insofar as the former exercises coercion, even though nonviolent, it cannot be equated to biblical nonresistance, which forbids any coercive measure. The full discussion involves many pages but the following brief statement constitutes a pivotal point: "In justice to Mr. Gandhi it must be said that while he confuses the moral connotations of non-resistance and non-violent resistance, he never commits himself to pure non-resistance. He is politically too realistic to believe in its efficacy."[28]

In concluding this chapter, Professor Niebuhr, who is not a pacifist, makes the following urgent plea, no doubt reflecting the influence of the Gandhian movement:

> There is no problem of political life to which religious imagi-
> nation can make a larger contribution than this problem of

---

[26] Ibid., 158.
[27] Charles Freer Andrews, *Mahatma Gandhi's Ideas* (New York: The Macmillan Company, 1930), 122.
[28] Reinhold Niebuhr, *Moral Man and Immoral Society* (New York: Charles Scribner's Sons, 1960), 243.

developing non-violent resistance. The discovery of elements of common human frailty in the foe and, concomitantly, the appreciation of all human life as possessing transcendent worth, creates attitudes which transcend social conflict and thus mitigate its cruelties.... Secular imagination is not capable of producing them; for they require a sublime madness which disregards immediate appearances and emphasizes profound and ultimate unities. It is no accident of history that the spirit of non-violence has been introduced into contemporary politics by a religious leader of the orient.... If the mind and the spirit of man does not attempt the impossible [the peace of the world], if it does not seek to conquer or to eliminate nature but tries only to make the forces of nature the servants of the human spirit and the instruments of the moral ideal, a progressively higher justice and more stable peace can be achieved.[29]

In the field of political theory Dr. Joan V. Bondurant has taken a fresh look at the teachings and efforts of Gandhi. Her study, published in 1958, is entitled *Conquest of Violence,* with the subtitle, *The Gandhian Philosophy of Conflict.* In the preface the author identifies herself as a "Westerner whose basic predispositions are rationalist and humanist and who shares with some of Gandhi's severest critics an abiding suspicion of religious systems and of obscurantist approaches." Dr. Bondurant thus approaches the investigation with a purpose that suggests the possibility that Gandhi still has something to offer to the field of political and social theory. This thought is specifically spelled out in the author's preface:

In times such as ours when conflict is the order of the day and the potential of technology offers more to fear than to hope, social and political theory face their gravest challenge. Theoretical political systems have grown increasingly suspect and intellectual formulations tend less to challenge than repel. But there is rapidly developing a demand hitherto neglected by social and political theory. This is the demand for solutions to the problem of conflict—not for theoretical systems of end-structure aimed at ultimately eliminating conflict, but for ways of conducting conflict when it arises: ways which are constructive and not destructive. Such a

---

[29] Ibid., 254–56.

demand must be met by a theory of process and of means, and not of further concern for structure, for pattern, and for ends. Basic to such a theory is a philosophy of action.[30]

And again Dr. Bondurant writes, "The problem of human conflict is perhaps the most fundamental problem of all time. In this age when the physical sciences have outstripped the more slowly advancing social sciences, it is one of undeniable urgency, and one which already attracts social scientists in many disciplines. This essay on 'satyagraha' and political thought is an effort to focus attention on yet another direction in which solutions might be sought."[31]

The concluding paragraph of the book contains the following significant statement:

> The search for constructive, creative means has been pressed forward in fields of enquiry peripheral to the study of politics. The political philosopher who would pursue the search for an adequate technique of action can view the Gandhian philosophy of conflict as little more than a point of departure. He must bring to bear upon this central problem the findings of his colleagues regarding conflict on very different levels of human experience. The complexities of modern society, the advances in techniques of human organization, the intensifying of pressures created by the human mind and spirit which continue to press beyond the known to ever-extending frontiers of the unknown—these complexities, advances, and pressures demand that the search be carried into yet other dimensions. . . . The Gandhian experiments suggest that if man is to free himself from fear and threat alike, he must pause in his flight from violence to set himself the task of its conquest.[32]

Bondurant suggests that there may be other levels of human experience that may provide creative and constructive means for

---

[30] Dr. J. V. Bondurant is Associate Editor of the Indian Press Digests; Research Political Scientist at the Institute of International Studies, University of California, Berkeley; and Lecturer in Political Science at the University of California, Berkeley. Since 1944, Dr. Bondurant has spent a total of four years in India, during which she traveled extensively throughout that country (author information from back of title page).

[31] Joan V. Bondurant, *Conquest of Violence* (Princeton, NJ: Princeton University Press, 1958), v.

[32] Ibid., vii–viii.

the conquest of violence. She asserts further that the "complexities, advances, and pressures" of society "demand that the search be carried into yet other dimensions."[33]

In view of the almost desperate appeal for an alternative to violent conflict on one hand, and the potential within peace-minded people on the other, it seems appropriate that one area of this search may be that proposed in this study. As seen above, Gandhi constitutes a challenge to Christendom as a whole, since—in terms of self-sacrifice and spiritual perception—he objectified the New Testament ethic. Because his nonviolent technique demonstrated pragmatically the power of nonviolence and brought about certain desirable ends, it challenges the pacifist element within Christendom by implying a way for Christian love to find more adequate expression. To some who espouse the nonresistant interpretation of the New Testament ethic, its absolutist limitation seems to inhibit the spiritual dynamic which ought to be channeled toward desirable social and political ends by means consistent with that ethic. It is ultimately the purpose of this investigation to locate the areas of compatibility between the New Testament ethic as interpreted by the Mennonite Church, and the doctrine of nonviolence as evolved by Mohandas K. Gandhi, and to provide in a single document a comparative statement of the distinctive features of each school of thought as regards philosophy as well as practical application. It is projected that an examination of this kind may result in some contribution to the discovery of constructive alternatives to violence in conflict situations.

Frank R. Moraes, editor of the leading daily newspaper in India, *The Times of India,* in reviewing the influence of Gandhi in India since his assassination in 1948, reports some of his observations in *Foreign Affairs* of January 1958, under the title, "Gandhi Ten Years After." He clearly documents the conspicuous ways Gandhi's influence seems to have waned. For example,

> Looking back over the past ten years from January 30, 1948, when the Mahatma was assassinated, it would be pharisaical to pretend that Gandhi's ideas and teachings survive and shine as vividly as they did in his lifetime. Like Hinduism, Gandhism is much more than a way of life, for just as

---

[33] Ibid., 232.

the mere observance of caste, ritual and the institution of the joint family does not constitute Hinduism, so also the adoption of ascetic habits, verging on the masochistic, does not in itself generate the "soulforce" which is Gandhism. Paradoxically enough, while Hinduism is beginning to shed its outer habiliments such as caste and the joint family, the present-day exponents of Gandhism, with rare exceptions, prefer the facade to the faith. The result is a general debasing of Gandhian gold.[34]

In mentioning particularly the waning of regard for the doctrine of nonviolence, which played such a conspicuous role in the gaining of independence from the British crown, he cites the frequently recurring use of physical force by the Congress government:

In the ten years of independence there have been more police firings on workers, students, and other demonstrators, admittedly obstreperous, than there were in the ten comparatively quiescent years between 1932 and 1942 when the British *raj* held sway. According to a survey carried out by the central office of the Socialist Party, the police have opened fire on over a thousand occasions in the past ten years. In all, 840 persons were reported to have been killed, and 3,136 injured. These figures have not been controverted by the Government. Of non-violence, save as an expression of India's foreign policy, there is therefore little evidence inside India—which is not to say that a state of turmoil persists (it does not)—but that authority as represented by those in charge of law and order is more trigger-happy in independent than it was in British-ruled India.[35]

Whatever else this observation may mean or imply, it does seem to raise a question about the generalization sometimes made that nonviolence is a method peculiar to Hindu culture and therefore practicable only in that context. Apparently it is no more natural in this than in any other part of the world. It is inferred that Gandhi brought something of a high order of personal ideal-

---

[34] Frank R. Moraes, "Gandhi Ten Years After," *Foreign Affairs* 36 (January 1958), 253–54.
[35] Ibid., 257–58.

ism and discipline that inspired the movement. Moraes suggests that it is necessary to help India today to see through the eyes of a younger generation the significance of the father of modern India, Mohandas K. Gandhi. Indian students, often frustrated socially and economically, find themselves prey to political tensions. It is the intention of the contemplated study to provide for Christian students primarily an opportunity to look objectively at the doctrine of nonviolence both in the light of the philosophy and practice of Gandhi and his followers, and in the light of the New Testament. It is the personal conviction of this investigator that in the land where the most notable experiment in nonviolence as a political technique has been demonstrated, and where Christian truth is less concealed by accretions of tradition, the opportunity to further the pursuit of the meaning of nonviolence should not be neglected. Inasmuch as Gandhi acknowledged a measure of influence on his thinking by Jesus Christ, and particularly by his Sermon on the Mount, it should serve both the Christian and the non-Christian student of Gandhi to consider this relationship.

V. Procedure in collecting and treating data

General statement

In general the sources used in this investigation have been primary published sources. Investigation followed the steps of the inductive method involving gathering data, analyzing and interpreting the data, and formulation of conclusions supported by the data. In execution of this research the investigation was guided by authorities in the field of historical research such as Barzun and Graff,[36] and Gottschalk.[37]

To insure objectivity and validity in the collection and selection of data, the following criteria were applied wherever their use was indicated:

1. Are the data representative of the concept or event they describe?
2. Are the sources cited true to their original form?

---

[36] Jacques Barzun and Henry F. Graff, *The Modern Researcher* (New York: Harcourt, Brace and Company, 1957).
[37] Louis Gottschalk, *Understanding History: A Primer of Historical Method* (New York: Alfred A. Knopf, 1958).

3. Do the authorities cited have recognized standing in their respective fields?
4. Do the names of authorities appear frequently in connection with major works and activities in their field?
5. Do the authorities cited occupy a high level of professional status?
6. Is it the consensus of professional opinion that the publications and scholastic efforts of the authorities cited make a significant contribution to their respective fields?

Following critical examination, data were classified and organized in a design to facilitate orderly collation, description, analysis, and synthesis. All pertinent data have been presented in an expository form. Where indicated, analysis has been supported with corroborating data from recognized scholars.

As a guide in the investigation, the following scheme of questions was drawn up as suggested by the material, and the requirements of the problems under investigation.

Sub-problem 1:
To analyze the basic writings of Mohandas K. Gandhi pertaining to his concept of nonviolence for the purpose of discovering the origin and fundamental characteristics of his concept.

As a first step, the investigator identified pertinent works of Gandhi, by examining the writings and records of public addresses and collections of letters, as they are found in the bibliography of Jagdish S. Sharma as described under "delimitations" above in this outline.

As a second step, pertinent books, articles, letters, and addresses were used to answer such questions as the following:

With regard to historical development:
1. What was the social and religious setting in which Gandhi grew up?
2. What formal education did he have?
3. What were the circumstances that brought him into public life?
4. What were his contacts with Christian thought?
5. To what sources did Gandhi attribute his views?

6. Were his interpretations consistent with traditional interpretations of the Hindu scriptures?
7. What differences in interpretation appear?
8. What does he say with regard to ideas on nonviolence from the New Testament?

With regard to the philosophy of nonviolence:

1. How did Gandhi define nonviolence?
2. What terminology did he use, and why?
3. How is nonviolence related to his total scheme of thought?
4. What are the component parts of Gandhi's view of nonviolence?
5. What are the dynamics in his concept of nonviolence?

With regard to technique:

1. What nonviolent techniques are described and sanctioned?
2. When and where did Gandhi apply or sanction nonviolence in a personal conflict situation?
3. When and where did Gandhi apply or sanction nonviolence in an intra-group conflict situation?
4. When and where did Gandhi apply or sanction nonviolence in an international conflict situation?
5. According to his own criteria, what efforts in nonviolent coercion were successful? which unsuccessful?

Sub-problem 2:

To analyze the official documents and authorized writings of the Mennonite Church with a view to discovering the origin and fundamental characteristics of the doctrine of nonresistance.

To answer this sub-problem, the investigator identified official documents and pronouncements, and authorized writings of the Mennonite Church. In addition, articles in the *Mennonite Quarterly Review* and other pertinent pamphlets and books were examined. Investigation was guided by the following questions:

With regard to the historical development of the doctrine of nonresistance:

1. What is the historical origin of the Mennonite Church?

2. What is the first formulation of the doctrine of nonresistance?
3. What are the sources of the doctrine?
4. What are the sources of the doctrine relating to the historical contexts in which the doctrine was reiterated?
5. Has there been any modification of the doctrine?
6. What is the official statement of the doctrine at the present time?
7. What is unique about the doctrine as distinct from other Christian traditions?
8. How is the doctrine distinct from other pacifist positions?

With regard to the philosophy of nonresistance:
1. What is the official definition of the doctrine of nonresistance?
2. What terminology is used and why?
3. How is the doctrine of nonresistance related to the total scheme of thought?
4. In what areas of human behavior is the doctrine of nonresistance exercised?
5. What dynamics for this behavior are described?

With regard to technique:
1. What forms of action are sanctioned?
2. In what ways has the church given direction with regard to interpersonal conflict situations?
3. In what ways has the church given direction with regard to intra-group conflict situations?
4. In what ways has the church given direction with regard to international conflict situations?
5. What evidence is there in the literature with regard to unsolved problems in the application of the doctrine of nonresistance?

Sub-problem 3:
To compare modes of application in social and political conflict situations.

To answer this sub-problem, the investigator identified pertinent references to conflict situations in which nonviolent techniques have been applied under the direction and with the sanction of M. K. Gandhi. Application of the steps of satyagraha as identified and described by Krishnalal Shridharani has been examined and illustrated from historical accounts.

As a second step, the investigator identified pertinent references to conflict situations in which nonviolent techniques have been applied at the direction or with the sanction of the Mennonite Church or an authorized agency of the same, or by an individual or group, consistent with the doctrine of nonresistance. An attempt was made to extract illustrations of nonresistance in action and to compare them with the pattern of satyagraha.

In identifying each mode of nonviolent action, the following questions have been considered.

1. What was the nature of the action taken?
2. What problem prompted the action?
3. Why was this particular form of action taken?
4. With what immediate purpose was it designated?
5. What dynamics were considered to be effective in the action?
6. What effect was anticipated?
7. What effect was observed? upon the enemy? upon participants?
8. What evidence is there with regard to ideological sanction?
9. What evidence is there of success or failure?

From this data, a comparative analysis reveals the similarities and differences in modes of application of Gandhian nonviolence (satyagraha) and Mennonite nonresistance.

Sub-problem 4:
To discover lines of demarcation between the two views and explore areas of common thought and technique.

An effort has been made to produce a summary of findings that have emerged, showing the similarities and the differences in both philosophy and technique, as represented in Gandhian satyagraha and Mennonite nonresistance respectively. Findings relate to the following major categories: (1) the nature of ultimate reality and authority, (2) the nature of morality, and (3) the definition of nonviolent action (including dynamics and application).

These findings suggest operational implications for cooperative social action.

Chapter 2

The literature of pacifism

As a basic guide to the literature in the field of pacifism, "A Select Bibliography of Notable Books for Pacifists"[1] has been used. This bibliography of fifty-one titles was published under the auspices of the Fellowship of Reconciliation[2] in its official monthly magazine of March 1, 1960. The selection was made from a larger bibliography of more than five hundred titles on the subject of pacifism. All titles were recommended by a panel of twenty-one scholars in the field. Those items recommended by a minimum of eight persons were included in the select list. A perusal of these writings reveals the breadth of contemporary concern for finding an alternative to violence in dealing with conflict situations.

While there appear in the literature many references to the nonviolence of Mohandas K. Gandhi, and to Christian nonresistance as interpreted by the Mennonite Church, no document, published or unpublished, deals exclusively with a comparative analytical study of these two schools of thought. The related literature as examined provides a survey of the field and particularly indicates the context in which the subject for this study is set.

The titles are herewith grouped according to their general content:

Practical pacifism and nonviolence

In *Stride toward Freedom,* Martin Luther King describes the first successful large-scale application of nonviolent resistance to an American social problem. He writes from the standpoint of personal involvement in the movement for desegregation of public transportation in Montgomery, Alabama. Though he did not originate the movement, he became a leader of it. He was prepared for this

---

[1] William Robert Miller, comp., "A Select Bibliography of Notable Books for Pacifists," *Fellowship* 28 (March, 1960), 21.
[2] The Fellowship of Reconciliation is a religious organization based on the belief that love, such as that seen preeminently in Jesus, must serve as the true guide of personal conduct under all circumstances. The office of the Fellowship is in Nyack, New York.

leadership because of personal concern and because of an ideology that could provide direction to the movement. The ideological preparation is described in a chapter entitled "Pilgrimage to Nonviolence," in which he mentions the influence of the writings and work of Mohandas K. Gandhi, and summarizes by saying:

> Gandhi was probably the first person in history to lift the love ethic of Jesus above mere interaction between individuals to a powerful and effective social force on a large scale. Love for Gandhi was a potent instrument for social and collective transformation.

> It was in this Gandhian emphasis on love and nonviolence that I discovered the method for social reform.... Gandhi resisted evil with as much vigor and power as the violent resister, but he resisted with love instead of hate.[3]

The Montgomery movement described in *Stride toward Freedom* represents an attempt at a synthesis of Gandhian technique and Christian motivation. The account provides an insight into the ideological and practical problems encountered in the application of nonviolent coercion.

In the literature on nonviolence, the work of Gandhi most frequently referred to is his *Autobiography,* subtitled *The Story of Experiments with Truth.* This self-portrait of the Indian leader reveals the relationship between his personal commitment and social action in his life. This long work was written originally in his mother tongue, Gujarati, and later translated into English. It first appeared serially in the newspaper Gandhi founded and edited for many years, *Young India.* This autobiography terminates in 1920, when Gandhi had twenty-eight years of life and intense activity ahead of him, nor does it include the experiments with satyagraha in South Africa, which are described in another volume entitled *Satyagraha in South Africa.*[4] In later life Gandhi expressed himself mostly in editorials and essays and public addresses. These have been collected by his colleagues and biographers, and by students of his thought and life. Among the collections especially relevant to

---

[3] Martin Luther King, *Stride toward Freedom* (New York: Harper and Brothers, 1958), 97–98.

[4] M. K. Gandhi, *Satyagraha in South Africa* (Ahmedabad: Navajivan Press, 1950).

this study are the following: *Satyagraha*,[5] a systematic and concise outline of the origin, practice, and prospects of nonviolence, by R. R. Diwakar; and *Satyagraha*,[6] a later publication of the Navajivan Press comprising a very large collection of the writings of Gandhi on this subject.

A major interpretive study of satyagraha is Krishnalal Shridharani's work *War without Violence*.[7] The subtitle describes this as a study of *Gandhi's Method and Its Accomplishments*. The unique feature of Shridharani's presentation is its systematic ordering of the methods of applied satyagraha which are described and arranged in the order in which they would be employed to accomplish a desired objective. To some extent the author appears to ignore the religious and personal dynamics conceived by Gandhi. The presentation is objective, however, even though the author was a close follower of Gandhi in the Indian independence movement. Speaking as an exponent of nonviolence, he says, by way of introduction of the subject, "Satyagraha has to be compared to and contrasted with war, since the former aspires, as it were, to be an effective substitute for the latter. In other words, war furnishes us with a yardstick to measure and appraise Satyagraha. The utility, effectiveness, and limitations of Satyagraha are to be judged in the light of the utility, effectiveness, and limitations of war."[8]

Satyagraha is, therefore, to be thought of as an alternative to war, a technique with an exacting discipline and aggressive purpose comparable to organized warfare. As the former, it has characteristics that meet the criterion of the classic essay of the philosopher William James entitled "The Moral Equivalent of War," which is referred to frequently in the literature on pacifism. In tracing militarism historically, James concludes that "militarism is the great preserver of our ideals of hardihood, and human life with no use for hardihood would be contemptible."[9]

He remarks that in view of this strong urge for the qualities of the military type of man, any moral equivalent of war will have

---

[5] R. R. Diwakar, *Sayagraha* (Chicago: H. Regnery Company, 1948).
[6] M. K. Gandhi, *Satyagraha* (Ahmedabad: Navajivan Press, 1951).
[7] Krishnalal Shridharani, *War without Violence* (New York: Harcourt, Brace and Company, 1939).
[8] Ibid., xxx.
[9] William James, *Memories and Studies* (London: Longmans, Green and Company, 1911), 276.

to fulfill the ideals of hardihood. James writes, "We must make new energies and hardihoods continue the manliness to which the military mind so faithfully clings. Martial virtues must be the enduring cement; intrepidity, contempt of softness, surrender of private interest, obedience to command, must still remain in the rock upon which states are built."[10] The essay is significant in this insight into an element of human nature that supports the military appeal.

Richard B. Gregg has written what is considered a classic psychological interpretation of nonviolence, *The Power of Nonviolence,* in which he explains nonviolence primarily with respect to psychological dynamics, as stated in his preface: "I have tried to test the idea of nonviolence with the recent findings of psychology, military and political strategy, political theory, economics, physiology, biology, ethics, penology, and education."[11] Thus the discussion is enriched with and supported by many references to scholars in these separate fields, as well as to factual historical data. In dealing with the subject of war as a means of mass resistance, he quotes Captain B. H. Liddell as a military authority for defining the essential purpose of war: "The true aim in war is the mind of the enemy command and government, not the bodies of their troops, that the balance between victory and defeat turns on mental impressions and only indirectly on physical blows."[12] Then by comparison he shows that "the object of nonviolent resistance is partly analogous to the object of war, namely, to demoralize the opponent, to break his will, to destroy his confidence, enthusiasm, and hope,"[13] and besides, an additional constructive element, "nonviolent resistance demoralizes the opponent only to re-establish in him a new morale that is finer because it is based on sounder values."[14] The author demonstrates how mental and physical discipline is necessary in nonviolence as in violence, and concludes the book with an outline of training in nonviolent technique. Illustrative examples are drawn not only from the Gandhian experiments in India and Africa, but also from European and American history. The book represents

---

[10] Ibid., 287–88.
[11] Richard B. Gregg, *The Power of Nonviolence* (Philadelphia: J. B. Lippincott Company, 1934), 12.
[12] Ibid., 88.
[13] Ibid., 89.
[14] Ibid.

a serious attempt to assess and to explore the psychological and political potential in the method of nonviolence.

Nonviolence in an Aggressive World is a discussion of nonviolence in relation to the economic and political problems of the United States in the period between the two world wars. The author, Dr. A. J. Muste, reared in the Christian tradition, at one time renounced all forms of religion and identified himself with Marxist-Leninist thought. Subsequently returning to Christian faith, he became a leader in the Christian pacifist movement. His treatise does not rest on consideration of a few proof texts from the Bible but rather on the basic principles of Christian truth. It is his thesis that "Christian pacifism arises out of and is bound up with the very essence of the Christian world view."[15] At the center of this worldview is the love of God which is the source of all divine activity among humanity. The author asserts, "It must follow that every human organization and institution will be able to endure and to function in the degree that this divine, creative element of love, of fellowship, is embodied in it and promoted by it."[16] Muste proposes genuine Christian pacifism as a revolutionary strategy in solving political and social injustices but insists that it must be pacifist throughout. If in any manner or degree, whether for purposes of efficiency or expediency, there is resort to violence, there will be a perpetuation of violence. In support of this argument he analyzes many social and political revolutions, and particularly that of Lenin and Stalin in Russia. His comment in this connection is: "We have seen that the Communist movement, aiming at the realization of the prophetic ideal of justice, freedom and brotherhood, has nevertheless become a force of evil rather than good, because it succumbed to the belief that evil dictatorship is the road to democracy, violence to peace."[17] In conclusion, he returns to a consideration of the Christian church, which he believes to be the divine instrument of social justice, and to the exercise of its revolutionary function in an exclusively nonviolent manner. The state, he declares, is forcing the church

---

[15] A. J. Muste, *Nonviolence in an Aggressive World* (New York: Harper and Brothers, 1940), 11.
[16] Ibid., 12–13.
[17] Ibid., 172.

"to choose between being pacifist or cease to make any claim at all to the name of Christian."[18]

From a nonreligious approach is the book *Defense in the Nuclear Age*,[19] by Commander Sir Stephen King-Hall. This eminent British military man with a nationwide reputation as a commentator on defense questions writes from the standpoint of service experience in two world wars, on the admiralty staff, and at two staff colleges (army and navy). He proposes that the only solution to the H-bomb deadlock is nuclear disarmament followed by a national education program for nonviolent resistance. He is explicit in stating that the proposition is made on the basis not of morality but of expediency. The book is divided into two parts; the first is a historical treatment of the nature of war and its evolution from conflict over things to conflict of ideology; the second part is in reality a hypothesis about the outcome of the nuclear disarmament and nonviolent resistance program. Commander King-Hall points out that nuclear disarmament is one idea that has emerged in an effort to break through the present thought-barrier—the concept that a stockpile of nuclear weapons is the best military deterrent. In considering the security nuclear armament is supposed to represent, he points out its equivalent potential for destruction.

While this book is primarily important for its political implications, it has considerable value in the field of education. It is through the medium of education in its broadest sense that such a program of nonviolent resistance could be effective.

Another brief discussion that represents the thought of a scientist on the subject of war and pacifism is the book *Is Peace Possible?*[20] by Kathleen Lonsdale, which deals with the implications of the expanding world population and technical advancement with regard to freedom, justice, and peace.

Of the books that present some of the practical implications of living the pacifist life are the following:

---

[18] Ibid., 199.
[19] Stephen King-Hall, *Defense in the Nuclear Age* (Nyack, NY: Fellowship Publications, 1959).
[20] Kathleen Lonsdale, *Is Peace Possible?* (Harmondsworth, England: Penguin, 1957).

For More than Bread[21] is an autobiographical account of twenty-two years' work with the American Friends Service Committee, the relief and service agency of a Historic Peace Church known as the Society of Friends. The author, Dr. Clarence E. Pickett, gives an informal history of the range of humanitarian activity engaged in by the Friends in direct commitment to the way of love. Dr. Pickett describes the help given to needy people during strikes in West Virginia, distribution of food and caring for refugee children following World War I, marshaling relief in this country during the Great Depression, investigating the inhumane treatment of Jews during World War II, mediation for conscientious objectors, establishing ambulance units, assisting in immigration. The account demonstrates how personal service can influence, for good and for peace, the relationships of nations and peoples. It shows the concrete application of a positive program of love in action.

Others are *Humiliation with Honor*,[22] by Vera Brittain, and *Journal*,[23] by George Fox. The latter is the autobiography of the founder of the Religious Society of Friends. An account of the day-to-day thought and activity of a conscientious objector imprisoned during World War II is found in the book *Diary of a Self-Made Convict*,[24] by Alfred Hassler. Another classic of the Friends tradition is *Journal and Other Writings*,[25] by John Woolman, which reveals the spiritual thought of one who took an active part in the antislavery movement in colonial America. A more recent book, *Christians in the Arena*,[26] is a small collection of biographical sketches of contemporary persons who have courageously expressed their faith in the way of love, particularly as opposed to war and totalitarian tyranny. Their experiences illustrate some of the practical problems of the application of the love ethic, as well as the positive results of costly self-suffering.

---

[21] Clarence E. Pickett, *For More than Bread* (Boston: Little, Brown and Company, 1953).

[22] Vera Brittain, *Humiliation with Honor* (New York: Fellowship Publications, 1943).

[23] George Fox, *Journal* (New York: Dutton, 1924).

[24] Alfred Hassler, *Diary of a Self-Made Convict* (Nyack, NY: Fellowship Publications, 1958).

[25] John Woolman, *Journal and Other Writings* (New York: Dutton, 1952).

[26] Allen A. Hunter, *Christians in the Arena* (Nyack, NY: Fellowship Publications, 1958).

One of the recent collections of Gandhi's writings is *The Gandhi Reader,* edited by Homer A. Jack. This compact chronicle of Mohandas K. Gandhi records some of the practical difficulties he encountered in his program of nonviolence. *The Gandhi Reader* comprises biographical material, writings, and records of speeches by Gandhi himself, as well as writings by his friends, colleagues, and students. The compiler has had a lifelong interest in Gandhi, which took him to India, where he personally interviewed persons who lived and worked closely with the Indian leader. His book represents research in five hundred volumes, newspapers, and magazines. He observes, about Gandhi, that "his legacy consisted not of personal possessions, but of a dramatic life and penetrating ethical insights. . . . His life and teaching were one."[27] It is this close correlation between Gandhi's life and his doctrine that confronts the researcher with the difficulty of isolating the dynamic of the ideal from the dynamic of the personality.

Recognizing that Gandhi's greatest contribution was in the field of methodology, the author has included a generous representation of the documentary material dealing with nonviolence. It is for this reason, in addition to its overall value as a source volume, that it was selected from among many such collections.

Religious basis of Christian pacifism

Of particular interest in this category are the writings of Leo Tolstoy; it was his book *The Kingdom of God Is Within You,*[28] that, among Christian sources, was especially identified by Gandhi as of singular inspiration to him in the formulation of his doctrine of nonviolence. It represents a polemic against the compromise of the church as well as an exposition of the New Testament ethic. His final work, *The Law of Love and the Law of Violence,*[29] is his spiritual last testament, exhorting individuals to make a commitment to Christ and criticizing the widespread superficiality of much of Christendom.

---

[27] Homer A. Jack, *The Gandhi Reader* (Bloomington, IN: Indiana University Press, 1956), 5.

[28] Leo Tolstoi, *The Kingdom of God Is Within You* (Boston: L. C. Page and Company, 1905).

[29] Leo Tolstoy, *The Law of Love and the Law of Violence* (New York: Rudolph Field, 1948).

Love, the Law of Life[30] represents the philosophical reflections of Toyohiko Kagawa, noted for his varied and extensive humanitarian services for the poor in his native Japan. The individual units of this book deal with love and its implications in moral and ethical categories. The dominant thesis is that the human conscience, when informed by divine love, is the most reliable criterion for personal social action. Of interest to the student of pacifism are his ideas about adherence to love in commerce and industry, as applied to the capitalist, the laborer, the employer and the employee, the owner and the tenant. Love, he declares, is the most reliable criterion for social action, as it has the ultimate sanction of the God of the universe. Love is the law of life.

The authority of this work derives from the fact that it represents the thought informing one who identified himself with the law of love and served his fellowmen and women with true self-sacrifice. His extraordinary ministry has been witnessed by many observers. The book does not give a documentary account of Kagawa's activities; this is found elsewhere. *Love, the Law of Life,* however, reveals his basic philosophy.

Of particular significance with reference to Christian nonresistance are the studies of the biblical sources. One by Gerald Heard deals with the Sermon on the Mount of Jesus: *The Code of Christ.*[31] This is an exposition of the seven beatitudes interpreted from the standpoint of one who considers these basic principles of the law of God as applicable to the follower of Christ. In the individual chapters he expounds each principle, showing its meaning for human society. The work is instructional and inspirational and clarifies the basic motivations of Christian pacifism.

A Testament of Devotion, by Thomas R. Kelly, is a reflective devotional work dealing with the most profound dynamics of Christian pacifism. The nature of social responsibility is one of its themes. In this connection, Kelly contends that "social concern is the dynamic life of God at work in the world."[32]

---

[30] Toyohiko Kagawa, *Love, the Law of Life* (Philadelphia: The John C. Winston Company, 1929).
[31] Gerald Heard, *The Code of Christ* (New York: Harper and Brothers, 1941).
[32] Thomas R. Kelly, *A Testament of Devotion* (New York: Harper and Brothers, 1941), 111.

Christ and the Christian, by the theologian Nels F. S. Ferré, shows God's method of dealing with humanity as essentially one of self- giving and self-sacrifice, demonstrated preeminently in Jesus Christ. This self-giving love is identified by the Greek term *agape,* which he uses throughout his book. Ferré uses data from biblical and classical tradition in support of his thesis, and the result is a document in which the agape theme emerges predominant. It is shown to be the normative pattern for the Christian's behavior, individually, and especially for the collective action of the church vis-à-vis the world. He states that the true church comprises those "who know and live the 'Agape' life." The ultimate purpose of God in history is "full creative harmony of 'Agape,' God with man and man with men."[33]

Recognized as a standard work in the field of pacifism is the exegetical and historical study by G. H. C. Macgregor, Professor of Divinity and Biblical Criticism, entitled *The New Testament Basis of Pacifism.* MacGregor justifies the use of the New Testament on the grounds that the ethical standards here represented reach a higher plane than those of the Old Testament. In examining pertinent teachings of Jesus, he shows their implications in individual and collective application. He finds that the basic ethic of Jesus can be summarized as follows: "Evil can be truly conquered only by the power of truth and goodness and self-sacrificing love."[34] His treatise embodies the wider application of this basic ethic as it emerged in the contemporary Jewish-Roman antagonism of Jesus' own time. In summary he declares, "The Pacifism which led Jesus to the Cross is so integral a part of His whole attitude toward the life of individuals and of the nation alike, that it must also be recognized to be an integral part of any ethic which can in the full sense of the word claim to be Christian."[35]

Another similar work is *The Dagger and the Cross,* by Culbert G. Rutenber, in which the student of Christian pacifism finds a discussion of the biblical sources from the perspective of neo-Reformation theology. Following a review of pertinent literature with special

---

[33] Nels F. S. Ferré, *Christ and the Christian* (New York: Harper and Brothers, 1958), 239.
[34] G. H. C. Macgregor, *The New Testament Basis of Pacifism,* rev. ed. (Nyack, NY: Fellowship Publications, 1960), 39.
[35] Ibid., 50–51.

reference to differing points of view, Rutenber notes that Christian pacifism has been nurtured pretty largely within the matrix of liberal theology, with the decline of which the question of the biblical foundations of pacifism emerged.

He examines, first of all, the New Testament sources and then those of the Old Testament, explaining that the latter is understandable only in the light of the former. His method is to select the statements in the biblical documents that pertain to military and police functions, and then to compare the various interpretations given. The discussion is illustrated with examples from literature and history. Concerning practical involvement in conflict situations, Rutenber finds Gandhian nonviolence as a possible measure, compatible with Christian commitment. At the same time, he recognizes that it may not always be effective. Effectiveness is not, however, the ultimate criterion by which Christians are to judge their actions; "God asks us to be faithful before he asks us to be successful in any such sense as war is successful."[36] Rutenber thus defines Christian pacifism in terms of its origin in the Christian revelation and finds its dynamic in Christian commitment.

The Theological Basis for Christian Pacifism[37] supports the same conclusion. This small book comprises four lectures of Dr. Charles E. Raven, former chancellor of Cambridge University, delivered at Union Theological Seminary and at Boston University in 1950. Raven demonstrates—by copious references to other theologians, biblical sources, and the tradition of the Christian church—that pacifism is the logical consequence of acceptance of the divine revelation of Jesus Christ. Recognizing the possible cost of full commitment to this ideal, he still finds it much more tenable philosophically than the compromise of dialectical theology.

The churches and Christian pacifism

A historical review of Christian pacifism readily reveals the fact that within Christendom there are widely differing views with regard to the social application of the love ethic of Jesus Christ. According to Roland H. Bainton in his work *Christian Attitudes toward War and*

---

[36] Culbert G. Rutenber, *The Dagger and the Cross* (Nyack, NY: Fellowship Publications, 1958), 116.

[37] Charles E. Raven, *The Theological Basis of Christian Pacifism* (New York: Fellowship Publications, 1951).

Peace,[38] three distinct views with regard to war are identified. These are the just war, the crusade, and pacifism.

In the category of the just war would be found the point of view represented by the school of thought identified with Professor Reinhold Niebuhr. In his book *Moral Man and Immoral Society*, Niebuhr deals with the dilemma encountered by the confrontation of an absolute Christian ethic of love and the world of pragmatic necessity. As a possible solution he postulates the recognition of a "basic difference between the morality of individuals and the morality of collectives, whether races, classes or nations."[39]

In his historical treatment of human society in its social and political dimensions, he points up the difficulties involved in the assumption that an absolute morality, whether religious or rational, may be applied with success to the complexities of society. Niebuhr advises that one face the situation realistically and suggests that the only way to resolve the conflict, at least in part, is to think in terms of a dualism of ethics: namely, one ethic for the individual and another for society. The former may derive from religious or rational assumptions, but the latter will be found in the human predicament itself.

In consideration of the dilemma of the Christian pacifist, Niebuhr defends the position of nonresistance as being clearly the ethic of Jesus Christ. He rejects the position only because of its idealism.

The same conclusion is borne out by the German scholar Ernst Troeltsch, whose monumental work in the sociology of the Christian religion, *The Social Teaching of the Christian Churches*, traces the development of the Christian church in its influence on, as well as its response to, society as a whole. Troeltsch demonstrates the thesis that the Christian movement has divided itself into three sociological types: the church type (highly structured institution), the sects (schismatic), and mysticism (individualistic). Pacifism is generally found within the sects, though not exclusively. The author's conclusion is: "All Christian-Social work is in a problematic condition. It is problematic in general because the power of thought

---

[38] Roland H. Bainton, *Christian Attitudes toward War and Peace* (New York: Abingdon Press, 1960).
[39] Reinhold Niebuhr, *Moral Man and Immoral Society* (New York: Charles Scribner's Sons, 1932), ix.

to overcome brutal reality is always an obscure and difficult question."[40] By this he does not mean to imply that Christianity is of no consequence, but rather that its essence is personal and inner rather than social.

Among other historical studies which trace the thought and practice of the Christian church particularly in relation to political conflict and war is *The Early Church and the World,* by C. John Cadoux, which begins with an analytical study of the teaching of Jesus and the apostles. Following an examination of the biblical material and the interpretations by the early church fathers, Cadoux traces the thought and practice of the church prior to the time of the Roman Emperor Constantine. He finds that the teaching of Jesus was clearly that of nonresistance and that "the early Christians took Jesus at his word and understood his inculcations of gentleness and nonresistance in their literal sense."[41] He proceeds to show, however, that the historical record up to the time of Constantine in the fourth century AD reveals the gradual acceptance of military service by the Christian community.

The sign of the cross became an imperial military emblem. This transition is shown to have come about as a result of a combination of factors—for example, no clear differentiation between the military and the police functions of the army, the Old Testament record of sanctioned warfare, and the uncritical mind of uninformed Christians. The change took place in spite of the doctrine of some of the theologians of the period.

The history of this period shows a clear capitulation on the part of the Christian community to the principle of resistance, thus deviating from the principle of nonresistance as understood originally to be the norm of Christian behavior.

Based somewhat on this study of Cadoux is a later work by G. J. Heering, entitled *The Fall of Christianity.* He identifies the period of Constantine as the turning point in Christian compromise with the state. Heering's conclusions are, briefly, that this compromise is related to the following:

1. too close alliance with the state;

---

[40] Ernst Troeltsch, *The Social Teaching of the Christian Churches,* trans. Olive Wyon (New York: Harper and Brothers Torchbooks, 1960), 1012.
[41] C. John Cadoux, *The Early Church and the World* (Edinburgh: T. and T. Clark, 1952), 256.

2. dominance of political expediency and the nationalist idea;
3. suppression of primitive Christian values and the false exegesis of the New Testament concurrent with it;
4. lack of a critical and reformatory Christian sociology for today; and
5. power of age-long tradition, maintained both naturally and artificially.[42]

These observations are made from a historical perspective.

The Church, the Gospel and War, edited by Rufus M. Jones, is a symposium of essays by American and British churchmen and authors. Under this general heading, the essays fall into two groups: first, the theological basis for pacifism, and second, a historical survey of the attitudes toward war as represented by the Christian church.

The authors demonstrate with the use of historical data and theological reasoning that nonparticipation in war is the only position consistent with a commitment to the Christian revelation. In content the book is selective rather than exhaustive. Its purpose is to serve as a prophetic voice, eliciting serious consideration of the subject by persons committed in faith to Jesus Christ. The thrust of the argument is implied in the editor's statement in the introduction: "Readers . . . will find it difficult to continue believing that the Church which Christ founded and informs by His living Spirit can go on blessing and supporting wars of the modern type."[43] Another book of this nature, *Not by Might,*[44] by A. J. Muste, a leader in the Christian pacifist movement for many years, gives an appraisal of the postwar international scene, and sets forth a proposal for the adoption of Christian principles as a radically new foreign policy for the United States.

Another brief history of Christian pacifism is that of Geoffrey F. Nuttall, comprising a series of five lectures under the heading *Christian Pacifism in History.* In these lectures delivered at a conference of the Fellowship of Reconciliation at St. John's College in York,

---

[42] G. J. Heering, *The Fall of Christianity,* trans. J. W. Thompson (New York: Fellowship Publications, 1943), 179.
[43] Rufus M. Jones, ed., *The Church, the Gospel and War* (New York: Harper and Brothers, 1948), xii.
[44] A. J. Muste, *Not by Might* (New York: Harper and Brothers, 1947).

England, in August 1957, Nuttall identifies five distinct avenues of approach to Christian pacifism. These approaches found expression historically as follows:

1. The Christians in the first three centuries of the church were pacifist primarily because of the fear of idolatry; service in the Roman army involved worship of the Roman deities.
2. Certain sects in the Middle Ages, because of the law of Christ as found in the Sermon on the Mount, withdrew from military activity.
3. Swiss Anabaptists and Dutch Mennonites in the sixteenth century saw the ministry of suffering as the alternative to coercion.
4. English Quakers in the seventeenth century were motivated in their pacifism by the concept of the dignity of humankind.
5. Christian pacifists of the twentieth century see pacifism as the means of redemption of a wicked social order.[45]

In all these historical studies there are allusions to the non-resistant tradition of the Mennonite denomination, and there are occasional references to the nonviolence of the Gandhian tradition. Each is referred to as typical or representative of a distinct point of view. The observations of these writers will thus help the investigator to identify the distinctive features of each school of thought, and to assess the meaning of each.

Psychology, sociology, and pacifism

Authors whose writings are included in this category see love in human society as a dynamic that is more healthful, and ultimately more constructive, than the hate upon which the institution of war is predicated. One of these authors from whom Mohandas K. Gandhi derived insight and direction was Henry David Thoreau, whose classic essay *Civil Disobedience* is referred to frequently in the literature about Gandhi. The essence of civil disobedience is, according to Thoreau, "action from principle,—the perception and the performance of right,—changes things and relations; it is

---

[45] Geoffrey F. Nuttall, *Christian Pacifism in History* (Oxford, England: Basil Blackwell, 1958), 3.

essentially revolutionary."[46] On this ground the citizen would be justified in engaging in civil disobedience where the state required support for or obedience to an action violating moral principle. It was this idea that appealed to Gandhi.

In his book *The Art of Loving,* Erich Fromm makes a contribution to thinking in the area of pacifism in presenting an analytical study of the complex human phenomenon of love. In the major chapter dealing with the theory of love, he identifies types of love as they are observable in relation to objects of love. Love in its finest form is an integrating whole.

In analyzing contemporary Western society, he observes that it is not conducive to the development of love, which has become a marginal phenomenon of present-day Western society. In support of this he says, "Not so much because many occupations would not permit of a loving attitude, but because the spirit of a production-centered, commodity-greedy society is such that only the nonconformist can defend himself successfully against it."[47] Faith in the possibility of love as a socially acceptable phenomenon is a rational faith, based on insight into the very nature of humankind. Fromm says: "Those who are seriously concerned with love as the only rational answer to the problem of human existence must, then, arrive at the conclusion that important and radical changes in our social structure are necessary, if love is to become a social and not a highly individualistic marginal phenomenon."[48] In conclusion, for further consideration of the social implications of this study, he directs the reader to an earlier book, *The Sane Society.*[49] Here he diagnoses the "cultural neuroses" of contemporary society and points the way to a society in which human love and creativity can flourish. Both books together represent the author's analysis of the nature of the human dilemma as well as of the potential for reconstruction.

In the same vein are the studies of Pitrim A. Sorokin. *Altruistic Love*[50] is a sociological analysis of five hundred persons nominated by the public as "good neighbors," and of thousands of saints of the

---

[46] Henry David Thoreau, *Walden* (contains the essay "On the Duty of Civil Disobedience") (New York: The New American Library, 1960), A Signet classic, 228.
[47] Erich Fromm, *The Art of Loving* (New York: Harper and Brothers, 1957), 132.
[48] Ibid.
[49] Erich Fromm, *The Sane Society* (New York: Rinehart and Company, 1955).
[50] Pitrim A. Sorokin, *Altruistic Love* (Boston: Beacon Press, 1950).

Roman Catholic and Greek Orthodox Churches. While the study is not statistically designed, it does reveal some data that would suggest further enquiry into the function of altruistic love. *The Ways and Power of Love*[51] is a sociological study of the types, factors, and techniques of moral transformation. The import is that love is a force which ought to be motivated and directed in the solution of the problem of social hostility.

Another study pertaining to the meaning of love and its power for the reconstruction of the individual and society is *Love against Hate*, by Karl and Jeanetta L. Menninger.[52] In this psychological study, the authors describe the basic conflicts of men and women. They show the many forces in the complexity of modern civilization that frustrate the love needs of humanity. Their hypothesis is that recognition of basic needs and freer expression of love would overcome the impulse to hate. When this adjustment takes place in the more intimate social relations, the same drive will, it is projected, tend to promote more amicable relations in the larger social units, and interrelations. Education needs to take into account that love and hate are both realities in human nature and consequently in all human relations.

Lewis Mumford in his book *In the Name of Sanity,* says, "We must uphold love and reason as more precious than life itself,"[53] and gives as his personal opinion that "the chief enemy of peace is the spirit of unreason itself: an inability to conceive alternatives, an unwillingness to reconsider old prejudices, to part with ideological obsessions, to entertain new ideas or to improvise new plans."[54] He concludes, asserting in a prophetic fashion that "now that power has over-reached itself, love offers the only alternative that will lead us back to life: The Sermon on the Mount has thus become the new Mount Everest that calls forth the human spirit today. Nothing less than that 'impossible ascent' remains as a practical alternative to our yielding to the destructive and inhuman forces that threaten our whole civilization."[55]

---

[51] Pitrim A. Sorokin, *The Ways and Power of Love* (Boston: Beacon Press, 1954).

[52] Karl Menninger and Jeanetta L. Menninger, *Love against Hate* (New York: Harcourt Brace and Company, 1959).

[53] Lewis Mumford, *In the Name of Sanity* (New York: Harcourt, Brace and Company, 1954), 7.

[54] Ibid., 206.

[55] Ibid., 241.

Causes and effects of war

In finding ways and means to prevent or avoid war, or to see it in proper perspective, it is necessary to probe into the causes of war. It is said that war begins in the minds of men. The authors considered in the books in this group have attempted to expose the real causes of some of the conditions that have impelled the United States and other countries into war.

In *The War Myth in United States History,* the author, C. H. Hamlin, exposes with documentary evidence incidents of fictional propaganda, deliberate misrepresentation, and illegal negotiation prompted by political and economic motives, which have been used to stimulate artificially a militaristic mentality in connection with the major wars engaged in by the United States up to the end of World War I. The thesis of the author is that the United States, like other countries, has been guilty of the use of the myth "that wars are defensive against an offensive enemy."[56] This, he asserts, is the war myth of every country.

Cry, the Beloved Country, by Alan Paton,[57] appears in the bibliography of pacifist literature not as a formal study but as a novel depicting a kind of social situation that breeds explosive tensions. It deals particularly with interracial tension in South Africa and is intended to elicit humanitarian concern and action. It demonstrates the absurdity of inhumanity and rationalized self-interest. In this method of presentation of social and economic abuse, the author uses an educational technique that can transform the attitudes of a people.

A resource work related to the whole problem of interracial tension is *An American Dilemma,* by Gunnar Myrdal. This two-volume analytical study is based on comprehensive research by many persons into the interracial problem in the United States. In the introduction, the author explains that "the practical purpose of the study is to construct, in a preliminary way, bases for rational policy. . . . The theoretical analysis will stress interrelation and trends."[58] The specific problems investigated are color, region,

---

[56] C. H. Hamlin, *The War Myth in United States History* (New York: Vanguard Press, 1927), 9.

[57] Alan Paton, *Cry, the Beloved Country* (New York: Charles Scriber's Sons, 1948).

[58] Gunnar Myrdal, *An American Dilemma* (New York: Harper and Brothers, 1944), lvi.

urban-rural residence, social class, education, sex, and age. Trends emerge and are identified as they obtained up to the time of World War II. It was noted that the greatest strides toward emancipation took place in the times of war. The findings, though to some extent dated, represent thorough research.

In his book *Ends and Means,* Aldous Huxley addresses himself to the urgency for a new mentality on the question of dealing with international tensions as follows: "The malleability of human nature is such that there is no reason why, if we so desire and set to work in the right way, we should not rid ourselves of war. . . . War is not a law of nature. . . . It exists because men wish it to exist. . . . We can wish otherwise than we actually do."[59]

The author then identifies and discusses the causes of war and makes the observation that the Christian civilizations of the West have sanctioned war, in contrast to the Buddhist and Hindu civilizations of the East. He attributes this to a basic belief about the nature of reality. The former, from the belief of human sinfulness and divine indignation, tend to sanction war, while the latter, emphasizing more mystic communion with God and less sense of sinfulness, tend to abhor hatred and the war method. The questions raised in this book seem to be related to basic questions of the nature of reality.

In another work, *An Encyclopedia of Pacifism,* Aldous Huxley gives brief explanatory discussions of terms and subjects relevant to pacifism. It was written before World War II and is to that extent limited in scope and data. The author's perspective is that of one who would expose the powerful realities of economic and political motivation obscured by patriotic propaganda. Of the opinion that the economic as well as the psychological system of modern societies needs to be changed, he postulates that these desirable changes would come about if "men and women specifically pledged to put pacifist principles into action in all the circumstances of life in personal relations, in economic relations, in politics, in education."[60]

In the book *War and Civilization,* extracts are collected on the subject of war from Arnold J. Toynbee's multivolume work, *A Study of History.* Toynbee asserts that "militarism has been by far the

---

[59] Aldous Huxley, *Ends and Means* (New York: Harper and Brothers, 1937), 105.
[60] Aldous Huxley, *An Encyclopedia of Pacifism* (New York: Harper and Brothers, 1937), 104.

commonest cause of the break downs of civilization."[61] He observes that war has occurred historically in a cyclical pattern and with increasing intensity and frequency. From the perspective of the whole sweep of human history, the successes achieved by the sword have been uneasily retained by the sword; in Toynbee's words, "Our survey has revealed the suicidal importunity of a sword that has been sheathed after having once tasted blood."[62] Therefore, as a historian, in view of the futility of and the unprecedented potential for destruction inherent in modern armameOnts and all that they represent, he appeals for a "renunciation of war as an instrument of policy."[63]

In the history of the United States there have always been efforts to restrain a rising militarism. Professor Merle Curti in *Peace or War: The American Struggle 1636-1936*[64] traces the history of these internal struggles. The total period is treated in shorter periods relating to major war efforts in United States history. He demonstrates that in each period there were individuals and organizations who sought to promote peaceful negotiations as opposed to armed conflict. Each chapter is documented with copious footnotes. The author finds justification for the observation that peace efforts achieved some notable goals. It is a fact of history, however, that in the larger objective of eliminating war, peace movements have failed. Two of the reasons suggested are the diverse philosophies that divide pacifists and the oversimplification of the obstacles to be overcome. By way of positive inference the author insists that ultimate success will depend on securing greater justice in all categories of human relationships, and in finding effective ways for curbing the forces that make war seem of value or of profit to powerful groups. Thus, according to Professor Curti the peace movement must concern itself with philosophical bases and its educational task.

---

[61] Arnold J. Toynbee, *War and Civilization* (New York: Oxford University Press, 1950), 130.
[62] Ibid., 164.
[63] Ibid., 143.
[64] Merle Curti, *Peace or War: The American Struggle 1636-1936* (New York: W. W. Norton & Company, 1936), 374.

With regard to provision for the conscientious objector in time of universal military conscription, *Conscription of Conscience*[65] is a comprehensive survey by Mulford Q. Sibley and Philip E. Jacob. It is designed to tell the story and to analyze the problem of the conscientious objector in World War II, and is limited to the United States during the period 1911–1947. Of particular relevance to the present study are the references to the Mennonite Church in relation to the state during this period of war. The survey of the Civilian Public Service program provides data showing the types of service rendered by conscientious objectors. Problems dealt with in the course of organization and administration reflect the underlying philosophy of the participants.

An inference drawn from the perusal of this body of literature is that the two schools of pacifist doctrine, one identified with Mohandas K. Gandhi, and the other with the Mennonite Church, represent distinct types. Inasmuch as Gandhi led a singular and successful independence movement in India, he and the technique he evolved have attracted the attention of a wide spectrum of humanitarian people searching for an alternative to war. It would appear from the thought represented in this body of literature that some form of nonviolent technique for the settling of disputes is the only method consistent with the highest rational, humanitarian, and religious ideals.

As Professor Curti pointed out in *Peace or War*, one of the major causes of failure in the peace movement throughout history has been the diverse philosophies that divide pacifists. It is with a view to facilitating understanding between the two schools that the investigator has projected the present research.

---

[65] Mulford Q. Sibley and Philip E. Jacob, *Conscription of Conscience* (Ithaca: Cornell University Press, 1952).

Chapter 3

Gandhian nonviolence: Satyagraha

I. History of satyagraha

Family of Mohandas K. Gandhi

MOHANDAS K. GANDHI was born on October 2, 1869, into a Hindu family of the Vaishnava sect.[1] His family lived in Porbander in the Gujarat area northwest of Bombay, where they were socially and politically important. The grandfather, the father, and an uncle had each served as prime minister at various times in several of the Kathiawar states. The Gandhis were Vaishyas by caste and were traditionally grocers by trade.

Gandhi wrote that his father was not particularly religious by nature and that there was little formal religious exercise by way of instruction in their home. The mother, on the other hand, was extremely devout in her own religious practice; she kept the fast days and visited the temples regularly. The lasting impression she made on him was that of saintliness. Strict vows were taken and kept, even in spite of illness or other interference. She would not take her meals unless she had first observed her daily prayers. This unflinching discipline was to appear also in her son.[2]

Dhirendra Mohan Datta[3] notes the maxim that was to influence his whole life and thought, learned in his childhood: "He learned from his mother and neighbors the Indian maxim . . . *Ahimsa Paramo Dharamah* [There is nothing higher than Truth]. Though this is universally acknowledged among the Hindus in all parts of India, it is most rigidly practiced by the Vaishnavas and particularly the

---

[1] The Vaishnava sect is one of the three great divisions of modern Hinduism in which Vishnu is identified with the Supreme Being; the Vaishnavites worship Vishnu exclusively, regarding him as creator, preserver, and destroyer of the universe. Theos Bernard, *Hindu Philosophy* (New York: The Philosophical Library, 1947), 201.

[2] M. K. Gandhi, *The Story of My Experiments with Truth* (Ahmedabad: Navajivan Publishing House, 1940), 4.

[3] Dhirendra Mohan Datta, *The Philosophy of Mahatma Gandhi* (Madison, WI: University of Wisconsin Press, 1953), 9.

Jains."[4] Likewise Charles Freer Andrews, a close personal friend of Gandhi for fifteen years in the period of his political activity, makes a similar observation: "The young boy's mother was a devout Hindu, who had a deep religious faith penetrating and inspiring her whole personal life and character. From his mother more than anyone else the child gained his religious nature. It becomes clear from his autobiography that no one so profoundly affected him in childhood as she did."[5]

As a child, he had a great fear of ghosts, and an old servant woman of the household recommended as a remedy the repetition of *Ramanama* (literally, the name of Rama). In later years, this was to become a very important part of Gandhi's personal religious life, but at this stage he recalls that he had more faith in the servant than in her cure. Nevertheless he began repeating Ramanama to overcome his fear of ghosts and spirits. In his autobiography Gandhi says: "I think it is due to the seed sown by that good woman Rambha that today Ramanama is an infallible remedy for me."[6] The repetition of the holy name had become a permanent part of his devotional life.

While these instances of religious devotion made some impression on him, there was little formal instruction. He recalls that during his school days up to his sixteenth year he was "taught all sorts of things except religion."[7]

Nevertheless there were certain circumstances and events that seem to have been significant in stimulating his reflection and inquiry about things religious. Their effect reveals something of the moral sensitivity of the young boy.

In his first year of high school, during the visit to the school of the inspector, Mr. Giles, the class was given a spelling exercise. When the teacher noticed that Mohandas had misspelled a word, he suggested a source of help by an appropriate gesture in the

---

[4] Jainism is a monastic reform movement stressing very rigid discipline. The five major vows for the monks were (1) do not steal, (2) do not lie, (3) do not kill, (4) abstain from sexual intercourse, (5) renounce all worldly things—especially property. These vows figured significantly in the discipline of Gandhi. Hermann Jacobi, "Jainism," *Encyclopaedia of Religion and Ethics* (New York: Charles Scribner's Sons, 1926), 3:465–74.

[5] Charles Freer Andrews, *Mahatma Gandhi's Ideas* (New York: The Macmillan Company, 1930), 13.

[6] Gandhi, *The Story of My Experiments with Truth,* 4.

[7] Ibid.

direction of his neighbor. Mohandas refused to comply and as a result was the only one in the class with a mistake in the exercise. Concluding the account of this episode Gandhi said: "The teacher tried later to bring this stupidity home to me, but without effect. I never could learn the art of copying."[8]

His response to two plays illustrates this moral sensitivity. He said they impressed him with the nature and value of duty. In the play *Shravana Pitribhakti Nataka,* there was a portrayal of extra-ordinary filial piety. His response to this was to take the example of the self-giving hero, Shravana, as normative for himself. Likewise, the play *Harischandra,* which portrayed the nobility of truthfulness, constituted a living challenge for him. He expressed his sentiments as follows: "Why should not all be truthful like Harischandra? was the question I asked myself day and night. To follow Truth and to go through all the ordeals Harischandra went through was the one ideal it inspired in me.[9]

Three other incidents, which in themselves may not be particularly significant, give an insight into the sensitive spirit of the young lad. Meat-eating was forbidden according to the moral code of the Gandhi family. Yet for a period of time Mohandas secretly shared meat meals with a friend. This involved lying to his mother in order to explain his lack of appetite for meals at home, causing him no little conflict, and he decided to refrain from meat-eating until he was older and responsible to no one but himself in regard to his diet.

He recalls that at the same period he took to smoking. The first step was to smoke the cigarette butts thrown away by his uncle. Then he and a friend began to steal money from the household servants in order to buy cigarettes. The stealing soon led to mental conflict that became so intolerable that he and his friend planned suicide. But, at the critical moment, they decided that, rather than committing suicide, they should give up smoking, which they did.

Another act of stealing, in which he took some of his father's gold in order to pay off his brother's debt, brought him into real despair. He saw that the only way out was to confess the theft, ask his father's forgiveness, and make suitable retribution. He wrote

---

[8] Ibid., 5.
[9] Ibid., 6.

out his confession and handed it to his ailing father, waiting with trepidation for his reply. His father's unexpected tears were ample evidence of his forgiveness, and Mohandas was greatly relieved. He felt at once his father's love, which seemed then more than human. Of this experience he wrote later: "This was, for me, an object lesson in *Ahimsa*. . . . When such *Ahimsa* becomes all embracing, it transforms everything it touches. There is no limit to its power."[10] Nanda in his biography of Gandhi observes: "The adolescence of Mohan was no stormier than that of many of his contemporaries; adventures into the forbidden land of meat-eating and smoking and petty pilfering were, and are not uncommon among boys of his age. What was extraordinary was the way his adventures ended."[11]

Another factor in his early environment that appears to characterize his later thought is found in the attitude of tolerance toward religions other than Hinduism. During the time of his father's illness, there were many visitors, among them Parsis, Muslims, and Jains. Gandhi's father listened sympathetically to them all as they discussed religious matters very seriously. The effect on young Gandhi was to inculcate in him a respect for all faiths. The exception was Christianity. His contact with Christianity was such that he developed a dislike for it, precipitated by hearing some Christian missionaries berating the Hindu gods in a public gathering.[12]

According to his own statement, the most important religious conviction to emerge from the various religious forces that played on him in this period was that "morality is the basis of all things and that truth is the substance of morality."[13] A Gujarati didactic stanza of Shamal Bhatt gripped his mind, and its precept "return good for evil" became a guiding principle for him. He quotes a translation of the stanza as follows:

> For a bowl of water give a goodly meal;
> For a kindly greeting bow thou down with zeal;
> For a simple penny pay thou back with gold;
> If thy life be rescued, life do not withhold.
> Thus the words and actions of the wise regard;
> Every little service tenfold they reward.

---

[10] Ibid., 20.
[11] B. R. Nanda, *Mahatma Gandhi* (Boston: Beacon Press, 1958), 22.
[12] Gandhi, *The Story of My Experiments with Truth*, 24.
[13] Ibid., 25.

But the truly noble know all men as one,
And return with gladness good for evil done.[14]

Formal education

Gandhi's formal education consisted of primary and secondary schooling in the city of Rajkot. In his thirteenth year he was married and as a result missed one year of school. He writes with much regret about the early marriage practice of the Hindus. His brother discontinued his studies entirely because of his own early marriage. Mohandas returned to school and passed the matriculation examination in 1887. His father had died the previous year, and the future of the family seemed to depend quite heavily on him. He had received the highest education of the four sons. In order to fulfill the hopes for public service the family had for him, Mohandas was sent to Bhavnagar for college studies. As the instruction was in English, he felt woefully handicapped, and consequently, at the end of the first term, returned to his home.

At this point a friend and adviser of the family, in whom they had a great deal of confidence, proposed that Mohandas go to England. It appeared the quickest and surest way to succeed to the *Diwanship*[15] of his deceased father. The three years of study involved in becoming a barrister, and abroad at that, would give him the qualifications and prestige necessary for this post. There were financial obstacles and caste prejudices to be overcome, but in September 1888, he sailed for England. Before going he made a vow, for the satisfaction of his mother, that he would have nothing to do with wine, women, or meat while he was abroad. His caste leaders, considering the trip abroad to be a violation of the Hindu religion, formally excommunicated him from the caste.

In England he was confronted with the problem of adapting himself to a new culture. He took great pains to find out what clothing he should wear. He made efforts to learn the art of dancing, taking special tutoring. He wanted to become an "English gentleman." But, after three months of rather extravagant efforts along this line, he settled down to more serious concerns. "Drapers and dance halls could not turn him into an English gentleman, but only

---

[14] Ibid.

[15] A diwan is a prime minister of a native state. *The Oxford English Dictionary* (Oxford: Clarendon Press, 1933), 3:298.

an English gentleman-about-town. His brother was straining the slender resources of the family, perhaps incurring debts to enable him to continue his studies in England. As he brooded over it all, he realized the folly of chasing the will-o'-the-wisp of an English gentleman."[16]

In reference to his study of law he recalls, "It took me nine months of fairly hard labor to read through the Common Law of England. For Broom's *Common Law,* a big but interesting volume, took up a good deal of time. Snell's *Equity* was full of interest, but a bit hard to understand. White and Tudor's *Leading Cases* from which certain cases were prescribed, was full of interest and instruction. I read all with interest. Williams' and Edwards' *Real Property,* and Goodeve's *Personal Property.*"[17]

He passed his examination and was called to the bar on the tenth of June, 1891. On the eleventh he was enrolled in the high court and the following day sailed for India. In spite of the discipline of the study and his success, he did not feel professionally or socially confident. He continued to compare himself with a famous Indian legal figure, Sir Pherozshah Mehta, and felt lost when he considered the fact that in his study he had not acquired any knowledge of Hindu or Muslim law. He recalled: "I had serious misgivings as to whether I should be able even to earn a living by the profession."[18] This same state of anxiety that had pursued him throughout his study in England persisted when he took up his work in India.

In his autobiography, he refers to other experiences that, while not a part of his formal education, were significant elements in his education in terms of his later political and social activity. Two such experiences are his contact with vegetarians and his introduction to many religious books. He became a convinced vegetarian and an active participant in the work of a vegetarian society. In this way he became acquainted with Sir Edwin Arnold, the author of *Light of Asia* and *The Song Celestial,* two books that moved him deeply. The former dealt with Buddhism, and the latter was a translation into English of the Hindu religious classic, the Bhagavad Gita. With regard to

---

[16] Nanda, *Mahatma Gandhi,* 28.
[17] Gandhi, *The Story of My Experiments with Truth,* 24.
[18] Ibid., 58.

the significance of these religious contacts, Nanda observes: "If any subject seemed to strike a vital chord in him it was religion."[19]

It was because of a contact with two brothers who were Theosophists that Gandhi realized how meager his knowledge of the Hindu religion was. On their suggestion he undertook to read Sir Edwin Arnold's translation of the Bhagavad Gita, and he was enthralled by the depth of meaning and the beauty of the translation. He mentions the following passage as having made a deep impression upon him:

> If one ponders on objects of the sense, there springs,
> Attraction; from attraction grows desire,
> Desire flames to fierce passion; passion breeds
> Recklessness; then the memory—all betrayed—
> Lets noble purpose go, and saps the mind,
> Till purpose, mind, and man are all undone.[20]

It was from this passage, to which Gandhi refers again and again, that he perceived the significance of the doctrine of nonattachment, which we shall note later. The same brothers recommended the reading of *Key to Theosophy*, by Madame Blavatsky, which he did read. He did not join the Theosophical Society, as these friends had hoped he would, but was stimulated to undertake further reading in Hinduism, which increased his respect for the religion of his fathers.

About this same time, he met a Christian vegetarian gentleman in a vegetarian restaurant. In the course of their acquaintance, this gentleman was instrumental in erasing some of the prejudice against Christianity that Gandhi had acquired from his experiences with Christians in his hometown of Rajkot. At the suggestion of this friend, he purchased a Bible and read it (especially the Old Testament) somewhat ploddingly. With regard to the New Testament, he had a different impression. He was especially moved by the Sermon on the Mount, with the injunction of Jesus, "But, I say unto you, that ye resist not evil: but whosoever shall smite thee on thy right cheek, turn to him the other also."[21] The similarity of the

---

[19] Nanda, *Mahatma Gandhi*, 30.
[20] *The Song Celestial or Bhagavad-Gita*, trans. Edwin Arnold (London : K. Paul, Trench, Trübner, 1900); quoted in Gandhi, *The Story of My Experiments with Truth*, 48.
[21] Gandhi, *The Story of My Experiments with Truth*, 49.

teaching of the Gita, the didactic poem of Bhatt, and the Sermon on the Mount, greatly appealed to him. He sought to synthesize what he had understood from these three sources, and the result was the conception of complete renunciation as the highest form of religion.[22]

Another book he recalled reading at this time was *Heroes and Hero Worship*, by Thomas Carlyle. The chapter that impressed him most, apparently, dealt with "The Hero as Prophet"; it consisted of an examination of the character of the prophet Mohammed, his bravery and his austere living.

With this introduction to religious studies and acquaintance with occidental vegetarianism, Gandhi acquired, in addition to his formal law education, two areas of interest he was to pursue even more seriously in the future. He was now returning to his native land to find his place in the courts. Slight of stature and rather timid by nature, with no unusual intellectual capacity, he did not appear to have the potential for the place of leadership in Indian affairs that was to become his. As Nanda observes: "Here was an earnest but diffident young man with a definite but limited range of interests. Not even the partial observer could have detected in this young barrister-at-law any promise of distinction when he sailed for India. He did not seem to be out for a brilliant career, least of all in law or politics."[23]

Louis Fischer comments in the same vein but more analytically:

> Gandhi's two years and eight months in England came at a formative phase of his life and must have shaped his personality. But their influence was probably less than normal. For Gandhi was not the student type; he did not learn essential things by studying. He was the doer, and he grew and gained knowledge through action. Books, people and conditions affected him. But the real Gandhi, the Gandhi of history, did not emerge, did not even hint of his existence in the years of schooling and study. . . . But only when it was touched by

---

[22] Ibid.
[23] Nanda, *Mahatma Gandhi*, 31.

the magic wand of action in South Africa did the personality of Gandhi burgeon.[24]

Gandhi was at the threshold of a public career that would be unique in many ways, but especially for the experiment and development of the weapon of Satyagraha.

His return to India from England

Upon return to India, he found his brother had made every provision within his power for Mohandas's happy adjustment both professionally and domestically. He had arranged for a meeting with the eminent lawyer of Bombay, Dr. Ferozshah Mehta, and others of the law profession. He had equipped their home with furnishings that would appeal to Mohandas, who had acquired a taste for things Western while abroad. There had even been some adaptation in the family diet. This enhanced standard of living was designed not only to please Gandhi but also to add the prestige his profession would demand. All these measures increased the financial and personal pressure on Mohandas to succeed as a barrister.

Mohandas was naturally of a shy disposition and faced with trepidation the urgent problem of achieving some success in his vocation. He felt particularly under strain as he contemplated starting his work in Rajkot, his native town. The following statement shows this rather clearly: "I had hardly the knowledge of a qualified *vakil* (pleader) and yet I expected to be paid ten times his fee! No client would be fool enough to engage me."[25] The result was that he went to Bombay to gain some experience in the high court, with the intention of returning to Rajkot at an appropriate time in the future. While there, he set out to qualify himself further by a study of Indian law, which had not been a part of his formal study in England. During his residence of several months in the city he had few clients—and his early performances in court were most disappointing to him. He attempted to get a position as an English teacher, but this did not materialize. He continued in law. He had some professional experience, but he could scarcely be considered successful. Consequently he returned to Rajkot. Here, too, he was to suffer disappointment, attributing the measure of

---

[24] Louis Fischer, *The Life of Mahatma Gandhi* (New York: Harper and Brothers, 1950), 28.

[25] Gandhi, *The Story of My Experiments with Truth,* 66.

success he enjoyed rather to family prestige than to professional competence. It was at this period that an offer came from a business firm in Porbander, the place of his birth, to serve its interests in connection with a major lawsuit in South Africa. If he accepted the offer, it would engage him for a year and give him ample financial remuneration. Also, this trip abroad would afford him the prospect of relief from the disappointments and frustrations he was experiencing in his native land. This, no doubt, had a strong appeal to him. Accepting the offer, he proceeded to South Africa, landing at Durban, Natal, in May 1893.

Louis Fischer points up the significant fact of his relationship with Raychandbhai while in Bombay. Gandhi was impressed by the religious learning and spotless character of this jeweler-poet, saying, "No one else has ever made on me the impression that Raychandbhai did." But, as Fischer points out,

> Gandhi did not accept Raychandbhai as guru. Hindus believe that every man should acknowledge a guru, a superior person, near or far, living or dead, as one's teacher, guide or mentor. . . . "The throne has remained vacant," he said. For a Hindu this is tremendously significant and for Gandhi it is endlessly revealing. With all his diffidence he was spiritually independent. Ideas came to him through books but chiefly through his own acts. He remade himself by tapping his own inner resources.[26]

In South Africa 1893–1914

The period in South Africa is important because it is here that the encounter with the grim realities of interracial injustices activated and challenged Gandhi. Soon after his arrival in South Africa, he discovered the limitations that circumscribed Asians and Africans, and the personal humiliation they experienced. The greatest tragedy to Gandhi seemed to be that his countrymen and women had accepted their circumstances without revolt. He soon became involved in efforts to bring about understanding and a measure of reform. As a result, he was rapidly thrust into leadership of the Indian community. Thus the spirit of the reformer became awakened

---

[26] Fischer, *The Life of Mahatma Gandhi*, 40.

and intensified, and South Africa was to become for him a place of preparation for his larger service to his motherland, India.

It is not within the scope of this study to delineate the social and political situation in South Africa during that period. What is significant is the emergence of the method of reform that became identified as satyagraha. The critical moment came when the government of South Africa proposed the Asiatic registration act, a measure for controlling the Indian population. The proposed ordinance required all Indian men, women, and children over eight to register with the authorities, submit to fingerprinting, and obtain a certificate they were to carry with them at all times. A person found without the certificate could be imprisoned, fined, or deported. This act applied not only to the poorer indentured laborers but to persons of wealth and property as well. This greatly incensed the Indian community, and a mass protest meeting was convened at the Imperial Theatre in Johannesburg, in September 1906. A resolution Gandhi had helped to draft was read and adopted. The adoption took the form of a religious vow, which Gandhi stressed was one that must not be broken regardless of the consequences. The pledge meant that no one would submit to the registration ordinance. Gandhi, who had the greatest regard for the significance of a religious vow, impressed upon the assembled crowd the meaning of what it had done, and challenged the people with his own determined stand: "There is only one course open to those like me, to die but not to submit to the law. It is quite unlikely, but even if everyone else flinched leaving me alone to face the music, I am confident that I would not violate the pledge."[27]

The movement thus launched had still to discover ways and means of achieving its ends. In the years between 1906 and 1914, Gandhi was completely engrossed in the implementation of the pledge. Some measure of reform was achieved, but this was by no means the most significant. As Nanda observes:

> The Gandhi who left South Africa in 1914 was a very different person from the callow diffident youth who had arrived at Durban in 1893. South Africa had not treated him kindly; it had drawn him into the vortex of the racial problem created by the domination of the Dark Continent by the white races.

---

[27] Nanda, *Mahatma Gandhi*, 94–95.

The tug of war which followed had matured Gandhi, given him his own original political philosophy and also helped him forge a new technique of social and political agitation, which was destined to play a great part in Indian politics in the next thirty years.[28]

How then did Gandhi and his colleagues proceed to guide the agitation? And how did this weapon of nonviolent agitation take form and substance?

Origins of satyagraha

During the resistance movement against the Asiatic Law Amendment Ordinance, the term *passive resistance* was at first used. As the struggle continued, however, it became clear to Gandhi that this term was inadequate. The concept and the form of the resistance was more positive and dynamic than the adjective *passive* connotes. Through the newspaper *Indian Opinion,* which became the voice of the movement, Gandhi extended an invitation for suggestions for a more acceptable term. The word *sadagraha* ("firmness in conduct") was submitted. It appealed to Gandhi, but he amended it to satyagraha ("firmness in truth"); *satya,* derived from the Sanskrit root *sat,* meaning "truth," and *agraha,* derived from another Sanskrit root, *graha,* meaning "grasp," formed satyagraha, meaning literally, holding on to truth.[29]

In his first book, *Hind Swaraj* (Indian Home Rule), published in 1909, Gandhi describes satyagraha as follows: "The gospel of love in place of that of hate. It replaced violence with self-sacrifice. It pits soul-force against brute force."[30] Convinced of the justice of the cause of the minority groups against the forces of imperialism, racism, and nationalism, Gandhi saw the possibility of overcoming these evils by utilizing and appealing to soul force. In 1908, when he was asked by his first biographer, Doke, about the origin of satyagraha, he mentioned the influence of Shamal Bhatt's poem, the Sermon on the Mount, and the Bhagavad Gita. In all three of these he saw the teaching of good for evil and became more confirmed in this opinion after reading Tolstoy. Nanda records:

---

[28] Ibid., 125.
[29] Joan V. Bondurant, *Conquest of Violence: The Gandhian Philosophy of Conquest* (Princeton, NJ: Princeton University Press, 1958), 12.
[30] M. K. Gandhi, *Hind Swaraj* (Ahmedabad: Navajivan Publishing House, 1938).

When I read in the Sermon on the Mount such passages as "Resist not him that is evil, but whosoever smiteth thee on thy right cheek turn to him the other also," and "Love your enemies and pray for them that persecute you, that ye may be sons of your Father which is in heaven," I was simply overjoyed, and found my opinion confirmed where I least expected it. The *Bhagavad Gita* deepened the impression, and Tolstoi's *The Kingdom of God is Within You* gave it permanent form.[31]

Datta points out what may have been a reason for this particularly strong appeal of Tolstoy's book. He says: "It should be noted that Tolstoi's spiritual interpretation of Christianity, the presence of God within, brought Christianity near to the Vedantic idea of man; his emphasis on the Sermon on the Mount and the conquering of hatred by love and evil by nonresistance seemed to Gandhi to be in exact conformity with Buddhist and Jain teachings about *ahimsa* put into social practice."[32] In course of his public service in South Africa, Gandhi continued to read many books about different religions. A friend by the name of Coates gave him material about Christianity. But the book that seems to have added the most to his thinking during this period was John Ruskin's *Unto this Last,* presented to him by an English friend, H. S. L. Polak. This Gandhi declared to be "the one book that brought about instantaneous and practical transformation in my life."[33] James K. Mathews notes this enthusiasm for Ruskin's work and points out that the book itself seems to have served as a catalyst: "It is hard for a reader to find in the essays just what Mr. Gandhi found. It was a characteristic of his to bring to a work much of his own thinking and find justification for the same there."[34] Gandhi summarized the points of special interest to himself, saying that the good of any one individual is contained in the good of all. And that as everyone had equal right to earn his livelihood, it mattered little whether he did so as a lawyer or as a barber. Each was of equal value from a utilitarian point of view. However, in terms of personal satisfaction, the life of the tiller of

---

[31] Nanda, *Mahatma Gandhi*, 95.
[32] Datta, *The Philosophy of Mahatma Gandhi,* 13.
[33] Gandhi, *The Story of My Experiments with Truth,* 220.
[34] James K. Mathews, "The Techniques of M. K. Gandhi as Religious" (PhD diss., Columbia University, New York, 1957), 56.

the soil and the life of the handicraftsman were most rewarding.[35] The inspiration derived from this book (and these particular ideas) led him to translate it into Gujarati under the title *Sarvodaya* ("the welfare of all"). It seems also that another concrete outcome was the establishment of Phoenix Farm. Thus did he attempt to put his idealism into practice. Moreover, *Sarvodaya* was to become a symbol of many experiments and efforts to promote the welfare of oppressed millions of his fellow countrymen and women in India.

Yet another influence in this period was an essay of the American Henry David Thoreau, *Civil Disobedience.* While in prison in South Africa for his revolutionary activities, Gandhi was in correspondence with Tolstoy, who sent him a copy of the essay, which appears to have been for him more a confirmation of what he already believed and was practicing than an initiation of any new ideas. The agitation had taken the form of civil disobedience, and it was motivated by the belief that a higher moral order could be appealed to in defiance of an unjust action of a state. Natesan cites the following statement of Gandhi in 1933:

> The statement that I had derived my idea of civil disobedience from the writings of Thoreau is wrong. The resistance to authority in South Africa was well advanced before I got the essay of Thoreau on Civil Disobedience. But the movement was then known as Passive Resistance. As it was incomplete I had coined the word *satyagraha* for the Gujarati readers. When I saw the title of Thoreau's great essay, I began the use of his phrase to explain our struggle to the English readers.[36]

While all these data indicate some influence on Gandhi, no one source can be judged to have been a major factor in awakening his social consciousness or in giving direction to the reformations he pursued. Gandhi was sensitive to the sufferings and frustrations of the oppressed and sought to find justice and freedom by methods that would be at once practical and moral. As his ideas developed, they took form and force, as well as vocabulary, in the dialectic of the circumstances and his intellectual pursuits. As he looked back

---

[35] Gandhi, *The Story of My Experiments with Truth,* 220.
[36] B. Natesan, "Gandhi and Thoreau," *Gandhi Marg* 2 (July 1958), 219.

over the development of satyagraha, he claimed to stand firmly in the tradition of Hinduism.

This is confirmed by most observers and students of Gandhi. Radhakrishnan, for example, said: "Entirely abjuring the use of any physical violence for attaining political ends; he has developed this new technique (of *satyagraha*) in the history of political revolution, a technique which does not inure [sic] the spiritual tradition of India but arises out of it."[37]

Throughout his life Gandhi was loyal to Hinduism, the religion of his fathers. He believed that since he was born a Hindu, he should remain a Hindu. But more than that, he appreciated the tolerance and scope for self-expression that seemed to him to be unique to Hinduism. "Not being an exclusive religion," it enables its followers to respect all other religions and to assimilate what they wish from them.[38] Also, he believed that the essence of truth was to be found beyond the form and content of any of the known religious systems. Hinduism, which he "prized above all others," was one of the many approaches to truth. True religion holds the devotee close to truth and changes his nature from within and purifies him. Thus human nature "finds full expression" in realizing the "true correspondence between the Maker and itself."[39]

While taking a position within the framework of Hindu tradition, he was not limited by adherence to any dogma or ritual as such, but sought the realization of truth as his own conscience led him. He asserted the final authority of his "moral sense" and "spiritual growth." For this reason, he found the accommodation and flexibility of Hindu tradition to his liking.

Into Indian politics

The first important work by Gandhi was a pamphlet entitled *Hind Swaraj, or Indian Home Rule.* It was written aboard ship while he was traveling from England to South Africa in 1908, and appeared first in installments in the columns of *Indian Opinion.* It was an answer to the Indian "school of violence and its prototype in South Africa." Gandhi said he felt violence was no remedy for India's ills, and that

---

[37] S. Radhakrishnan, ed., *Mahatma Gandhi: Essays and Reflections on His Life and Work* (London: George Allen and Unwin Ltd., 1939), 15.

[38] M. K. Gandhi, *Hindu Dharma,* ed. Bharatan Kumarappa (Ahmedabad: Navajivan Publishing House, 1950), 5–6.

[39] M. K. Gandhi, *My Religion* (Ahmedabad: Navajivan Publishing House, 1958), 3.

her civilization required the use of a different and higher weapon of self-protection. Satyagraha had been tested to some extent in South Africa, and it gave him confidence to suggest its use for India. In a preface to the 1921 edition of this pamphlet, he said of its message: "It teaches the gospel of love in place of that of hate. It replaces violence with self-sacrifice. It pits soul force against brute force."[40] Thus, several years before returning to his native land, he had formulated an approach to the problem of Indian home rule. The document was a critique of Western civilization, a castigation of English imperialism, and an appeal to Indian self-respect. It proposed passive resistance or soul force as the agent of liberation, and the necessity of developing the virtues of citizenship.

On his return to India in 1915, he took up a temporary residence at Tagore's school at Shantiniketan, and then established his own ashram at Sabarmati in western India, across the river from the city of Ahmedabad. Here Gandhi made his headquarters as he rose to leadership in the renascence of modern India. The ashram consisted of several simple whitewashed huts set in a pastoral environment overlooking the river. From a settlement of thirty members in the beginning, it grew gradually to 230, as more people gathered around the Mahatma.

1. Sabarmati Ashram. Some of the most active leaders in the independence movement began their careers at Sabarmati. The ashram was a symbol of the life of self-sacrifice Gandhi wished to inculcate in the minds of the leaders of the freedom movement. The monastic-like discipline of the ashram is interestingly described by Reginald Reynolds in *A Quest for Gandhi*.[41] Many who rallied to Gandhi's leadership seemed to have had the impression that the sole object of the freedom struggle would be the evacuation of British government, but Gandhi insisted that the major concern should be the uplift of the masses and preparation for responsible nationhood. Louis Fischer remarks that this approach "stood the Indian National Congress on its head" and meant trouble for Gandhi. But as he said, "Gandhi wanted a new Indian today, not just

---

[40] Homer A. Jack, ed., *The Gandhi Reader* (Bloomington, IN: Indiana University Press, 1956), 104.
[41] Reginald Reynolds, *A Quest for Gandhi* (New York: Doubleday and Company Inc., 1952), 5–13.

a new India tomorrow."[42] The Indian National Congress had been formed on December 28, 1885, and serving as a channel of Indian public opinion, it ultimately became the instrument of resurgent national aspirations. To this movement Gandhi brought a new emphasis: "Gandhi craved for his country a cultural regeneration and spiritual renaissance which would give it inner freedom and hence, inevitably, outer freedom, for if the people acquired individual and collective dignity they would insist on their rights, and then nobody could hold them in bondage."[43] It was this larger function which Gandhi envisaged for the Congress, and which characterized his whole career.

2. *Benares incident.* In a startling address, Gandhi gave expression to this point of view at the opening ceremonies in February 1916 of the Hindu University Central College in Benares. Before a glittering assemblage, including the viceroy, maharajas and maharanis, and other nobility, Gandhi spoke freely about everything that burned in his reformer's mind. The audience became unruly, and some of the dignitaries left the platform before the meeting was adjourned. But the Gandhi fame began to spread and to capture the imagination of the masses.[44]

3. *Champaran indigo problem.* In December of the same year, at the annual convention of the Congress, Gandhi's attention was drawn to the problem of the Champaran indigo farmers in north Bihar. The subsequent investigation, negotiation, and jail-going constituted the first satyagraha experiment in India, and is considered to have been one of the purest instances of it. It engaged Gandhi for almost a year. The significance of this success to the aspirations of Indians is summed up by Babu Rajendra Prasad, who was later to become the first president of the Republic of India. Writing about the Champaran reform, he said:

> The seed of Indian Swaraj has been truly sown in Champaran and the freedom which the poor, helpless down trodden tenants of Champaran have secured against the educated, ever-vigilant and wealthy planters, living under the protecting wings of the powerful government, is but a precursor of that larger freedom which, Indians, trampled under the

---

[42] Fischer, *The Life of Mahatma Gandhi,* 131.
[43] Ibid., 132.
[44] Ibid., 133–37.

heels for centuries, are going to achieve in their struggle for Swaraj.[45]

4. Ahmedabad mill workers' strike. Before the Champaran work was completed, Gandhi was called to assist in negotiation in a mill strike in his home city of Ahmedabad. It was here that another "first" transpired, his first fast. At his suggestion, the mill workers had gone on strike against their employers. He felt their grievances justified this action. Some of the mill owners were his personal friends. After two weeks of the strike, the workers were becoming discouraged and restless and were about to capitulate, and at this point Gandhi decided to fast until a settlement was made. He said that his motive was to encourage the workers, not to coerce the mill owners. He said: "As a Satyagrahi I knew that I might not fast against them, but ought to leave them free to be influenced by the mill-hands' strike alone."[46] The result of the fast was that a system of arbitration was established in the mills, which provided for the participation of both owners and workers. The system was functioning satisfactorily up to 1948.[47]

5. Kheda satyagraha. The next satyagraha campaign was conducted in Kheda[48] district, Gujarat, where Gandhi led the movement for the remission of taxes for peasants who had suffered a crop failure. It took the form of a pledge not to pay the taxes even if it should mean being dispossessed of their land. Eventually the authorities conceded to a compromise, whereby payment was required from the rich but not from the poor. This settlement had the effect of arousing an awareness of "strength and dignity on the part of the peasant." In spite of this measure of success, Gandhi did not consider the Kheda achievement a satyagrahi success. He referred to it as a Himalayan miscalculation or Himalayan blunder, because participants did not exercise proper restraint and became destructive—pulling up railroad tracks, derailing trains, and burning telegraph offices.[49]

---

[45] Babu Rajendra Prasad, *Satyagraha in Champaran* (Madras: S. Ganesan, 1928), 266.
[46] Jack, ed., *The Gandhi Reader,* 156.
[47] Fischer, *The Life of Mahatma Gandhi,* 157.
[48] M. K. Gandhi, *Gandhi's Autobiography: The Story of My Experiments with Truth* (Washington: Public Affairs Press, 1948), 531–38.
[49] M. K. Gandhi, *Satyagraha,* ed. Bharatan Kumarappa (Ahmedabad: Navajivan Publishing House, 1951), 365-66.

6. Rowlatt Act.[50] The passing of the Rowlatt Act by the government of India on March 18, 1919, precipitated a crisis and a turning point in Gandhi's attitude toward the British authorities. It was a disappointment to Indian nationalists who had anticipated more liberal legislation in the direction of dominion status for India.[51] It did not seem a fair reward for the service that half a million Indian solders had rendered in France in support of England during the war of 1914–18. Gandhi prepared to direct a civil disobedience campaign on the pattern of that in South Africa. It actually took the form of a *hartal*—a complete suspension of economic activity. This was Gandhi's first act against the British government as such. It was a nationwide appeal for action against the British authority in India, and the struggle continued in one form or another until the end of British rule in 1947.[52]

Of Gandhi's general popularity at this time, Nanda says: "Gandhi was swept to the top in 1919–20 because he had caught the imagination of the country. . . . Gandhi was now the Mahatma . . .; with his voluntary poverty, simplicity, humility and saintliness he seemed a Rishi (sage) of old who had stepped from the pages of an ancient epic to bring about the liberation of his country.[53]

The hartal Gandhi called for in April 1919 spread widely throughout the country and demonstrated how effective the populace could be. Gandhi had told the viceroy that the satyagraha campaign "constitutes an attempt to revolutionize politics and restore moral force to its original station." But he had not anticipated the anarchy that ensued. In Bombay, in Ahmedabad, and other places where Gandhi addressed the people, he remonstrated with them for burning buildings, forcibly taking weapons, stopping trains, cutting telegraph wires, and plundering shops and private homes. As penance he undertook a seventy-two hour fast and asked the people to fast for twenty-four hours.[54]

---

[50] The Rowlatt Act gave arbitrary powers to the authorities to arrest, confine, imprison, or otherwise punish persons who were suspected of being concerned in movements prejudicial to the security of the State. Editor's note in Gandhi, *Satyagraha,* 102.

[51] A dominion was a self-governing colony or autonomous state within an empire.

[52] Fischer, *The Life of Mahatma Gandhi,* 176.

[53] Nanda, *Mahatma Gandhi,* 212.

[54] Fischer, *The Life of Mahatma Gandhi,* 178–79.

On April 18 he called off the movement. But an unforgettable incident had taken place in Punjab: the Jallianwalla Bagh massacre, in the city of Amritsar. There, at the command of British Brigadier General Reginald Dyer, an unauthorized public gathering was fired on, with the intent to enforce due respect for authority. According to official British Raj reports, 379 persons were killed and 1,137 wounded as they tried to escape from the confines of the partly enclosed meeting ground. The whole incident fanned latent hatred for the ruling power. Fischer states that "Jallianwalla Bagh quickened India's political life and drew Gandhi into politics."[55] The Hunter Commission, which investigated the Jallianwalla Bagh incident, wavered in its criticism of official action; and when subsequently the House of Lords declined to condemn General Dyer, Gandhi took what Radhakrishnan described as the "great decision of his life to refuse to co-operate with the British Government." He quotes part of Gandhi's letter of August 1, 1920, to the viceroy:

> Half of India is too weak to offer violent resistance, and the other half is unwilling to do so. I have therefore ventured to suggest the remedy of non-cooperation, which enables those who wish to dissociate themselves from Government, and which if unattended by violence and undertaken in an ordered manner, must compel it to retrace its steps and undo the wrongs committed; but, whilst I pursue the policy of non-co-operation, insofar as I can carry the people with me, I shall not lose hope that you will yet see your way to do justice.[56]

Our purpose now is to examine the doctrine of nonviolence Gandhi applied to the realization of nationhood, which from the earliest stages of application in South Africa came to be known as satyagraha.

II. Metaphysical presuppositions

In the foyer of the Gandhi Memorial Museum and Library in New Delhi, India, there is inscribed the following statement of Mr. Gandhi: "My devotion to Truth has drawn me into the field of politics and I can say without the slightest hesitation and yet in all humility

---

[55] Ibid., 184.
[56] Radhakrishnan, ed., *Mahatma Gandhi,* 29.

that those who say that religion has nothing to do with politics do not know what religion means."

This declaration suggests that Gandhi was called on to defend his involvement and his unique philosophy in politics, because he was assailed either as an impractical idealist in politics, or primarily a political opportunist misusing religion. At any rate, his own testimony would indicate that he became involved and continued to be sustained in his political activities on the basis of an essentially religious point of view. In so doing he did not claim to be originating philosophy, but in his own words, "I have simply tried in my own way to apply the eternal truths to our daily life and problems."[57] These eternal truths he claimed to find primarily through the Hindu religion, though he claimed to have derived insights and inspiration from other religions as well. He called himself an orthodox—Sanatani—Hindu. Mathews, in his investigation of the satyagraha techniques of Gandhi, has shown that "the determinative force in Mr. Gandhi's life and work was Hinduism. . . . He was born a Hindu, lived according to the presuppositions of Hinduism and died a Hindu."[58]

The implication of this conclusion is, according to Mathews, twofold: (a) it is a corrective to a misleading view that Gandhi was strongly Christian, and (b) it is a clue to a clearer understanding of the man and his work.

At the same time, Gandhi was not a learned Hindu and was not versed in all the intricacies of Hindu philosophy. At least Datta, commenting on one of Gandhi's philosophical explanations, said, for example:

> This paragraph shows to an expert in Indian philosophy that Gandhi is using the words *advaitist, dvaitism* and similarly *anekantavadi* and *syadvadi* without the precise knowledge of the meanings of those terms in technical philosophical discussions. But being aware that he is being dialectically driven beyond his depth he confesses, frankly enough, that he has been using words in his own sense, not like the learned.[59]

---

[57] M. K. Gandhi, *Harijan,* March 28, 1936.
[58] Mathews, "The Techniques of M. K. Gandhi as Religious," 196.
[59] Datta, *The Philosophy of Mahatma Gandhi,* 25.

Thus with this word of caution, and considering Gandhi a practicing Hindu by persuasion, the student may be prepared to understand his thought. As his basic ideas are few and as these are frequently repeated, it is possible to identify them. As this study pertains to his concept of satyagraha, we are concerned with the metaphysical presuppositions that support it. That these were religious in nature there is no doubt. Dhawan finds that "his political philosophy and political technique are only corollaries of his religious and moral principles. For him politics bereft of religion is a death trap because it kills the soul, for politics like other human activities must be governed by religion or irreligion."[60] What, then, are the religious and moral principles that govern the technique of satyagraha?

Concept of God

The nucleus of Gandhi's thought was his idea of God, according to Datta. He did not claim to have originated any philosophical system or even any principles. He took what he understood as "the eternal truths" and tried to apply them to life.

Gandhi used many terms—pronouns, adjectives, and verbs—suggestive of the idea of a personal God. Yet to identify God in this way would have been, according to Gandhi, to misunderstand God's full nature. He was familiar with the thousand names of God which he was taught to use as a child, but none seemed as appropriate as Truth. At best the names and the attributes ascribed to God were partial insights into the real nature of God. In one editorial he summarized some of his understanding of God. To him God was truth, love, conscience, morality, and fearlessness. God was a personal God to those who needed a personal God. He was embodied to those who needed his touch. God was long-suffering and allowed his creatures free will, but he was also their tyrant. His existence was perceived by faith.[61] Thus the God of Gandhi's conception corresponds to the needs of humanity. He is personal, with personal attributes, to those who may realize him best in that way. Yet Gandhi thought of these as merely approaches to God. He believed that every search, if persistently and honestly pursued, would lead ultimately to one

---

[60] Gopinath Dhawan, *The Political Philosophy of Mahatma Gandhi* (Ahmedabad: Navajivan Publishing House, 1946), 41.

[61] M. K. Gandhi, *Hindu Dharma,* ed. Bhamaran Kumarappa (Ahmedabad: Navajivan Publishing House, 1958), 54.

ultimate reality. This applied to all who sought truth through the various religions or through intellectual disciplines. Ultimate reality, however, was universal. He himself employed the name Rama for this "all-powerful essence" with its many-sided approaches. Also, to Gandhi this belief in the oneness of God implied the unity of all humankind, as is seen in the following statement: "I believe in absolute oneness of God and therefore also of humanity. . . . I believe in the essential unity of man and for that matter all that lives."[62] He perceived this as the clue to the ultimate success of satyagraha. All being essentially a unity could only mean that in the dialectic between truth and untruth, between good and evil, truth would ultimately prevail. Eventually Gandhi came to express his faith in the brief creed "Truth is God." He describes this as the resolution of a search of more than fifty years, during which time he held God is truth. This new concept meant to him that "Truth was the substance of reality."[63] Datta's comments on the significance of this change in Gandhi's thought, "but let it not be forgotten that this was an extension of his early faith in God and not a relinquishing of anything that was vital in it."[64] And in the same context, Datta describes some of the factors that may have contributed to this solution. He proposes that such a view was more encompassing and could therefore command broader sympathy; it disarmed those who were skeptical of traditional theistic beliefs.

What this meant in actual experience for Gandhi was the realization of God through reason and intuition. When asked, "What then is Truth?" his reply was, "A difficult question, but I have solved it for myself by saying that it is what the voice within tells you."[65] The intuitive dimension is expressed in a statement he made in a discussion of the exercise of prayer: "It is faith that steers us through stormy seas, faith that moves mountains and faith that jumps across the ocean. That faith is nothing but a living, wide-awake consciousness of God within."[66] In an interview with Basil Matthews in 1936 concerning his religious practices, a question was asked about the seat of authority. Gandhi, saying "It lies here,"

---

[62] M. K. Gandhi, *Young India* (1927–1928) (Madras: Ganesan Press, 1935), 421.

[63] M. K. Gandhi, *Autobiography: The Story of My Experiments with Truth* (Boston: Beacon Press, Inc., 1947), 87.

[64] Datta, *The Philosophy of Mahatma Gandhi*, 36.

[65] Gandhi, *Hindu Dharma* (1958), 60.

[66] Ibid., 104.

pointed to his breast. But he went on to say that he subjects every scripture ultimately to reason, He said: "I cannot let a scriptural text supersede my reason. . . . I cannot surrender my reason whilst I subscribe to divine revelation. . . . But you must not misunderstand my position. I believe in Faith also, in things where Reason has no place, e.g., the existence of God."[67]

The fullest realization of God came, according to Gandhi, in service to humankind, particularly to the poor and needy. In 1936 he wrote in *Harijan:* "Man's ultimate aim is the realization of God, and all his activities, social, political, religious, have to be guided by the ultimate aim of the vision of God. The immediate service of all human beings becomes a necessary part of the endeavor, simply because the only way to find God is to see Him in His creation and be one with it."[68]

Varma sees in this idea of God a relationship to his humanity. In true Hindu tradition, Gandhi considered each human being as well as each living creature a part or a "spark" of God. Especially did he advise service to the poor and suffering as the best way to realize God. In fact, he used a special term, *Daridranarayan,* God of the poor or God appearing in the hearts of the poor, to describe this experience.[69]

For Gandhi, God was not some remote reality residing somewhere beyond the clouds, but God was nearer, he said, than "fingernails to the flesh"; and in the same context, he specified, "God is in every one of us and therefore, we have to identify ourselves with every human being without exception."[70] Benay Gopal Ray comments that this pantheistic attitude of Gandhi is a direct outcome of his Vaishnava mind. The motto of a Vaishnava is *Vasudevah sarvamidam* or "Everything is He." But this reality is not a spirit but rather the essence of law. Ray says that in this conception, "He is the synthesis of the various laws. All natural laws are divine laws. Laws of logic are His laws, and He cannot override any of them."[71]

---

[67] Ibid., 54.
[68] M. K. Gandhi, *Truth Is God,* comp. R. K. Prabhu (Ahmedabad: Navajivan Publishing House, 1959), 30.
[69] V. P. Varma, *The Political Philosophy of Mahatma Gandhi and Sarvodaya* (Agra: Lakshmi Narain Agarwal Publishers, 1959), 59.
[70] Benay Gopal Ray, *Gandhian Ethics* (Ahmedabad: Navajivan Publishing House, 1958), 20.
[71] Ibid.

It is this concept of God as law which seems to be inherent in the formula or equation that Gandhi stressed, namely, Truth is God.

Datta explains what this meant to Gandhi in practice. It meant that though he was a lover of God, he was not satisfied with mere abstract contemplation or the observance of ritual. It meant expecting God to "rule the heart and transform it." In other words, "acceptance of God means to allow love, truth, reason to rule the heart and remove selfishness, ill will, ignorance and unreason, and all the passions like anger, greed, and lust that follows therefrom. Therefore the essence of religion is morality."[72] Morality meant the observance of law, and this law centered in God. In a 1928 editorial in *Young India,* he wrote, "There is orderliness in the universe, there is an unalterable law governing everything and every being that exists or lives. It is not a blind law; for no blind law can govern the conduct of living beings. . . . That Law then which governs all life is God."[73]

Again in similar words, in *Harijan,* 1946, he said, "God is not a person. He transcends description. He is the Law-maker, the Law and the Executor."[74] From these statements it may be deduced that God for Gandhi was transcendent, immanent, dependable, and dynamic—in essence, cosmic moral law.

Concept of the human

After tracing traditional and modern views of humankind in Hindu philosophy, Datta summarizes the distinctive characteristics of Gandhi's view. His observation is that Gandhi utilized the new positive ideas of modern India by assimilating them in thought, living them in his life, and giving them social and political shapes. "His notion of the presence of God in man amounts to belief that man has free will, reason, conscience, and love. Man is the maker of his destiny. If he chooses to use his reason correctly and guides his life by listening to the dictates of his conscience (the inner voice of God) and lives with his fellow beings with love in his heart, he can realize God and bring heaven on earth."[75]

He believed also that the highest level of fulfillment of humanity was no easy matter, but would take time and discipline.

---

[72] Datta, *The Philosophy of Mahatma Gandhi,* 42.
[73] Gandhi, *Truth Is God,* 7.
[74] Ibid., 22.
[75] Datta, *The Philosophy of Mahatma Gandhi,* 70.

The struggle involves the body and the spirit and may continue into another lifetime. For he believed in the inexorable *karma*.[76] He declared his strong desire to attain ultimate liberation from the karma and *sanskara*, though it was not an easy matter to overcome the effect of past deeds. He was hopeful and was comforted in the belief that there was the prospect of rebirth, if his ultimate goal of liberation were not achieved in this life.[77] Gandhi believed that this struggle was depicted allegorically in the Bhagavad Gita. The battle of Kurukshetra described therein was for him a symbolic representation of the struggle between good and evil in the human heart. The battlefield was the human soul, wherein Arjuna, representing higher impulses, struggles against evil. Krishna is the "dweller within," ever whispering to a pure heart. This, Gandhi asserted, described the duel that went on in the human heart.[78]

III. Ethical principles

Gandhi affirmed again and again that his chief concern was the pursuit of truth. This, as we have noted, he understood to be realized through both reason and faith. He conceived of truth as ontological and not to be enjoyed for its own sake, not as a subject for intellectual exercise, but to be worshiped. And this worship, for Gandhi, took the form of service to one's fellow men and women. When asked by Radhakrishnan about his religion and its bearing on life, for a contribution to a symposium on Indian philosophy, he replied: "Realization of Truth is impossible without a complete merging of oneself in, and identification with, this limitless ocean of life. Hence, for me, there is no escape from social service, there is no happiness on earth beyond or apart from it."[79]

Again, Roland W. Scott, in his study of *Social Ethics in Modern Hinduism,* says with regard to Gandhi's unique contribution: "He achieved an original contribution in his distinctive alliance of ethical belief with social activity, and the forceful awareness of human values on a scale, and to a degree, unique in modern Indian history. . . . Morality for him was equivalent to religion, when it was understood as

---

[76] Karma is the law of causality, and Sanskara is the effect of Karma. Bernard, *Hindu Philosophy,* 172, 192.

[77] Gandhi, *Hindu Dharma* (1958), 124.

[78] Fischer, *The Life of Mahatma Gandhi,* 32.

[79] S. Radhakrishnan and J. J. Muirhead, eds., *Contemporary Indian Philosophy* (New York: The Macmillan Company, 1936), 21.

man's duty to man. Unselfish service of others was the moral law of the universe."[80] Thus there is a close relationship between metaphysical presuppositions and ethical principles. In essence, the devotion attached to the object of belief, namely, truth, was equivalent to the individual devotee's involvement in right social action.

This relationship between metaphysical belief and social action is important, for the reason pointed out by Radhakrishnan:

> The Bhagavadgita exalts the idea of action as the way to God, but Schweitzer reminds us that such action was to be empty of all motive. . . . If Gandhi and Tagore today adopt an ethical view of life, it is certainly to be traced to their contact with the Christian West. The whole development of Indian thought is described as gradual weaning from "world and life negation" to the more rational "world and life affirmation."[81]

With this understanding of the relationship between ethical behavior and metaphysical belief, it is our purpose to investigate the norms or principles of ethical behavior. Datta observes, "Though the different systems of Indian philosophy differed widely on metaphysical questions, there was a great unanimity among them in Ethics."[82] He goes on to say that there is also unanimity about those basic virtues that everyone should try to practice. These five cardinal virtues were harmlessness (ahimsa), truthfulness (satya), nonstealing (asteya), chastity (brahmacharya), and nonacceptance (aparigraha). Gandhi accepted these five virtues and interpreted and applied them to the conditions of his time as he understood them. It is therefore appropriate to examine his definition and employment of them.

Ahimsa

Literally, ahimsa means "noninjury." It was thus used in the Upanishads, in Buddhism, in Jainism, and in the orthodox laws of Manu. The Jains went so far as to apply the restriction to all living things that moved. Even speaking of killing, or thinking of it, was taboo.

---

[80] Roland W. Scott, *Social Ethics in Modern Hinduism* (Calcutta: Y.M.C.A. Publishing House, 1953), 89.

[81] S. Radhakrishnan, *Eastern Religions and Western Thought* (New York: Oxford University Press, 1940), 68.

[82] Datta, *The Philosophy of Mahatma Gandhi,* 86.

Manu allowed the killing of sacrificial animals.[83] Gandhi, on the basis of his reading of books of Hinduism and also of other religions, conceived of ahimsa in positive terms, equating it to love in many statements but defining it as "the largest love," or "the greatest charity." In his own definition of ahimsa, Gandhi said, "I accept the interpretation of *ahimsa,* namely, that it is not merely a negative state of harmlessness but it is a positive state of love, of doing good even to the evil-doer."[84] He likened it to the love spoken of by Paul in the New Testament, expressed in the Greek term *agape,*[85] meaning self-sacrificing love. But ahimsa, for Gandhi, went beyond the Pauline application to include not only humankind but all creation.[86] Ahimsa is also the way to truth. Gandhi maintained that without ahimsa, it would be impossible to find truth. In fact, ahimsa and truth are so closely related that he compares them to two sides of a coin. Ahimsa is the means and truth is the end.[87] In this same context, he said that this relationship between ahimsa and truth implies that humanity's chief or supreme duty is ahimsa. Every means, however noble and good its end, must also be subject to the criterion of ahimsa: nonviolent, self-sacrificing, love.

Satya

The second cardinal virtue or ethical principle is inherent in the concept "Truth is God." The same Sanskrit word *satya* also means "truthfulness."[88] In Gandhi's use, satya as a behavioral principle means there should be "Truth in thought, Truth in speech, and Truth in Action."[89] Observance of truth in thought was conceived of as the pursuit of right knowledge. When truth is sought sincerely and devotedly, it will ultimately be realized, though in the process it may appear at times different to different persons. Gandhi illustrated this by likening the variety of conceptions of truth to the variety of leaves on a tree. Humanity is always limited, however, and cannot expect to attain or achieve absolute truth or truthfulness.

---

[83] T. W. Rhys Davids, "Ahimsa," *Encyclopedia of Religion and Ethics,* ed. James Hastings (New York: Charles Scribner's Sons, 1926), 1:231.
[84] Quoted in Clarence Marsh Case, *Non-Violent Coercion* (New York: The Century Company, 1923), 363.
[85] 1 Corinthians 13.
[86] M. K. Gandhi, *For Pacifists* (Ahmedabad: Navajivan Publishing House, 1949), 5.
[87] Gandhi, *Hindu Dharma* (1958), 224.
[88] Datta, *The Philosophy of Mahatma Gandhi,* 94.
[89] Gandhi, *Satyagraha,* 39.

The test of truth is to apply it to practical problems of life. For example, "If we once learn how to apply this never-failing test of Truth, we will at once be able to find out what is worth doing, what is worth seeing, what is worth reading."[90] The acceptance of this principle and its fulfillment engages one in self-examination and self-discipline. Gandhi said that the realization of truth involved self-suffering. By this he meant "single-minded" devotion and "indifference to other interests."[91] In the practical working of satya, the individual acknowledges error or departure from truth and is then free to make another approach to truth. Truthfulness or satya liberates the individual from selfish interests. It is therefore true devotion to truth. Gandhi's perception is made explicit in the following editorial statement in Young India: "A Satyagrahi, whether free or incarcerated, is ever victorious. He is vanquished only when he forsakes truth and nonviolence and turns a deaf ear to the Inner Voice."[92] Satya is therefore enunciated as a basic ethical principle requiring the pursuit of truth with all truthfulness in thought, speech, and deed—an important principle in the discipline of the satyagraha worker.

Asteya

Asteya is the third cardinal virtue and literally means "non-stealing." It is compatible with nonviolence, for to appropriate without permission that which belongs to another is to deal violently with him. As with the previous principles, Gandhi amplified it, or one may say, made certain inferred applications. In this case, non-stealing meant also to desist from exploitation in any form. In an editorial dealing with a problem of crime, he stated that the one who amasses wealth greedily and unfairly is just as guilty of robbery as any thief. A facade of respectability might shield him from the law, but he is a thief nonetheless.[93] On another occasion, addressing himself to the residents of the Ashram from Yeravda Prison, he advised, "One who follows the observance of 'Nonstealing' will bring about a progressive reduction of his own wants. . . . One who observes the principle of 'Non-stealing' will refuse to bother himself about

---

[90] Ibid.
[91] Ibid.
[92] Ibid., 236.
[93] Ibid., 351.

things to be acquired in the future."[94] Thus non-stealing or asteya as an ethical principle has personal as well as social implications and applications. It accounts no doubt to a great degree for the austerity that Gandhi observed personally and which he promulgated in the ashram and among satyagraha trainees.

Aparigraha

The fourth cardinal virtue or ethical principle, *aparigraha*, may be translated as "non-acceptance." Datta explains that in Hindu tradition it involved a vow of non-possession, especially for the hermits who resigned themselves to living on nature's wild fruits and on unsolicited gifts from others. But for ordinary persons ,it meant non-acceptance of any unnecessary thing.[95] In explaining the meaning of this principle, Gandhi compared it to the liberty of the birds, who have neither dwellings nor stores of food. They do not concern themselves about future needs. This, he said, should be the attitude of the "seeker after Truth" and the "follower of the law of love."[96] This emphasis on simplicity and austerity is directly related to his religious idealism, but there is also evidence that it was an operational necessity. It was a necessary discipline for effective satyagraha. Gandhi, in an editorial of 1914, early in his experience with satyagraha, said, "The use of this force Satyagraha requires the adoption of poverty, in the sense that we must be indifferent whether we have the wherewithal to feed or clothe ourselves."[97] Another very perceptive observation is made with regard to the relevance of this principle in the exercise of satyagraha: "Many sacrificers imagine that they are free to receive from the people every thing they need, and many things they do not need, because they are doing disinterested service. Directly this idea sways a man, he ceases to be a servant, and becomes a tyrant over the people."[98]

---

[94] M. K. Gandhi, *From Yeravda Mandir* (Ahmedabad: Navajivan Publishing House, 1930), 19–22.
[95] Datta, *The Philosophy of Mahatma Gandhi*, 99.
[96] Gandhi, *Satyagraha*, 46.
[97] Ibid., 35.
[98] Ibid.

This principle of non-acceptance, non-possession, or selfless action Gandhi understood to be the chief message of the Bhagavad Gita.[99]

Brahmacharya

The fifth cardinal ethical principle, *brahmacharya,* is literally "continence." Etymologically, it means the way of life dedicated to Brahma or God. Datta points out that in Hindu tradition the general meaning of the term is "a life of celibacy which was regarded essential both for a student of the Vedas and also for one who would devote himself to the realization of God. Along with celibacy were associated all kinds of self-restraint."[100] According to the laws of Manu, abstinence from sexual relations is essential for a male student up to twenty-five years of age. Then from twenty-five to fifty, every able-bodied man should marry and rear a family. This is the period of the householder, during which brahmacharya took the form of marital loyalty and self-control. Beyond fifty years of age, religious duty requires absolute self-control. Gandhi took a brahmacharya vow as early as 1899, when he was thirty years of age and when their family consisted of four sons. This decision was really a measure to limit the size of the family. But like other ideals, it also underwent some transformation. As Nanda said, "Finally Gandhi came to the conclusion that Brahmacharya in the narrower sense of sexual restraint was impracticable without the Brahmacharya in the widest sense—the control of all the senses in deed, word, and thought. It was not a question of the disciplining of one appetite but all appetites; it was a rule of life."[101]

In Gandhi's view, brahmacharya vows were found to be difficult only because other than sexual desires were allowed free satisfaction. He considered the restraint of the palate absolutely essential, and therefore provided for this in the ashram discipline.[102] The discipline of brahmacharya appealed to Gandhi as a desirable aspect of the training of the satyagraha, because in the sublimation of natural desires higher creative energies were released. Also, the disciplined behavior of a satyagrahi in time of crisis or nonviolent

---

[99] Mahadev Desai, in introductory remarks to M. K. Gandhi, *The Gita according to Gandhi* (Ahmedabad: Navajivan Publishing House, 1956), 10.
[100] Datta, *The Philosophy of Mahatma Gandhi,* 100.
[101] Nanda, *Mahatma Gandhi,* 84–85.
[102] Gandhi, *Hindu Dharma* (1958), 226–27.

action required a previous conditioning to which brahmacharya contributed.

Abhaya

To the five cardinal virtues Gandhi added a sixth, *abhaya* ("fearlessness"),[103] an important part of the armament of the satyagrahi, for without fearlessness, without courage, the satyagrahi could not meet the demands of satyagraha. Those alone can follow the path of passive resistance who are free from fear, whether about their possession, their honor, their physical welfare, or life itself.[104] Thus fearlessness appears as a value rather than a moral teaching and therefore is not directly an ethical principle. It makes possible the fulfillment of ethical principles.

Sarvodaya

Sarvodaya was the term used for the comprehensive program of social uplift. It emerged from the reading of Ruskin's *Unto this Last* and means literally "the welfare of all." Gandhi was concerned not only about the political liberation of India but also about the liberation from poverty, disease, superstition, untouchability, and lethargy. In these concerns Gandhi was taking his place in the stream of modern Hinduism, in the tradition of Ram Mohan Roy, which stressed the affirmation of life in contrast to the fatalistic indifference characteristic of traditional Hinduism.[105] Sarvodaya comprised the total program of social betterment and was also described as the "Constructive Program." In 1940 he described the constituent social efforts as follows: (1) Hindu-Muslim unity, (2) removal of untouchability, (3) prohibition, (4) *khadi* (use of homespun cloth), (5) other village industries, (6) village sanitation, (7) basic education, (8) adult education, (9) uplift of women, (10) education in hygiene and health, (11) propagation of national language, (12) cultivating one's own language, (13) working for economic equality.[106]

---

[103] Datta, *The Philosophy of Mahatma Gandhi*, 102.
[104] Gandhi, *Satyagraha*, 55.
[105] D. S. Sarma, "The Nature and History of Hinduism," *The Religion of the Hindus*, ed. Kenneth W. Morgan (New York: The Ronald Press Company, 1953), 42–46.
[106] Mathews, "The Techniques of M. K. Gandhi as Religious," 113.

Sarvodaya represented the comprehensive social concern that should characterize the ideal satyagrahi. "He will strive for the greatest good of all and die in the attempt to realize the idea."[107]

Thus the ethical principles inherent in Gandhi's concept of satyagraha appear to be the five traditional Hindu cardinal virtues expanded and interpreted, with fearlessness as a supporting ideal. Sarvodaya, while not limited to its significance in satyagraha, is the larger frame of reference for the satyagrahi. It represents an ethic of social concern, in itself an innovation in modern Hindu thought.

IV. Satyagraha (An exposition)

Definition
Krishnalal Shridharani has defined satyagraha as follows:

> The word means insistence on truth. . . . The concept has come to be applied to all the organized and concerted activities coordinated in a pattern under the control of a pledge of nonviolence. In most cases, these mass actions have been extralegal and extra-constitutional; they have outgrown parliamentary procedure and become revolutionary. Thus Satyagraha becomes a form of direct action insofar as the people take the law into their own hands. In contrast to war or violent revolution, however, Satyagraha is nonviolent direct action.[108]

This definition was given in 1939 when British authority was still supreme in India. The present constitution of independent India provides for democratic political procedures but does not make any special reference to satyagraha as a political instrument. Gandhi's own definition of satyagraha appears in a statement made to the Hunter Committee,[109] an extract of which appeared in *Young India* on January 14, 1920. In this statement satyagraha is defined as "holding on to truth." It is regarded as "truth-force," "love-force," or "soul-force." The pursuit of truth does not permit the use of violence against one's opponent but instead "weans from error"

---

[107] M. K. Gandhi, *Sarvodaya* (Ahmedabad: Navajivan Publishing House, 1958), 4.

[108] Krishnalal Shridharani, *War without Violence* (New York: Harcourt Brace and Company, 1939), 4.

[109] A committee headed by Lord Hunter, Senator of the College of Justice of Scotland, appointed to investigate the Punjab disturbances of 1919. See Fischer, *The Life of Mahatma Gandhi*, 177–84.

by patience and sympathy. In the process, self-suffering becomes the force by which "truth is vindicated."[110] Joan V. Bondurant, a political scientist who approached her examination with what she described as a rationalist and humanist predisposition and with "a suspicion of religious systems and obscurantist approaches,"[111] has focused on the distinctive features of satyagraha as follows:

> Is Satyagraha no more than the generic term for all organized efforts in opposition? If this were so, the difference between Gandhian Satyagraha and mass-demonstration for a given political objective would be reduced perhaps to the factor of Gandhi himself. Such an analysis cannot, however, satisfy one who has troubled to examine the procedures and the progress, the assumptions and the behavior involved in Satyagraha movements of the Gandhi genre.[112]

The distinctive features of Satyagraha are, according to Bondurant, the precepts of truth, nonviolence, and self-suffering. Having thus identified these constituents of satyagraha, she evolves the following definition: "The discovery of truth, or the resolution of conflict arising out of differences of opinion as to what is truth, must be prosecuted through non-violent action. Action based on the refusal to do harm often requires dealing with violence which may be instigated by the opponent in a conflict. Self-suffering is this further means by which relative truth is tested."[113]

In "A Study of the Meanings of Non-violence," an attempt to classify and define distinct types, Gene Sharpe has identified Satyagraha as follows:

> The believer in satyagraha ... aims at attaining Truth through love and right action. Satyagraha is a matter of principle.... The Satyagrahi seeks to "turn the searchlight inward" and to (7) improve his own life so that he does no harm to others. He seeks to combat evil in the world through his own way of living, constructive work, and resistance, and action against what are regarded as evils. He seeks to convert

---

[110] Gandhi, *Satyagraha*, 6.
[111] Bondurant, *Conquest of Violence*, vii.
[112] Ibid., 5.
[113] Ibid., 31.

the opponent through sympathy, patience, truthfulness and self-suffering.[114]

It is clear from these statements that satyagraha is a principle of social action informing and controlling the conduct of social conflict, in which the end and the means thereto are consistent with the requirements of truth, nonviolence, and self-suffering. Evident also is the continuity between the constituent elements of satyagraha and the metaphysical presuppositions and the ethical principles identified above. Thus defined, the question remains, how does satyagraha become a force?

Dynamics of satyagraha

An analysis of the effectiveness of the campaigns and movements directed by Gandhi would reveal the influence of his personality, the susceptibility or otherwise of the opponents to the appeal, as well as the power of public opinion. The present investigation, however, does not purport to assume such an analysis. The dynamics to be described are those Gandhi believed inherent in the principle of satyagraha itself. As has been noted, satyagraha is a principle of so-cial action composed of basic ethics. Datta has shown these six basic principles to be ahimsa, satya, asteya, aparigraha, brahmacharya, and abhaya, each of which has been explained earlier in this chap-ter. Bondurant suggests three: truth, ahimsa, and self-suffering; to some extent asteya, aparigraha, and brahmacharya are included in her classification. Abhaya, fearlessness, is really not among the ethical principles but is a psychological factor necessary to—and to some extent a product of—any exercise of them. In explanation of her threefold classification, Bondurant said that it is necessary to separate from the overall ethical system associated with Gandhi what pertains strictly to satyagraha.[115] She finds confusion about the extent to which a satyagrahi needs to conform to the system of morals and values according to which Gandhi himself "ordered 'the good life.'" Especially mentioned are brahmacharya and aparigraha. Whether complete or partial dismissal of these requirements is justified may be questioned in the light of the importance Gandhi

---

[114] Gene Sharp, "A Study of the Meanings of Non-violence," part 3, *Gandhi Marg* 4, no. 2 (April 1960), 139–40.
[115] Bondurant, *Conquest of Violence*, 12.

attached to the power of discipline and nonattachment to family, possessions, or social status.

It is not possible to measure the strengths of the dynamics that operated. But in Gandhi's writings we find enunciated again and again the dynamics he considered inherent in the operation of satyagraha. Neither can the absolute or independent significance of each be evaluated, for they operated simultaneously and inter-relatedly. Also, it must be observed that for Gandhi, satyagraha operated in the context of a particular historical and cultural situation, and directly or indirectly under his own leadership. The strength of his own personality must account for a great deal of the success of satyagraha as a whole, and of any of its contributing elemental principles.

An estimate of the leadership of the author of satyagraha and his personal influence in the satyagraha experiments is beyond the scope of this study. But it would be unrealistic not to take it into account. Bondurant suggests that Gandhi matched the qualifications of the charismatic leader as defined by Max Weber—that is, one who seems to be endowed with supernatural, superhuman, or at least specifically exceptional powers or qualities, on the basis of which he is accorded the place of leadership. It is, of course, patent that Gandhi denied any claim to these special endowments. He claimed to be a seeker after truth and stoutly resisted efforts to put him on a superior plane. Nevertheless, in the estimate of his countrymen and women he held an unusually secure place of leadership both politi-cally and religiously. Louis Fischer, in describing Gandhi's influence in India as late as 1942, after twenty-five years of public service, said: "Gandhi had more than influence, he had authority which is less yet better than power. Power is the attribute of a machine; authority is the attribute of a person. Statesmen are varying combinations of both. . . . Gandhi's rejection of power enhanced his authority. Power feeds on the blood and tears of its victims. Authority is fed by service, sympathy and affection."[116]

Varma confirmed and combined the observations by both Bondurant and Fischer, when he said that Gandhi's "power and authority were really charismatic because they were based on his

---

[116] Louis Fischer, *The Life of Mahatma Gandhi* (London: Jonathan Cape, 1951), 407.

own moral and spiritual discipline."[117] Thus, though recognizing the prestige and power of the protagonist of satyagraha, it must be noted that for Gandhi himself this power, and more, resided in satyagraha. For it was in devotion to truth through nonviolence that the satyagrahi became pure and released into human affairs the power of ultimate truth. In other words, the power of Gandhi as a person was in essence the power of satyagraha and therefore was potentially available to anyone who, like Gandhi, devoted himself to the pursuit of truth. His conviction was that satyagraha as an operational principle is infallible.[118] What were the dynamics inherent in the concept of satyagraha? And how did they operate in the motivation and discipline of the satyagrahi? How did they operate in effecting change?

1. The dynamic of truth. In the discussion of truth above, it was noted that it is not an abstraction or merely an ethical principle, though it is that also; it is the ultimate cosmic reality that is dynamic. The realization of truth and the realization of God are one and the same thing. The process involves both faith and reason. The first qualification set down for the would-be satyagrahi is that "he must have a living faith in God." That God is defined as truth allows individuals of any theistic or atheistic commitment to participate. But faith in God (Truth) means faith in a moral authority over the universe. A practical interpretation of this is reflected in the statement Gandhi made in *Harijan*, July 20, 1947: "This God [Truth] is a living Force. Our life is of that Force. That Force resides in, but is not of the body. He who denies the existence of that great Force, denies to Himself the use of that inexhaustible Power and thus remains impotent."[119] Truth (satya) is a potential for the opponent as well. Therefore, faith in the ultimate triumph of truth is possible. It may involve adjustment by compromise, in that humanity is incapable of knowing the absolute truth.[120] The test of truth is to be applied from the very beginning of a satyagraha campaign by the identification of a clear case of injustice. Satyagraha cannot be applied legitimately in some selfish or evil purpose. Among the conditions

---

[117] V. P. Varma, *The Political Philosophy of Mahatma. Gandhi, and Sarvodaya* (Agra: L. N. Agarwal, 1959), 15.
[118] Mathews, "The Techniques of M. K. Gandhi as Religious," 147.
[119] M. K. Gandhi, *Harijan*, July 20, 1947.
[120] M. K. Gandhi, *Speeches and Writings of Mahatma Gandhi*, 4th ed. (Madras: Natesan, n.d.), 506.

set down by Gandhi for the success of satyagraha was that the "issue must be true and substantial."[121] Freedom and self-determination as a nation was such a true and substantial issue. To seek truth in such a situation was to be in league with truth, the ultimate power of the universe. Truth also governed the means to be applied in the struggle. In fact, Gandhi believed, "our progress towards the goal will be in exact proportion to the purity of our means."[122] Truth (satya) was dynamic in essence and in function, and could be depended on to operate on both sides of a conflict situation.

2. The dynamic of nonviolence. In the early stages of civil disobedience in India, Sir Chimanlal Setalwad of the Hunter Committee asked Gandhi, "Different individuals would have different views as to truth. Would that not lead to confusion?" Gandhi's reply indicates the relation between ahimsa and truth. He said: "That is why the nonviolence part was a necessary corollary. Without that there would be confusion and worse."[123] Ahimsa, in the conception of Gandhi, is not the traditional passivity of non-killing but requires positive self-sacrificing love. "Non-violence in its dynamic condition means conscious suffering. It does not mean meek submission to the will of the evil-doer, but it means the pitting of one's whole soul against the will of the Tyrant. Working under this law of our being, it is possible for a single individual to defy the whole might of an unjust empire."[124]

Ahimsa involves trust in the goodness of the opponent, and love toward even those who hate you,[125] and is the means to resolve the conflict.[126] It is the greatest force, because it appeals to the heart of the opponent, not merely to the intellect. "I observe," said Gandhi, "that unless I can reach the hearts of men and women, I am able to do nothing. I observe further that so long as the spirit of hate persists in some shape or other, it is impossible to establish peace or to gain our freedom by peaceful effort."[127] The target of

---

[121] Gandhi, *Satyagraha*, 181.

[122] M. K. Gandhi, *Amrit Bazar Patrika*, September 17, 1933, quoted in Gandhi, *Sarvodaya*, 6.

[123] Gandhi, *Satyagraha*, 29.

[124] M. K. Gandhi, *Young India*, August 11, 1920.

[125] Gandhi, *For Pacifists*, 6.

[126] Gandhi, *Satyagraha*, 42.

[127] M. K. Gandhi, "Non-violence the Greatest Force," *The World Tomorrow* 9, no. 5, (October 1926), 3.

ahimsa is not the physical body of the opponent but his heart or mind. It is in this respect analogous to violent warfare, as Richard Gregg points out, but it differs, of course, in the method used and in the ultimate objective. Violence is concerned with ends; means are secondary considerations. If the ends require the demoralization or destruction of the opponent, they are justified. Gregg shows this contrast in the following terms:

> The object of non-violent resistance is partly analogous to this object of war—namely, to demoralize the opponent, to break his will, to destroy his confidence, enthusiasm and hope. In another respect it is dissimilar, for non-violent resistance demoralizes the opponent only to re-establish in him a new morale that is finer because it is based on sounder values. Non-violent resistance does not break the opponent's will but alters it; does not destroy his confidence and enthusiasm and hope but transfers them to a finer purpose.[128]

Here is precisely the theory on which Gandhi based satyagraha. "If there is dogma in the Gandhian philosophy," said Bondurant, "it centers here: that the only test of truth is action based on the refusal to do harm."[129] In explaining how he expected the power of nonviolent means to move the opponent, Gandhi stressed four factors: (1) nonviolence is more effective than violence in that it lessens rather than increases violence; (2) nonviolence is a mental and moral weapon rather than a physical one; (3) nonviolence is disconcerting to the opponent prepared for physical force; (4) nonviolence does not destroy or humiliate the opponents but transforms and ennobles them.[130] Ahimsa is therefore a moral weapon informing and motivating the conduct of resistance against an opponent. It calls forth the energies of courage, persistence, and self-sacrifice on the part of the satyagrahi and softens the resistance of the opponent. Moreover, it was Gandhi's firm belief that it was a means of releasing divine approval and energy as well. The satyagrahi is engaged in a task in which he has divine sanction. In describing qualifications for the satyagrahi, Gandhi said, in *Harijan*, June 18, 1938: "He or she must have a living faith in non-violence. This

---

[128] Richard B. Gregg, *The Power of Non-Violence* (Philadelphia: J. B. Lippincott Co., 1934), 89.
[129] Bondurant, *Conquest of Violence*, 25.
[130] Gandhi, *For Pacifists*, 5.

is impossible without a living faith in God. A non-violent man can do nothing save by the power and grace of God. Without it he won't have the courage to die without anger, without fear and without retaliation. Such courage comes from the belief that God sits in the hearts of all and that there should be no fear in the presence of God."[131] Thus it is clear that the satyagrahi was urged to have faith both in the principle of ahimsa or nonviolence and in God, in order to guarantee courage and persistence in the face of suffering and possible death. There were instances when nonviolence turned into violence and thus the power of and respect for the movement was lost. It was Gandhi's firm belief that if ahimsa were maintained without compromise, it would ultimately effect the victory of right over wrong.

3. The dynamic of self-suffering. Krishnalal Shridharani shows that the concept of self-suffering had enhanced significance in the context of the Hindu tradition of sacrifice, of which it is a ritual form. He said:

> The far reaching assumption involved here is that suffer-
> ing self-imposed and borne in the spirit of sacrifice, is the
> most potent of appeals; that even the most whimsical of the
> gods cannot resist the power of suffering. Born of sacrifice,
> suffering is the human power which produces desired ends
> and defeats evil. . . . Down under all the complex and refined
> modern manifestations of the doctrine of non-violent direct
> action is the faith that desired ends may be attained through
> suffering, when it is voluntary and undertaken in the spirit
> of sacrifice.[132]

In the evaluation of Surendranath Dasgupta, "Gandhi's contribution lies in the fact that he applied this potentiality of suffering born through sacrifice to the social polity."[133] Gandhi expresses his own faith in the power of self-suffering: when in referring to the loss of thousands of lives in satyagraha, he asserts that self-suffering is the "chosen substitute for violence to others." It is justified, he says, because in the long run it results in the least loss of life, and

---

[131] M. K. Gandhi, *Harijan,* June 18, 1938.
[132] Shridharani, *War without Violence,* 169.
[133] Surendranath Dasgupta, *Indian Idealism* (London: Cambridge University Press, 1933), 1.

morally enriches the world.[134] In an earlier editorial, he regarded suffering as the requirement for national realization and thus appealed to patriotic aspiration as well. "No country has ever risen without being purified through the fire of suffering. . . . It is impossible to do away with the law of suffering which is the indispensable condition of our being. The way to do better is to avoid, if we can, violence from our side and thus quicken the rate of progress and to introduce greater purity in the methods of suffering."[135] Thus self-suffering was linked to religious tradition as well as to national loyalty. It was set forth as the most potent weapon in the arsenal of the satyagrahi when it took the form of the fast. Its use will be described later on in this chapter under application of satyagraha. But the fast as symbolic of self-imposed suffering depended, as did any kind of suffering, on other factors. Especially noted were the necessity of obedience to the laws of society and personal purity of character and intention. Only when an individual has scrupulously obeyed the laws of society does he have the right to judge which are just and which are unjust. And only then does he have the right to engage in civil disobedience.[136] Again, in the context of a discussion about national defense, Gandhi asserted: "For self-defense, I would restore the spiritual culture. The best and most lasting self-defense is self-purification."[137] Whereas, according to Gandhi, the effectiveness of satyagraha did not depend on the number of participants, it did depend to a large extent on arousing public opinion. Hence, we shall note the methods used under his direction for publicity (such as newspapers, personal contact with the masses, symbols and slogans). The importance attached to this aspect of satyagraha is indicated by the statement that "an awakened and intelligent public opinion is the most potent weapon of a Satyagrahi."[138] In summary, we may say that the element of suffering was considered an essential ingredient of satyagraha, because it elicited a response on the part of the masses. In India, tradition rendered it not only respectable but challenging. This is not to say that it was not resisted and even ridiculed, for to many

---

[134] M. K. Gandhi, *Non-Violence in Peace and War*, 3rd ed., vol. 1, ed. Mahadeo Desai (Ahmedabad: Navajivan Publishing House, 1948), 43–44.
[135] M. K. Gandhi, *Young India*, June 16, 1920.
[136] Gandhi, *Satyagraha*, 75.
[137] Ibid., 50.
[138] Ibid., 77.

of Gandhi's countrymen and women it seemed too idealistic and impracticable. Nevertheless, the self-imposed suffering dramatized injustice and evil and solicited goodwill and sympathy. It disarmed opponents psychologically. It constituted a challenge to satyagrahis, from whom it exacted sacrifice, courage, self-control, and action. It had most of the elements of violent warfare, according to Gregg, except destructive weapons.[139]

The power of self-suffering is dependent on the measure of discipline observed by the satyagrahis. In this connection is noted the importance of the principles cited above—asteya (non-stealing), aparigraha (non-possession) and brahmacharya (self-control)—as they contribute to the dynamics of satyagraha. Those who have renounced the attachments of family, physical, and social well-being, and who have conditioned their behavior over a period of time, are more apt to stand courageously in the face of violence.[140] "Like war with violence, war without violence also requires long discipline, organization, training and preparation."[141] Along with psychological conditioning, Gandhi recommended physical training; the latter was valuable in ensuring fearlessness and endurance under physical abuse, whether by the elements of nature, or by the might of others.[142] Thus we are led to the conclusion that satyagraha, as conceived by Gandhi, incorporated and depended for its success on many contributing factors. These elements, metaphysical and physical, mental and moral, united in the three ethical principles of truth, nonviolence, and self-suffering.

Application of satyagraha

By definition, satyagraha is a principle of social action operating in a conflict situation. It does not prescribe the specific forms in which the action should be conducted. It is within the rationale of satyagraha to employ forms or agents consistent with the principles of truth, nonviolence, and self-suffering, and these techniques, or modes of application, may be classified in various ways. As Gandhi envisioned satyagraha, its chief merit lay in the fact that it could be used by individuals, groups, and even by nations; it could be

---

[139] Gregg, The Power of Non-Violence, 125.
[140] Gandhi, For Pacifists, 17.
[141] Krishnalal Shridharani, My India, My America (New York: Duell, Sloan and Pearce, 1941), 275.
[142] Gandhi, Satyagraha, 94.

interpersonal, intragroup or international. Mathews in his study classified possible methods as follows: (1) techniques of preparation; (2) techniques of purification; (3) techniques of propaganda; (4) techniques of negotiation; (5) techniques of direct action; (6) techniques of constructive activity.[143] Whereas this classification may appear to convey a rather doctrinaire impression of Gandhian satyagraha, it does abstract very clearly the operational techniques applied in a variety of situations by Mr. Gandhi.

Krishnalal Shridharani's classification[144] takes still another form, in that it demonstrates to some extent the stages or phases through which a satyagraha effort may move. This structure commends itself for this particular study, which involves a comparison with Mennonite nonresistance, because the phases represent gradations in the degree and nature of the coercion employed. It is the use of coercion that forms the pivot of the problem of the comparison. The techniques employed will be defined briefly and historical examples given where necessary for clarity.

1. Negotiation and arbitration. Important are the clear and right cause, proper representation of the defendants before the authorities, and the use of the customary constitutional channels for appealing to the authority. "There can be no Satyagraha in an unjust cause."[145] When this primary phase fails, the next step is taken.

2. Agitation. This stage involves rousing public opinion and therefore requires dissemination of information and the stimulation of emotion. Use is made of the press (Gandhi edited *Indian Opinion* in South Africa; *Navajivan* and *Young India* in India, 1919; and *Harijan* from 1933), other literature, slogans, catchy songs, personal contacts, public meetings, speeches, discussions and debates, radio, drama, and the cinema. Symbols are used: the Congress cap, the spinning wheel, the wearing of homespun, and the use of the spinning wheel dramatized the economic issues. Fasting and prayer, while serving other purposes, too, contribute to rousing religious sentiments.

3. Demonstration and the ultimatum. In this stage, the "cause-consciousness" seeks expression. Processions and large public meet-

---

[143] Mathews, "The Techniques of M. K. Gandhi as Religious," 86–114.
[144] Shridharani, *War without Violence,* 5–42.
[145] Gandhi, *Satyagraha,* 56.

ings manifest the scope and strength of the cause. These demonstrations tend to draw out additional supporters. The demonstration precipitates a statement of the demands. This is then submitted to the authorities, specifying a time limit for their action. If this fails to get action, then the next stage is required.

   4. Self-purification. In preparation for more exacting activity, attention is given to the discipline of the satyagrahi. The movement begins to coalesce into a nonviolent army. Constitutional methods of representation and arbitration having failed, the next step is one of non-constitutional action, which may involve suffering and punishment. There is the possibility of the satyagrahis losing their restraint and becoming violent, or losing their courage and giving up the fight; hence the necessity for reflection and reaffirmation. Self-purification takes the form of fasting and prayer, the taking of vows or "the pledge." This procedure strengthens the satyagrahis and eliminates those who are not "fit" for the nonviolent army. This stage of self-purification is also an agent of persuasion, in that it demonstrates the seriousness and earnestness of the nonviolent army. The pledge specifies the object of the satyagraha and asserts the intention of the satyagrahi to "follow truth and refrain from violence to life, person or property."[146] In the first satyagraha against the Rowlatt Act in 1919, those who took the pledge were required to fast twenty-four hours. Indicative of the importance of the mental preparation of the satyagrahi is the list of qualifications set down originally in 1921 and reiterated in an editorial of 1939. Gandhi asserted that in satyagraha, it is not the number of participants that is important but the quality, for the appeal is to the heart and not to fear. The satyagrahi's purpose is to transform the opponents rather than to harm them. Qualifications set down for the satyagrahis are summarized briefly as follows: They must (1) have a "living faith in God"; (2) have faith in "truth and nonviolence" and in the "inherent goodness of human nature"; (3) be leading a "chaste life" and be ready to sacrifice "his life and possessions"; (4) be a habitual wearer of homespun cloth and a habitual spinner; (5) not use intoxicants; (6) subscribe willingly to all the satyagraha

---

[146] R. R. Diwakar, *Satyagraha: The Power of Truth* (Hinsdale, IL: Henry Regnery Company, 1948), 64.

rules; (7) if in jail, obey all the rules except those "devised to hurt their self-respect."[147]

Following the time of self-purification, some form of direct action is sought and applied. The circumstances suggested the form the action will take.

5. *Strike and general strike.* The strike in satyagraha is not different from that practiced generally in labor disputes. The general strike would involve the whole country or at least a large segment of the population. In some cases, it may be a sympathetic strike. Gandhi insisted that for a strike there should be a clear grievance, and that it should be carried on by the strikers without financial aid from any outside source. There should also be a clear predetermined statement of the minimum demand. The merit of a sympathetic strike lay in the measure of inconvenience and loss suffered by the sympathizers.

6. *Dhurna.* Dhurna is an ancient Indian practice that may be described as a sit-down strike. Creditors used this method to embarrass their debtors into payment; the former sat at the latter's doorstep until payment or promise of payment was received. It is useful to dramatize an injustice and rouse public sentiment. In the Indian movement, it was employed in Calcutta University to prevent students from going to class. It was in this instance a political boycott. Also, it was used against Indian government servants who continued to serve in the administrative posts of the British regime. Gandhi did not endorse this method.

7. *Economic boycott.* The economic boycott took the form of refusal to buy English goods, in the interest of promoting the national economy. The wearing of homespun clothing (khadi) and the promotion of hand spinning with the spinning wheel were concrete aspects of the boycott. There were also public burnings of foreign cloth.

8. *Nonpayment of taxes.* The call for nonpayment of taxes ushers in nonviolent direct action in its purely illegal and seditious stage. "Various have been the uses of the weapon in India. Sometimes it has been resorted to on a small regional basis, on other occasions as a large provincial measure, and then again it has been wielded by the entire nation." The reaction of the state was to arrest, to

---

[147] Gandhi, *Satyagraha*, 88.

confiscate property, to terrorize, and to shoot at sight if there were a mutiny. Gandhi urged extreme caution in using this weapon, as it depended on strong self-discipline on the part of the sufferers to prevent violence, especially when they would see government agents confiscating their property.[148]

9. Noncooperation. The exercise of the state authority is negated if the governed do not cooperate. Noncooperation is, therefore, a general term for a measure that inhibits the functioning of state authority. Noncooperation was not to be expressed in complete anarchy; it was to be orderly and to be effected through stages or phases. Gandhi recommended the following phases of noncooperation as representative of the movements of 1919–20 and 1930–32.

1. Surrender of titles of honor and the voluntary giving up of all honorary offices. This action would, on one hand, shatter the prestige of the opponent government and, on the other, make the business of administration a difficult affair.
2. Non-participation in government loans. This item of non-co-operation was aimed at unbalancing the monetary status of the government.
3. Boycotting of law courts by Congress and by litigants.
4. Boycott of government schools and colleges.
5. Boycott of the legislative councils. . . . By withdrawing from the legislatures, the leaders are likely to rob the government of such status as is bestowed by their participation.
6. Withdrawal from government service. The refusal on the part of Indians to accept or to continue in any civil post would bring the entire administration to a standstill.
7. Withdrawal of men from the army and the police.[149]

Diwakar summarizes the results of the first noncooperation movement of 1920.[150] When the Indian National Congress met in December of 1920, 30,000 Congress workers were in jail. Congress decided to enroll 50,000 new nonviolent volunteers. But at a village called Chauri-Chaura, some satyagrahis turned violent and brutally killed a subinspector of police, and in Bombay riots broke out in connection with the visit of the Prince of Wales. Gandhi asked Congress

---

[148] Gandhi, *Satyagraha*, 139–40.
[149] Shridharani, *War without Violence*, 30–31.
[150] Diwakar, *Satyagraha*, 79.

to call off the noncooperation movement and to engage in the Constructive Program. By March 1922, he himself was sentenced to a term of six years in prison. (He was released in February 1924.) While the movement had failed to achieve the goal of independence "in one year," Gandhi believed that an advance of thirty years had been effected.[151]

10. *Ostracism and social boycott.*[152] The technique of ostracism and social boycott did not originate with satyagraha but was used as a disciplinary measure under the caste system. Untouchables and those who broke caste rules were ostracized under certain conditions. They were forbidden to live in certain areas of the town or village, forbidden the use of certain wells, forbidden entrance to the temples. Gandhi was anxious to erase these evils from Hindu society. He saw, too, that the social boycott could be abused and thus bring satyagraha into disrepute. If social boycott or ostracism should be used, it must be with discretion and be applied only to certain privileges and not to essential services such as water supply or medical attention. "Privileges" were exemplified by occasions such as wedding feasts and dinner parties.

11. *Civil disobedience.* The technique of civil disobedience may take various forms, but in essence it amounts to disobedience to state regulations considered to be offensive or unjust. As indicated above in the history of the development of satyagraha, the phrase *civil disobedience* came to Gandhi's attention when he read Henry David Thoreau's essay with that title. At this time, Gandhi was already leading activity of this nature in the interests of the Indian community in South Africa. Gandhi defined civil disobedience as "civil breach of unmoral statutory enactments." If the disobedience is engaged in by an individual, it is a sort of vicarious suffering. When organized on a large scale, it may have the effect of partial or complete disruption of the government. The functioning of large-scale disobedience is defined as follows in an editorial of *Young India* in 1921. "Complete civil disobedience is a state of peaceful rebellion—refusal to obey every single State-made law. It is certainly more dangerous than an armed rebellion. For it can never be put down if the civil resisters are prepared to face extreme hardships. It is based upon an implicit belief in the absolute efficiency of innocent

---

[151] Ibid.
[152] Gandhi, *Satyagraha*, 148–49.

suffering. By noiselessly going to prison a civil resister ensures a calm atmosphere."[153] Civil disobedience is considered to be the right of every citizen and becomes, moreover, a sacred duty, if and when a state becomes lawless or corrupt. The relation between noncooperation and civil disobedience is very close. Gandhi described them as "branches of the same tree," which is satyagraha.[154]

An illustration of civil disobedience, a clear example, is the action against the salt tax, which was set in motion by Gandhi's dramatic Dandi march. Bondurant analyzes the movement and remarks that it contained all the elements of true satyagraha.[155] The offensive tax was imposed on salt by the British government of India, which also held a monopoly on the manufacture of salt. Gandhi selected this as symbolic of the total subjugation of India. He apparently saw the psychological value of making the salt tax a target. In this connection he said, "There is no article like salt, outside water, by taxing which the state can reach even the starving millions, the sick, the maimed and utterly helpless. The tax constitutes, therefore, the most inhuman poll tax the ingenuity of man can devise."[156] The march to the sea took on the character of a religious pilgrimage, with reverence and discipline. Gandhi selected seventy-eight inhabitants of the Sabarmati Ashram, who had been disciplined through the life of the ashram. They set out on foot to traverse 200 miles of country, carrying out their usual ashram discipline of spinning and prayer as they went. They were joined by thousands as they marched. When the pilgrimage ended at Dandi and the salt law was symbolically broken, a wave of enthusiasm spread throughout the country. The civil disobedience movement had begun, and many anticipated that it would be the final effort for independence.[157] Throughout the year, there was action and then retaliation by government repression: arrests, incarceration, beating, grid restrictions of various kinds. Civil disobedience manifested itself in manufacturing and using contraband salt, picketing liquor and opium shops, picketing foreign-cloth shops, plying the

---

[153] M. K. Gandhi, *Young India*, March 3, 1921.
[154] M. K. Gandhi, Extract from presidential address of All India Congress, Belgaum, India, December 1924. Gandhi, *Satyagraha*, 176.
[155] Bondurant, *Conquest of Violence*, 88–102.
[156] D. G. Tendulkar, *Mahatma: Life of Mohandas Karamchand Gandhi*, III (Bombay: Times of India Press, 1952), 16.
[157] Ibid., 40.

spindle (takli) and spinning wheel, burning foreign cloth. Students discontinued their studies in government schools, and government servants resigned their posts.[158]

By 1931, cessation of civil disobedience was agreed on by the viceroy and Gandhi. The specifications of the document drawn up at that time are indicative of the nature of civil disobedience; it prescribed the termination of

1. Organized defiance of the provisions of any law.
2. The movement for the nonpayment of land revenue and other legal dues.
3. Publication of any news-sheet in support of the civil disobedience movement.
4. Attempts to influence civil and military servants or village officials against the Government or to persuade them to resign their posts.
5. Boycott on English goods.[159]

12. Assertive satyagraha. The phase of assertive satyagraha is anticipated when the government is disabled through the effects of civil disobedience. It assumes that as the disabled regime gradually breaks down, satyagrahis would assume authority and occupy administrative posts. Though this occurred in some places and for some short periods of time, it was not significant in the satyagraha movement in India. As negotiations continued in the Indian experiment, resulting ultimately in the orderly transition from British to Indian authority, this phase of satyagraha remained untested.

13. Parallel government. Parallel government is the full realization of civil disobedience. The satyagrahis establish a new sovereignty by replacing the established order. Parallel government represents the taking over of all the functions of government, thus liquidating the previous regime.

14. Fasting. Fasting has been discussed above in reference to self-purification. However, as an active agent in nonviolent coercion, it deserves special examination. Gandhi regarded the fast as a powerful agent, to be used with discretion and discrimination. Fasts were personal or public. The public fast as an appeal for right thinking and right behavior was in reality purificatory, even as the

---

[158] Ibid., 41.
[159] Ibid., 71.

personal fast.[160] The principle of the fast is the "mortification of the flesh" and is "a condition of spiritual progress."[161] The exacting conditions of the fast for the individual, Gandhi set down in the following terms: "The mere fast of the body is nothing without the will behind it. It must be a genuine confession of the inner fast, an irrepressible longing to express truth and nothing but truth. Therefore, those only are privileged to fast for the cause of truth, who have worked for it and who have love in them even for opponents, who are free from animal passions and ambitions."[162] As the fast is essentially spiritual, "addressed to God," it quickens the spirit of prayer in the one who is fasting, and "awakens the sleeping conscience" of these for whose benefit the fast is undertaken.[163] Most of Gandhi's fasts were undergone in the interest of Hindu-Muslim unity or as penance for violence in the exercise of satyagraha. The one ordeal related directly to obtaining Indian independence was the twenty-one day fast of 1943 in the Agha Khan palace near Pune. The purpose was to resolve the deadlock that had stymied negotiations between the viceroy and the Indian leaders.[164] Civil disobedience had gone into effect without Gandhi's authorization; with his imprisonment it turned to violence. He was held responsible, but in prison was not allowed means of communication whereby he might halt the violence. The fast he undertook was called "political blackmail" by Lord Linlithgow, Viceroy of India. Gandhi replied: "It is on my part an appeal to the Highest Tribunal for justice which I have failed to secure from you. If I do not survive the ordeal I shall go to the Judgment Seat with the fullest faith in my innocence. Posterity will judge between you as a representative of an all-powerful government and me a humble man who tried to serve his country and humanity through it."[165]

   15. National defense. When asked whether satyagraha could be applied to defend a frontier in the event of an attack by an invader, Gandhi did not reply with any degree of optimism. In his opinion, India, having had some experience with nonviolent conflict, might conceivably attempt satyagraha in case of an attack. He did not anticipate the acceptance of satyagraha as a national policy. He

---

[160] M. K. Gandhi, *Harijan*, October 13, 1940.
[161] Gandhi, *Satyagraha*, 318.
[162] M. K. Gandhi, *Harijan*, April 15, 1933.
[163] Gandhi, *For Pacifists*, 24.
[164] Fischer, *The Life of Mahatma Gandhi*, 380–95.
[165] Ibid., 388.

did, however, project what he conceived of as the implication of satyagraha in such an event. There would be two possible ways to meet the aggressor, (1) "to yield possession but maintain non-co-operation," or (2) to offer themselves "unarmed as fodder for the aggressor's cannon." By way of further explanation he said:

> The underlying belief in either case is that even a Nero is not devoid of heart. The unexpected spectacle of endless rows upon rows of men and women simply dying rather than surrender to the will of an aggressor must ultimately melt him and his soldiery. Practically speaking there will be probably no greater loss in men than if forcible resistance were offered; there will be no expenditure in armaments and fortifications.[166]

In this investigation, we have reviewed the historical origins of Gandhian satyagraha and have examined documentary sources to ascertain, first of all, the metaphysical and ethical principles that unite in satyagraha. We have seen that these principles constitute the dynamic in satyagraha as a nonviolent weapon in conflict situations. The investigation has also led to the identification of the types of action that may be employed in satyagraha conflict.

Satyagraha as a principle of conducting conflict has much in common with any negotiation or arbitration carried out on a high level of objectivity. It is unique in the degree to which its principles of truth, nonviolence, and self-suffering are idealized. The realization of these principles in conflict situations depends on voluntary acceptance of them, and on the fortitude necessary to implement them. In its ideal form, as a moral weapon, it imposes moral obligations on the user, and delimits the purposes in which satyagraha may be used. Satyagraha thus informs and regulates the agent, the end, and the means to the end. When it tolerates or condones coercion that may involve harm, loss, or suffering to the opponent, the principles of truth, nonviolence, and self-suffering become in reality relative and not absolute. The ideal becomes subject to the pragmatic. Satyagraha as a technique of conducting conflict is therefore not absolutely nonviolent, but is a serious attempt to exert nonviolent resistance.

---

[166] M. K. Gandhi, *Harijan*, April 13, 1940.

Chapter 4

Mennonite nonviolence: Nonresistance

NONRESISTANCE IS AN IMPORTANT and distinctive doctrine of the Anabaptist-Mennonite tradition. As a representative of this tradition, the Mennonite Church of North America has been selected. The doctrine of nonresistance has been given a great deal of consideration by this denomination in the twentieth century, because of the two world wars and because of the implications of universal military conscription. The literature to be examined includes official documents of the denomination and treatises on the subject of nonresistance that have been recognized and authorized officially by the denomination. This period corresponds roughly to the period of the activity of M. K. Gandhi, with whose doctrine of satyagraha a comparison of nonresistance is herewith undertaken.

I. History of nonresistance

Nonresistance did not originate with the Mennonites, but the emphasis given to it by this particular denomination dates from the origin of the Anabaptist-Mennonite tradition in 1525. The Mennonites are direct descendants of the Anabaptists who emerged during the Protestant Reformation in the sixteenth century. Awakened to an interest in the study of the scriptures and the true nature of the church by Ulrich Zwingli in Zurich, Switzerland, they insisted on a radical reformation. To them this meant earnest personal discipleship, separation of church and state, baptism on confession of faith, a nonsacramental view of the Lord's Supper, and nonresistance to enemies.[1] Because of their practice of rebaptizing adults who had been baptized as infants, they were given the nickname "Anabaptists." This name was used to identify the movement until a leader named Menno Simons appeared in Holland (1496–1561). The movement had spread rapidly, in spite of severe persecutions by both Protestant and Catholic opponents in Germany, Holland, and to some extent in France. Because of the persecution and martyrdom

---

[1] Guy F. Hershberger, *War, Peace, and Nonresistance* (Scottdale, PA: Herald Press, 1946), 73.

of the early leaders, the movement disintegrated and deteriorated, falling into legitimate disrepute. Menno Simons, however, was able to give the kind of leadership that brought the movement to a new level of faith and discipline.[2] His followers became known as "Mennonites," and hence the name of the denomination under study.

With regard to the distinctive character of this branch of the Protestant Reformation, Roland Bainton says: "The word Reformation is usually referred to the Lutheran movement, the word Reformed to the Zwinglian and Calvinist. The word 'restored' would be the most appropriate to apply to those who by opponents were called Anabaptists. Their great word was 'Restitution.' Much more drastically than any of their contemporaries they searched the scriptures in order to recover the pattern of the early church."[3] The Anabaptists have not always enjoyed the most objective treatment by historians, but it would appear that their best intentions and efforts are being more fairly assessed. According to Littell, the Anabaptist movement is characterized as follows:

> There has been a marked change in writing about the Anabaptists in recent years. Many scholars are no longer content with sweeping generalizations about the movement based on polemical Lutheran and Reformed writings. In the newer writings, various schemes of classification have been attempted, to define various groupings among the radicals. . . . For working purposes, the Anabaptists proper were those in the radical Reformation who gathered and disciplined a "true church" (rechte Kirche) upon the apostolic pattern as they understood it.[4]

The term *Radical Reformation* is used to identify a major expression of the religious movement of the sixteenth century. George H. Williams says it is one that is "as distinctive as Lutheranism, Calvinism, and Anglicanism, and is perhaps comparably significant in the rise of modern Christianity."[5] Within the Radical Reformation

---

[2] Harold S. Bender, "The Mennonite Church," *The Mennonite Encyclopedia* (Scottdale, PA: Herald Press, 1955–59), 3:586–87.
[3] Roland H. Bainton, *The Reformation of the Sixteenth Century* (Boston: Beacon Press, 1952), 95.
[4] Franklin H. Littell, *The Anabaptist View of the Church* (Boston: Starr King Press, 1958), 17.
[5] George H. Williams and Angel M. Mergal, *Spiritual and Anabaptist Writers* (London: S.C.M. Press Ltd., 1957), 19.

movement there are, according to Williams, three distinct elements: the Anabaptists proper, the Spiritualists, and the Evangelical Rationalists. It is the Anabaptists proper who are the spiritual antecedents of the Mennonites.[6]

The earliest formulation of doctrine is called the Schleitheim Confession, dated February 4, 1527. According to John C. Wenger, "the Schleitheim Confession does not give a complete summary of Christian faith, but treats only of the unique emphases of the evangelical Anabaptists of that era or perhaps of the points which were particularly challenged, either by the opponents or by erring brethren within."[7] An English translation of the confession (originally written in German) appears in Wenger's *The Doctrines of the Mennonites* as Appendix I. The part that deals with the doctrine of nonresistance is as follows:

> We are agreed as follows concerning the sword: The sword is ordained of God outside the perfection of Christ. It punishes and puts to death the wicked, and guards and protects the good. In the Law the sword was ordained for the punishment of the wicked and for their death, and the same sword is now ordained to be used by the worldly magistrates.

> In the perfection of Christ, however, only the ban is used for a warning and for the excommunication of the one who has sinned, without putting the flesh to death—simply the warning and the command to sin no more.

> Now it will be asked by many who do not recognize this as the will of Christ for us, whether a Christian may or should employ the sword against the wicked for the defense and protection of the good, or for the sake of love.

> Our reply is unanimously as follows: Christ teaches and commands us to learn of Him, for He is meek and lowly in heart and so shall we find rest to our souls. Also, Christ says to the heathenish woman who was taken in adultery, not that one should stone her according to the law of His Father (and yet He says, As the Father has commanded me, thus I do), but in mercy and forgiveness and warning, to sin no more. Such

---

[6] Ibid., 31.
[7] John C. Wenger, "Brüderlich Vereinigung," *The Mennonite Encyclopedia*, 1:447.

an attitude we also ought to take completely according to the rule of the ban.

Secondly, it will be asked concerning the sword, whether a Christian shall pass sentence in worldly disputes and strife such as unbelievers have with one another. This is our united answer, Christ did not wish to decide or pass judgment between brother and brother in the case of the inheritance, but refused to do so. Therefore, we should do likewise.

Thirdly, it will be asked concerning the sword, Shall one be a magistrate if one should be chosen as such? The answer is as follows: They wished to make Christ king, but He fled and did not view it as the arrangement of the Father. Thus shall we do as He did, and follow Him, and so shall we not walk in darkness. For He Himself says, He who wishes to come after me, let him deny himself and take up his cross and follow me. Also, He Himself forbids the employment of the force of the sword saying, The worldly princes lord it over them, etc., but not so shall it be with you. Further, Paul says, Whom God did foreknow He also did predestinate to be conformed to the image of His Son, etc. Also Peter says, Christ has suffered (not ruled) and left us an example, that we should follow in His steps.

Finally, it will be observed that it is not appropriate for a Christian to serve as a magistrate because of these points:

The government magistracy is according to the flesh, but the Christian's is according to the Spirit; their houses and dwelling remain in this world, but the Christians' are in heaven; their citizenship is in this world, but the Christians' citizenship is in heaven; the weapons of their conflict and war are carnal and against the flesh only, but the Christians' weapons are spiritual, against the fortification of the devil. The worldlings are armed with steel and iron, but the Christians are armed with the armor of God, with truth, righteousness, peace, faith, salvation and the Word of God. In brief, as is the mind of Christ toward us, so shall the mind of the members of the body of Christ be through Him in all things, that there may be no schism in the body through which it would be destroyed. For every kingdom divided against itself will be destroyed. Now since Christ is as it is written of Him, His members must also be the same, that His body may remain complete and united to its own advancement and upbuilding.[8]

The significance of this statement of faith on the subject of nonresistance is more fully appreciated as it is recognized that the Anabaptists were considered heretics and as such were, because of their beliefs, subject to persecution and legal punishment by the state church. This was, therefore, a matter of immediate concern. The pursuit of their theological convictions was not an academic or theoretical exercise but was the search for truth in a situation that required it. At stake for them was their very survival. The document cited above indicates also that they took the life and teaching of Jesus to be their authority in this issue. They considered themselves to be primarily responsible to obey the will of God as they understood it in the biblical record. Guy Hershberger points out that "they accepted the Word of God as the only rule of faith and practice. Great emphasis was placed on discipleship, literal obedience to the commands of Christ, and faithfully following His steps. They searched the Scriptures diligently, and the way of life which they found there they lived within the brotherhood, and taught in their meetings, as well as in their missionary witness."[9]

They believed the church to be a brotherhood of believers who had experienced a spiritual regeneration. As such, they found themselves at issue with the state church and its practice of infant baptism. They insisted that baptism should be administered to adults who voluntarily expressed their faith in Christ and sought to conform their lives to the teachings of Christ. The believer's responsibility to the state was then a matter of secondary concern. In fact, believers were to desist from participation in any civil or military function of the state that conflicted with their primary loyalty to Christ. Bainton describes the position taken as follows:

The state was ordained because of sin, but the Church was created for the saved. These propositions entailed the dissolution of the whole structure of medieval society. Luther and Zwingli had never gone so far and recoiled the more be-

---

[8] Wenger, *The Doctrines of the Mennonites* (Scottdale, PA: Mennonite Publishing House, 1952), 74.
[9] Hershberger, *War, Peace, and Nonresistance,* 73.

cause the Anabaptists went on to say that the true Christian must not only foreswear an alliance with the state, but must have nothing to do with it, since the world is the world and remains without hope of ever being Christianized. Luther agreed that society cannot be Christianized, but nevertheless believed that Christians must accept the office of magistrate in order to restrain outrageous villainy.[10]

The Anabaptists insisted that the Sermon on the Mount be taken literally, and, since the state required the use of resistance and coercion, the Christian could not serve it unreservedly. The answer was to abstain from state service.

From the beginning of the movement, the Anabaptists suffered much persecution. Although many of the early leaders were annihilated, the faith persisted and spread throughout Switzerland, Germany, Holland, and to some extent in France. Modern research has brought to light much of the truth about the movement that had been obscured by its enemies, as well as by sympathetic scholars with inadequate evidence. Wenger sketches its history as it is understood by modern Anabaptist-Mennonite scholars. The continuity between the early Anabaptists in Zurich, Switzerland (also known as Swiss Brethren[11]), and the Mennonites of Holland and America is clearly demonstrated.[12] From the beginnings in Zurich under the leadership of Conrad Grebel, Felix Manz, and others, there was a proliferation into three main streams: (1) the original Swiss Brethren; (2) the Austrian branch, which added the Christian "community of goods" and became known as Hutterites after their leader, Jacob Hutter; and (3) the Dutch Anabaptists, who later came to be known as Mennists and Mennonites after Menno Simons. In addition to these three branches, there were offshoots of Spiritualism, Anti-trinitarianism, and the apocalypticism of the Munsterites. The latter brought disrepute on the whole Anabaptist movement. It was Menno Simons, emerging as a leader in Holland, who was able to salvage the good and bring order out of the confusion and chaos. In a brief biography in a collection of the writings of Menno

---

[10] Bainton, *The Reformation of the Sixteenth Century*, 99–100.
[11] Harold S. Bender, *Conrad Grebel* (Goshen, IN: The Mennonite Historical Society, 1950), xi–xii.
[12] John C. Wenger, *Even unto Death* (Richmond, VA: John Knox Press, 1961), 15–44.

Simons, Harold S. Bender summarized the significance of Menno Simons at this time as follows:

> It is not too much to say that the preservation of the Dutch and North German Anabaptists from complete annihilation or at least from absorption into the fanaticism of the Baten-brugers and Davidians, and their rallying around a Biblical standard of faith and life, was due in large measure to the fruitful labors of Menno Simons, who yielded himself heart and body and soul to his God, and took upon himself "the heavy cross" of his Lord in a faithful, unremitting devoted ministry until his death.[13]

Not only did Menno Simons bring about the reconstitution of the original intention and character of the Anabaptist movement, but his writings constituted the foundation of the Mennonite faith for generations to follow. His followers became known as Mennonites, thus perpetuating his name and the faith he represented. Among his literary works, the one that for practical purposes constituted a confession of faith is his Fundament-Boek. According to Krahn, "It is clear that the primary purpose of the Fundament-Boek in Menno's mind was to serve as a handbook for his fellow believers in matters of faith and practice in the church."[14] This document is the second in line historically, subsequent to the Schleitheim Confession, to set forth the beliefs of the Anabaptist-Mennonite church. Bender describes this document, along with other writings of this period, as follows:

> All of the writings of this period of Menno's life are sub-stantial doctrinal expositions dealing with fundamental doctrines such as repentance, faith, the new birth, holiness, and similar themes. They are not learned treatises but rather simply written books well adapted to the common man, and deal with the great issues of the hour. For this reason they were widely read and did splendid service in strengthening the faith of many who were disturbed and unsettled by the many conflicting currents of the day. It is no wonder that the

---

[13] Harold S. Bender, "A Brief Biography of Menno Simons," in *The Complete Writings of Menno Simons,* ed. John C. Wenger (Scottdale, PA: Herald Press, 1956), 16.
[14] Cornelius Krahn, "Menno Simons' Fundament-Boek of 1539–1540," *Mennonite Quarterly Review* 13 (October 1939): 225.

authorities were so anxious to suppress Menno's writings, and that they placed severe penalties upon those who read them or distributed them.[15]

The Fundament-Boek is addressed not only to the followers of Menno but to the magistrates and rulers and to the learned theologians. It contains pleas for justice and understanding, as well as an admonition to the rulers to recognize that they too are responsible to a higher authority for their actions. Krahn evaluates the significance of the Fundament-Boek as follows:

> When Menno wrote his Foundation Book four hundred years ago and circulated it among the churches of the brotherhood, without doubt he meant it to be a standard in matters of faith. There is also no doubt that through the centuries since that time, this book has had more influence in the history of Mennonitism than any other single volume except possibly the Martyrs' Mirror.[16] This is true not only of the Mennonites in Holland and North Germany, but also of the Mennonites in South Germany, in Switzerland, and in America and Russia. Repeated translations and reprints are a vivid testimony to the influence and power of this book.[17]

In this document there is no section dealing with nonresistance as such, but there are numerous statements that show that Menno Simons's concept of nonresistance is consonant with that of the Swiss Brethren and their belief as reflected in the Schleitheim Confession.

In an appeal to the representatives of the state, Menno reminds them that "it is Jesus of Nazareth whom you persecute and not us. Therefore awake, desist, fear God and His Word. For you and we shall all be called to appear before one Judge, before whom neither power, rank, splendor, fine speech, nor talents will count."[18] Expression is given here to the belief in the secondary

---

[15] Bender, "A Brief Biography of Menno Simons," 18.
[16] The Martyrs' Mirror was originally published in Holland in 1660; Part I contains accounts of Christian martyrs from the time of Christ to 1500; Part II, accounts of Anabaptist and Mennonite martyrs. The author was T. J. Van Braght. See Harold S. Bender, "Martyrs' Mirror," The Mennonite Encyclopedia, 3:527.
[17] Krahn, "Menno Simons' Fundament-Boek of 1539–1540," 230.
[18] Menno Simons, "Foundations of Christian Doctrine," in The Complete Writings of Menno Simons, ed. Wenger, 118.

authority of the state; that is, secondary to that of God as revealed in the scriptures. Nevertheless, in the very next paragraph is an expression of loyalty to the state. Menno Simons said: "We resist neither the emperor, the king, nor any authority in that to which they are called of God; but we are ready to obey to the death in all things which are not contrary to God and His Word. But so much mercy we request that under your gracious protection we may live, teach, conduct ourselves, and serve the Lord according to our consciences.[19] Menno Simons asserted the primary authority of the scriptures as the Word of God, and the necessity for liberty of conscience. In the same treatise, representatives of the state are challenged for their exercise of authority over the church, which Menno affirms is beyond the scope of their authority; the church has her own king. His charge is as follows:

> The almighty, eternal Father, through His eternal wisdom, Christ Jesus, has instituted and commanded according to His divine counsel, will, and wisdom, all things in His kingdom, that is, His church, relating to doctrines, sacraments, and life. But you are the ones who at the counsel and sugges-tion of the learned ones by your inhuman and cruel edict have changed, destroyed, and persecuted these, as if the almighty and eternal Word should yield to your command and authority, and as if the divine ordinances of the Son of God could be changed into a more acceptable form and a better use through the wisdom of men. . . . Acknowledge your superior, Christ Jesus, who is made to you a Prince and a Judge of God Himself.[20]

The state, according to Menno Simons, should limit itself to those earthly temporal matters that have been assigned to it by God as revealed in the scriptures, and not infringe on the province of the church, the realm of the "almighty king Jesus Christ." The principle of state-church relationship from the standpoint of the Mennonites he sets forth in this statement: "For with all our hearts we desire to render unto Caesar the things that are Caesar's and unto God the things that are God's."[21] To this he adds the declara-

---

[19] Ibid.
[20] Ibid., 119.
[21] Ibid., 120.

tion of a positive attitude toward civil responsibility: "We teach and exhort obedience to the emperor, king, lords, magistrates, yea to all in authority in all temporal affairs, and civil regulations in so far as they are not contrary to the Word of God."[22]

With regard to the use of weapons, Menno says, "Our weapons are not weapons with which cities and countries may be destroyed," and continues by describing those which the Christian does possess: "Christ is our fortress; patience our weapon of defense; the Word of God our sword; and our victory a courageous, firm, unfeigned faith in Jesus Christ. And iron and metal spears we leave to those who, alas, regard human blood and swine's blood about alike."[23] Thus in contrast to the material weapons which had been and were being employed against them, theirs were spiritual. The necessity of the civil use of the sword is acknowledged in this statement: "We teach and acknowledge no other sword, nor tumult in the kingdom or church of Christ than the sharp sword of the Spirit, God's Word. . . . But the civil sword we leave to those to whom it is committed."[24] These statements were obviously intended to counteract the prevalent suspicion that all Anabaptists had political aspirations and were threatening to set up a kingdom of God on the earth, with Jan of Leyden at Münster as king.[25] Hence Menno called on the state authorities to judge carefully, as "god-fearing" men, concerning the doctrine and behavior of his followers; and to judge not by what others say but rather by the Word of God. His plea was, "Again I say, Be not like those bloodthirsty, violent and cruel men. But examine the Scriptures with trembling. With Solomon pray for wisdom. Look to the Spirit, Word, conduct, and example of Christ, and pass an impartial, righteous sentence according to its truth, even as all princes and judges are commanded in the Scriptures."[26]

From these statements we may infer that for Menno Simons the authority for the individual Christian was the scriptures; truth was in the scriptures to inform and command both state and church, but each in its separate sphere. When the law of the state conflicted with the law of God as revealed in the scriptures or as

---

[22] Ibid., 200.
[23] Ibid., 198.
[24] Ibid., 200.
[25] Bender, "A Brief Biography of Menno Simons," 10.
[26] Menno Simons, "Foundations of Christian Doctrine," 201.

made concrete in the life of Jesus, the Christian was to obey the higher law of God.

The next document of significance in the history of the Anabaptist-Mennonite Church is the Dordrecht Confession. During the ministry of Menno Simons, the church became a well-defined unit. However, beginning in 1567 a number of schisms occurred.[27] By 1630 attempts to reunite the Mennonite groups culminated in a convocation of about fifty ministers at Dordrecht, Holland, in April 1632, which accepted a confession of faith originally drafted by Adriaan Cornelisz, bishop of the Flemish Mennonite Church in Dordrecht. This confession was subsequently adopted by Mennonites in Alsace and the Palatinate in Germany, and ultimately in the United States of America. It is the official statement of doctrine of the Mennonite Church in this study, and of it Wenger says, "Historically this confession of faith was used as a basis of instruction to classes of young people who were being prepared for baptism and church membership. At the present time in the *Mennonite Church* the chief significance of the Dordrecht Confession is undoubtedly its value as a symbol of the Mennonite heritage of faith and way of life."[28] Articles XIII and XIV of this confession deal with the doctrine of nonresistance and constitute the basis of later official statements of the denomination. These two articles are cited herewith; they will be referred to in later exposition.

Article XIII

Of the Office of Civil Government

We also believe and confess, that God has instituted civil government, for the punishment of the wicked and the protection of the pious; and further, for the purpose of governing the world, countries and cities; and also to preserve its subjects in good order and under good regulations. Wherefore we are not permitted to despise, revile, or resist the same, but are to acknowledge it as a minister of God and be subject and obedient to it, in all things that do not militate against the law, will, and commandments of God; yea, "to be ready to every good work"; also faithfully to pay it custom, tax, and tribute; thus giving it what is its due; as Jesus Christ taught,

---

[27] Wenger, *The Doctrines of the Mennonites*, 77.
[28] Ibid.

did Himself, and commanded His followers to do. That we are also to pray to the Lord earnestly for the government and its welfare, and in behalf of our country, so that we may live under its protection, maintain ourselves, and "lead a quiet and peaceable life in all godliness and honesty." And further, that the Lord would recompense them (our rulers), here and in eternity; for all the benefits, liberties, and favors which we enjoy under their laudable administration. Romans 13:1–7; Titus 3:1–2; 1 Peter 2:17; Matthew 17:27; 22:20, 21; 1 Timothy 2:1, 2.

Article XIV

Of Defense by Force

Regarding revenge, whereby we resist our enemies with the sword, we believe and confess that the Lord Jesus has forbidden His disciples and followers all revenge and resistance, and has thereby commanded them not to "return evil for evil, nor railing for railing"; but to "put up the sword into the sheath," or, as the prophet foretold, "beat them into ploughshares." Matthew 5:39, 44; Romans 12:14; 1 Peter 3:9; Isaiah 2:4; Micah 4:3.

From this we see, that, according to the example, life, and doctrine of Christ, we are not to do wrong, or cause offense or vexation to anyone; but to seek the welfare and salvation of all men; also, if necessity should require it, to flee, for the Lord's sake, from one city or country to another, and suffer the "spoiling of our goods," rather than give occasion of offense to anyone; and if we are struck in our "right cheek, rather to turn the other also," than revenge ourselves, or return the blow. Matthew 5:39, 1:23; Romans 12:19.

And that we are, besides this, also to pray for our enemies, comfort and feed them, when they are hungry or thirsty, and thus by well-doing convince them and overcome the evil with good. Romans 12:20, 21.

Finally, that we are to do good in all respects, "commending ourselves to every man's conscience in the sight of God," and according to the law of Christ, do nothing to others that we would not wish them to do unto us. 2 Corinthians 4:2; Matthew 7:12; Luke 6:31.[29]

This confession probably came to the American Mennonite church through Dutch Mennonites who came to Germantown, Pennsylvania. In 1725 it was adopted by the Lancaster and Franconia Conferences of the Mennonite Church as their official statement of belief. Subsequently, as new conferences were organized, it continued to be recognized by the conservative groups particularly. Today it constitutes the official statement of faith of the Mennonite Church, though its personal acceptance by members, either for baptism or for ordination, is not required.[30] In 1921 in the general conference of the Mennonite Church which was convened at Garden City, Missouri, the doctrines of the Dordrecht Confession were reaffirmed and restated. The restatement is entitled "Christian Fundamentals," the preamble of which states:

> This statement does not supersede the eighteen articles of the Dort [Dordrecht] Confession, which the Church still confesses and teaches. It is rather a restatement of that confession in the light of present religious contentions and teachings. It gives expression to some of the doctrines and practices of the early Church which at that time were not a matter of difference, but have since the time of the Dort Confession been questioned or denied by many church organizations. For the sake of preserving the faith and teaching the Gospel as given by Christ and His apostles the Church has confessed in this formal manner her faith in and practice of the Gospel of salvation in Jesus Christ.[31]

Article IX of this statement pertains to the definition of the church. It says, "We believe that the Church is the body of Christ, composed of all those who through repentance toward God, and faith in the Lord Jesus Christ, have been born again and were baptized by one Spirit into one body, and that it is her divinely appointed mission to preach the Gospel to every creature, teaching obedience to all His commandments."[32] Article X deals with the place of the church in

---

[29] Wenger, *The Doctrines of the Mennonites,* Appendix 2, 83.
[30] John C. Wenger, "The Dordrecht Confession," *The Mennonite Encyclopedia,* 2:92.
[31] Wenger, *The Doctrines of the Mennonites,* Appendix 3, 88.
[32] Ibid., 89.

social reconstruction in the following terms: "We believe that we are called with a holy calling to a life of separation from the world and its follies, sinful practices, and methods; further that it is the duty of the Church to keep herself aloof from all movements which seek the reformation of society independent of the merits of the death of Christ and the experience of the new birth."[33] Article XIII contains some specific statements with regard to individual Christians and their relationship to the state. It reads as follows:

> We believe that all Christians should honor, pray for, pay tribute to, and obey in all things those who are in authority in state and nation, provided however, that should instances arise in which such obedience would violate the higher law of God "we ought to obey God rather than man," that Church and State are separate, and while believers are to be subject to, they are not a part of the civil, administrative powers; that it is contrary to the teachings of Christ and the apostles to engage in carnal warfare.[34]

These are the only statements that pertain directly to the doctrine of nonresistance.

The next official statement of the denomination is in the form of a resolution adopted in August 1937 at its general conference at Turner, Oregon. The preamble refers to the previous documents, and to the world situation prior to World War II. It asserts that the ensuing statement is not an innovation but rather a reiteration and a reaffirmation of principles the denomination has held from its inception in Switzerland in 1525. Its content will be included in the exposition of the doctrine of nonresistance below. The full text appears as Appendix A at the end of this study.

In the year 1946, following World War II, the scholarly treatise *War, Peace, and Nonresistance,* by Guy F. Hershberger, was published. The first comprehensive and authoritative work on this subject, it represented the denomination in that it was published with the authorization of its Peace Problems Committee. This work examines the biblical foundations, the historical development, and the distinguishing features of biblical nonresistance as compared with other pacifist views, and describes some implications for the future.

---

[33] Ibid., 90.
[34] Ibid.

In 1950 a Study Conference on Nonresistance was convened at Winona Lake, Indiana, which brought together more than sixty delegates representing the various denominations of the Mennonite "family," of which the Mennonite Church of this study is one. The "convictions" of the conference were expressed in a "Declaration of Faith and Commitment,"[35] the content of which will appear in the exposition of nonresistance below. The declaration is evidence of the dynamic character of the nonresistant faith of contemporary Mennonites. There is acknowledgment of the tradition of nonresistance but also the recognition that "this faith must be repossessed personally by each one out of his own reading and obeying God's Word, and must ever be spelled out in life practice anew."[36] Five statements pertain to basic theological and ethical principles, and eight statements attempt to project the application of these principles to the social and political context. The latter section, dealing with application of the principles, is prefaced by this statement:

> These declarations of faith give no blueprint for peace nor do they assume that human endeavor alone can bring about a warless world within history, for only when men come under the Lordship of Christ can they make peace and fulfill the prayer of our Lord, "Thy Kingdom come. Thy will be done on earth as in heaven." They do, however, require certain attitudes, duties, and ministries of us, to which we do here by God's grace declare our adherence and our determination to undertake in His name.[37]

In the following year, the Mennonite General Conference affirmed its position as a denomination in "A Declaration of Christian Faith and Commitment with Respect to Peace, War, and Nonresistance," dated August 23, 1951, at Goshen, Indiana. A supplement to it, representing the same body meeting at Johnstown, Pennsylvania, in August 1961, deals with "The Witness to the State." These two statements are incorporated as Part I and Part II of the latest official

---

[35] *A Declaration of Christian Faith and Commitment* (Akron, PA: Mennonite Central Committee, Peace Section, 1950).
[36] Ibid., 7.
[37] Ibid., 3.

document of the denomination on the doctrine of nonresistance; the title is *Peace and the Christian Witness.*[38]

II. Metaphysical presuppositions

The Mennonite Church had its origin in the Protestant Reformation of the sixteenth century. It has been characterized as radical in that it purports to take the commandments of the Bible literally as normative for faith and practical living. In most matters, the beliefs and practices of the Mennonite Church do not differ from those of other denominations in the Free Church tradition. Gordon Kaufman, in a study of the emphases of the early Anabaptists, observed, "The Anabaptist movement began as a part of the Zwinglian reform in Zurich and therefore, as one would expect in general the Anabaptists agree with the Zwinglians in Theology. In the public debates which were often held between Anabaptist leaders and those of the Reformed Church, questions of theology usually played a very minor role."[39] A theology was implied, however, even though it was not formulated elaborately. J. C. Wenger prefaced a brief outline of the beliefs and teachings of the denomination with the statement that "the definitive Anabaptist-Mennonite theology is yet to appear,"[40] and expressed the opinion that the lack of theological treatises indicates the fundamental fact that Anabaptism and Mennonitism are more biblical than theological. The Bible, including both Old and New Testaments, constitutes the authority for the denomination and for the individual Christian in all matters of faith and practice. The confession of faith and other doctrinal statements are supported with numerous references from the Bible. Abraham Toews in his analytical study of Mennonite ethics observes that "from the time of Menno the Mennonites have tried to have their doctrine flow directly out of the Scriptures and thus keep it free from dogma."[41] An example of this approach to the problem of nonresistance is this statement by Edward Yoder in an apologetic treatise:

---

[38] *Peace and the Christian Witness* (Scottdale, PA: Herald Press, Mennonite Central Conference, [1961]).

[39] Gordon D. Kaufman, "Some Theological Emphases of the Early Swiss Anabaptists," *Mennonite Quarterly Review* 25 (April 1951): 75.

[40] John C. Wenger, *Glimpses of Mennonite History and Doctrine* (Scottdale, PA: Herald Press, 1949), 137.

[41] Abraham P. Toews, "The Problem of Mennonite Ethics" (ThD diss., Concordia Theological Seminary, St. Louis, MO, 1959), 407.

Nonresistant Christians seek to order their life and conduct according to the teachings of the Scriptures. The Scriptures, they believe, reveal to man the mind and the will of God, particularly His will for human beings who are His special creation and care. They hold that the fullest and completest revelation of God and His will were given to men in Jesus Christ His Son when He became flesh and dwelt among men. Therefore, Christ is the final authority for the faith of Christians, and the pattern of their way of life.[42]

On this basis the teachings of Jesus Christ, his personal example, and the teachings of the apostles become normative and constitute an absolute authoritative point of departure. Relativities of history and culture are not permitted to infringe on the clear commands of the scriptures. Jacob Nickel describes the process of this approach in the following terms: "Since Scriptures alone are held as authoritative, Mennonite ethics become backward, rather than forward looking. That is to say, it is oriented toward a period in history and toward a small minority, the Early Church, in it; and theoretically all ethical problems the group faces today must be solved in as nearly the same way as that early minority solved its problems in its day."[43] This scriptural (biblical) frame of reference is evident in the latest declaration on nonresistance, which begins with a statement of fundamental principles—described as "Basic Central Truths." The five basic central truths are as follows:

1. That one is our Master, even Christ, who is our only Savior and Lord, and to whom alone supreme loyalty and obedience is due. He is the basis of our faith and commitment to the nonresistant way of life, and in His strength alone do we hope to live in peace and love toward all men. "For other foundation can no man lay than that is laid, which is Jesus Christ."
2. That by the atoning and renewing grace of God which makes us new creatures in Christ, and through the power of the indwelling Spirit, we can live the life of holy obedience and discipleship to which all the children of God are called.

---

[42] Edward Yoder and Donovan E. Smucker, *The Christian and Conscription* (Akron, PA: Mennonite Central Committee, 1945), 4.

[43] Jacob W. Nickel, "An Analytical Approach to Mennonite Ethics" (ThD diss., Iliff School of Theology, Denver, CO, 1959), 165.

3. That redeeming love is at the heart of the Gospel, and that the life of love and peace is God's plan for the individual and the race.

4. That Christ has established in the church, which is His body, a universal community and brotherhood of the redeemed, within which the fullness of His lordship must be practiced and from which must go out into all human society the saving and healing ministry of the Gospel.

5. That war is altogether contrary to the teaching and spirit of Christ and the Gospel, and to God's will as revealed in His word; that therefore war is sin, as is all manner of carnal strife; that it is wrong in spirit and method as well as in purpose, and destructive in its results; and that if we profess the principles of peace and nevertheless engage in warfare and strife we become guilty of sin and fall under the just condemnation of God.[44]

A perusal of these five principles or truths reveals that they involve certain presuppositions about the nature of God, of humanity, and of society, and an acceptance of certain standards to judge the right and the good. That is to say, there are implied metaphysical presuppositions and ethical principles. The first of these to be defined will be the concept of God.

Concept of God

God for the Mennonite Christian is as he is revealed in the Bible, and especially in the historic person, Jesus Christ. The Dordrecht Confession states "that there is one eternal, almighty, and incomprehensible God, Father, Son, and the Holy Ghost, and none more and none other, before whom no God existed, neither will exist after Him. For from him, through him, and in him are all things. . . . And we further believe, that this God still governs and preserves the same, together with all his works, through his wisdom, his might, and the 'word of his power.'"[45]

Article II in "Christian Fundamentals," an addition to the above, reads: "We believe that there is but one God, eternal, infinite,

---

[44] *Peace and the Christian Witness*, 2.
[45] Wenger, *The Doctrines of the Mennonites*, Appendix 2, 78.

perfect, and unchangeable who exists and reveals Himself in three persons—Father, Son, and Holy Spirit."[46]

Summarizing the beliefs inherent in these statements, and in the biblical references given in support of them, it is noted that there is a Trinitarian view of God; God as Father, God as Son, and God as the Holy Spirit. Consistent with this view, Wenger outlines the beliefs about God under the three headings: (1) The Father, (2) Jesus Christ, (3) The Holy Spirit. According to this outline, the beliefs about God include the following: (1) God as Father—God is a Spirit and has personality. God is eternal, omnipotent, omnipresent, and omniscient. God is truthful and faithful, just and holy. God is loving. (2) Jesus Christ—As Son of God and Son of Man He is both divine and human. He appeared in the stream of history as the incarnation of God. He is eternal. On earth he performed miracles; lived sinlessly; taught the truth about God, man, sin, righteousness, and salvation; and proclaimed the coming of a spiritual kingdom and his own return. His death on the cross was a propitiation for the sin of the whole world. His resurrection from the dead was a historical fact which authenticated his doctrine and deity. (3) The Holy Spirit—He is the "one who convicts men of their sin and leads them to saving faith in Christ the Lord." He participated in the creation as well as in the redemptive history of Israel. The Holy Spirit "regenerates" and "sanctifies" the believers. He "leads" and "assures" and "comforts" the believers and intercedes to God in their behalf.[47]

This knowledge of God is available to the individual through faith and through the Bible, which is believed to be the inspired, authentic Word of God and therefore authoritative, "the only infallible rule for faith and practice."[48] Jesus Christ is the focal object of faith and authority. For example, to the question, "Why is Jesus Christ the Supreme Authority for the Christian's Faith and Life?" the answer given is: "Let the Scriptures answer the question before us. After His resurrection from the dead Christ declared, 'All authority hath been given unto me in heaven and on earth' (Matthew

---

[46] Ibid., Appendix 3, 88.
[47] Wenger, *The Doctrines of the Mennonites*, 2–9.
[48] "Christian Fundamentals," in *Mennonite Church Polity*, compiled by the Church Polity Committee of the Mennonite General Conference (Scottdale, PA: Mennonite Publishing House, 1952), 64.

28:18)."[49] Similarly, this faith in Jesus Christ as ultimate authority is expressed in the first of the "basic central truths": "That one is our Master, even Christ, who is our only Savior and Lord, and to whom alone supreme loyalty and obedience is due."[50] Thus Jesus Christ is and represents ultimate reality with authority and power, whose doctrine, life, death, and resurrection reveal the will of God in matters of truth, of right, and of good. Likewise, "the meaning of history is to be found in the redemptive work of Christ and His redemptive community which is the church."[51] Culmination of this redemptive activity will be "the personal return of the Lord Jesus to raise the dead, judge the world, and usher in the eternal state."[52] Thus Jesus Christ is believed to be the universal Lord.

Concept of the human

The Dordrecht Confession states that God "created the first man, the father of us all, Adam; whom he formed of the dust of the ground, and breathed into his nostrils the breath of life, so that he became a living soul, created by God in His own image and likeness, in righteousness and holiness, unto eternal life."[53] The belief is expressed in this statement that humanity came into being through the creative act of God, who made us in "His own image." On the basis of the biblical record, it is held that through disobedience on the part of the first parents, Adam and Eve, sin came into the world, "which has thus passed upon all man." Humanity henceforth in our natural state is sinful and therefore estranged from God, who is holy.[54] Because of its sinful nature, man is "spiritually dead," "subject to physical death," and "subject to the power of the devil; from this fallen condition is unable to save himself."[55] John C. Wenger, in *Glimpses of Mennonite History and Doctrine,* says this was also the belief of the early Anabaptist leaders: "The Anabaptists believed in the sinfulness of human nature and in man's total inability to deliver

---

[49] Edward Yoder, *Must Christians Fight?* 2nd ed. (Akron, PA: Mennonite Central Committee, 1943), 15.
[50] Supra, 152.
[51] *Peace and the Christian Witness*, 10.
[52] Wenger, *The Doctrines of the Mennonites,* 20.
[53] Ibid., Appendix 2, 78.
[54] Ibid., Appendix 2, 78.
[55] "Christian Fundamentals," in *Mennonite Church Polity*, 65.

himself from sin."[56] Also, in another work, *Introduction to Theology,* representing Mennonite belief, the same author says:

> A truly Biblical theology will acknowledge (1) that fallen man is depraved, a slave to sin; (2) that the sinner can usually reject any particular evil or choose any particular good, but he cannot of himself renounce sin as such and choose Christ apart from the enablement of the Holy Spirit; hence Salvation is wholly of grace; (3) that men are not mere creatures of heredity or environment, but are also responsible for themselves; their destinies are in their own hands, for they are able to accept or reject the grace of God when convicted by the Holy Spirit.[57]

This recognition of the personal responsibility of individuals applies not only to their personal acceptance or rejection of salvation as offered them in the grace of God, but applies to all decisions of a moral character. The standards of morality are found in the Bible, including the Ten Commandments of the Old Testament, the Sermon on the Mount, and other commands of Jesus and the apostles. Living in a way that conforms to these high standards is held to be possible, because God's grace comes to the individual believer in the person of the Holy Spirit. This belief is asserted as follows: "We believe in the deity and personality of the Holy Spirit, that He convinces the world of sin, of righteousness, and of judgment; that He indwells and comforts the believer, guides him into all truth, empowers for service and enables him to live a life of righteousness."[58] Thus, humans may be fundamentally changed in their nature by the gracious regeneration of God who will continue to enable them to live in obedience to the commands and spirit of Jesus Christ. In Mennonite literature, the favored term to identify this regenerated and reoriented status is *discipleship.* It has been described as a unique emphasis of the denomination, though the Mennonite Church does not claim exclusive use or understanding of it. Harold S. Bender, in his classic definition of the genius of Anabaptist vision, asserts: "First and fundamental in the Anabaptist Vision was the conception of the essence of Christianity as

---

[56] Wenger, *Glimpses of Mennonite History and Doctrine,* 140.
[57] John C. Wenger, *Introduction to Theology* (Scottdale, PA: Herald Press, 1954), 105.
[58] "Christian Fundamentals," in *Mennonite Church Polity,* 66.

discipleship: The focus of the Christian life was to be not so much the inward experience of the grace of God, as it was for Luther, but the outward application of that grace to all human conduct and the consequent Christianization of all human relationships."[59] This concept of the human—humanity's original nature, the necessity of human regeneration, and the possibility of realizing the will of God through disciplined living—is affirmed on the authority of the Bible. Obedience to the injunctions of scripture is expected to be costly, but warranted and tolerable by reason of the redemptive suffering of Christ.

Concept of society
The chief concern is that of the relationship between Christians and their environment. Individuals are members of the Christian community, members of society at large, and they are members of their denomination or "brotherhood." Mennonites use the term *the world* as it is used in the New Testament to designate human society or human culture as what stands separate from the church. The relationship has been described as the "noncontinuity of the church with the society in the midst of which the church stands."[60] In accommodating itself and witnessing to the culture in which it finds itself, the church may confront problems in language, ideas, beliefs, customs, social organization, technical processes, and values. This confrontation is approached critically, and all decisions are theoretically subjected to the authority of the Bible. Such an approach, and the attitude inherent in it, is characterized by Richard Niebuhr in his classification of types of Christian attitudes toward culture as "Christ Against Culture." He finds that "the Mennonites have come to represent the attitude most purely, since they not only renounce all participation in politics and refuse to be drawn into military service, but follow their own distinctive customs and regulations in economics and education."[61] The presupposition that appears to govern Mennonite thought and practice is that the culture of the world at large is basically sinful and demonic,

---

[59] Harold S. Bender, "The Anabaptist Vision," *Mennonite Quarterly Review* 18 (April 1944): 78.
[60] Leonard Verduin, "Menno Simons' Theology Reviewed," *Mennonite Quarterly Review* 24 (January 1950): 54.
[61] H. Richard Niebuhr, *Christ and Culture* (New York: Harper and Brothers, 1951), 56.

and that the church is called out to stand over against this world prophetically and redemptively. Wenger in his work *Separated unto God* (a title that clearly designates the Mennonite point of view) defines the cleavage as follows:

> There is a sense in which all men are brothers, namely, they all have a common ancestry; there is no race which is intrinsically better than another. But mankind is divided into two totally separate groups; those who by faith-surrender to Christ and to the obedience of faith have become children of God, with membership in His kingdom; and on the other hand, those who because they have never been converted are yet in the kingdom of this world, their fine manhood and decent moral character notwithstanding. This point of view is not held because of a narrow sectarianism but because of the plain teaching of Scripture.[62]

This strong cleavage between the kingdom of the world and the kingdom of God as a characteristic Mennonite view had its origin in the church's Anabaptist heritage. Robert Friedmann in fact demonstrates rather convincingly that this emphasis was the main concern of the early Anabaptists, the unique tenet of their theology. Their belief is identified in Friedmann's essay as "Kingdom theology" or "The Doctrine of the Two Worlds"; the two kingdoms are distinguished as follows: "The kingdom of God which is to come here and now, and the kingdom of darkness which rules over all those who do not see the light."[63] Friedmann points out that the kingdom theology implies a new set of values, a new outlook on history, and a social ethic. The content of these implications is further defined as follows in terms of a new set of values, an outlook on history, and a social ethic:

> The kingdom theory implies first a new set of values. Certainly the Sermon on the Mount is the best illustration: love, forgiveness, self-surrender, hating not even one's own persecutors, these values are so radically different that they seem paradoxical and unrealizable to an unregenerate

---

[62] John C. Wenger, *Separated unto God* (Scottdale, PA: Mennonite Publishing House, 1952), 186.
[63] Robert Friedmann, "The Doctrine of the Two Worlds," in *The Recovery of the Anabaptist Vision*, ed. Guy F. Hershberger (Scottdale, PA: Herald Press, 1957), 109.

mind. Rather they imply a different dimension, the world of the Spirit, in contrast with all secular this-worldly valuations. . . .

In the second place, kingdom theology has its own specific outlook on history. . . . The two realms, the kingdom of God and the kingdom of darkness, are engaged in a perennial struggle, a world drama, in which each person must choose and take his side. In the end the kingdom of God will triumph over the powers of darkness. . . .

Thirdly, the kingdom theology includes also a social ethic. . . . The horizontal man-to-man relationship belongs to the kingdom just as much as does the vertical God-man relationship. . . . The brethren, the body of believers, constitutes the realm; hence brotherly love, *agape*, is more than mere ethics. It is one of the basic qualifications of the kingdom here and now.[64]

Thus the Christians' relation to society as a whole begins with their position as members of the body of Christ, the group of believers. This is the realm that constitutes the kingdom of God of which Jesus Christ is Lord. Their loyalties and responsibilities in this kingdom take precedence over and govern their relationships in the larger context of the kingdom of the world. The state, representing the kingdom of the world, is to be honored, prayed far, supported by the payment of taxes, and obeyed in every way that does not conflict with the obligations of Christian discipleship. The biblical authority on which such decisions are made are statements such as the following: "Then render to Caesar the things that are Caesar's and to God the things that are God's;[65] We must obey God rather than men."[66] Again, in "The Anabaptist Vision," Bender states the belief that motivated the early Anabaptists in regard to their relationship to society:

> The Anabaptist vision was not a detailed blueprint for the reconstruction of human society, but the Brethren did believe that Jesus intended the Kingdom of God should be set up in the midst of the earth, here and now, and this they

---

[64] Ibid., 111–13.
[65] Luke 20:25 (RSV).
[66] Acts 5:29 (RSV).

proposed to do forthwith. We shall not believe, they said, that the Sermon on the Mount or any other vision that He had is only a heavenly vision meant but to keep His followers in tension until the last great day, but we shall practice what He taught, believing that where He walked we can by His grace follow in His steps.[67]

A similar belief is expressed by the Mennonite Church in a recent declaration pertaining to the church, the world, and the state. These statements are particularly relevant with regard to the problem of nonresistance. Under the title "The Christian Witness to the State," the following affirmations of belief are made:

> The church is the body of Christ, the community of believers, the gathered company, identified with the stream of forces issuing from the redemptive work of Christ, whom she acknowledges as the Lord of history and as her own supreme head, and under whose lordship she walks in obedient commitment and discipleship. The believers accept the new life in Christ as a binding imperative, as a glorious possibility, and as a blessed reality in which they live. They are laborers together with God for the redemption of the world which knows Him not. The meaning of history is to be found in the redemptive work of Christ and of His redemptive community which is the church.[68]

In regard to the world, the presupposition is asserted that:

> Outside the body of Christ are those who reject Christ and who stand in rebellion against God. The Scriptures speak of this non-Christian company as "the world," which is under the rule of principalities, of powers, of thrones, and of dominions. These terms suggest not only a degree of structure within the fallen social order, but also a degree of conflict among the units of the structure, and a certain rebellion against the will of God.

> This world does not recognize the lordship of Christ. In His death the powers even sought to destroy Him. His victory over the powers, however, is a demonstration of that lordship

---

[67] Bender, "The Anabaptist Vision," 78.
[68] *Peace and the Christian Witness,* Part 2: "The Christian Witness to the State," section entitled "The Church Accepts the Lordship of Christ."

to which every knee shall bow and which every tongue shall confess. Thus Christ is Lord both over the church which recognizes His lordship, and over the world which denies it.[69]

With regard to the state there are affirmations of two basic presuppositions. The first is a recognition of the function of the state as a "minister of God for good." This is defined in the following statement:

> The Scriptural view of the state is a twofold one. On the one hand it is a minister of God for good, whose function is the maintenance of order in this present world. Its ultimate source of power is the God of history Himself. As such, the Christian owes the state respect, obedience, and co-operation, with prayers for its rulers to the end that the people of God may "lead a quiet and peaceable life in all godliness and honesty." The primary function of the state is the maintenance of a stable society enabling the church to pursue her divine ministry of reconciliation and of prophetic witness under the lordship of Christ.[70]

The second function of the state is described as follows:

> It is clear, on the other hand, that the state is also an institution of this present evil world, and that as such it is at times an agent of the forces arrayed against the Lord of history. For this reason the Christian cannot always submit to the demands of the state. On the contrary, he must needs on occasion be in opposition to the state, as individual rulers or their acts come under the domination of the principalities, the powers, and the spiritual hosts of wickedness who are in rebellion against the lordship of Christ.[71]

From these presuppositions of a metaphysical nature we will examine the ethical principles that emerge and which are set forth as basic to the doctrine of nonresistance.

---

[69] Ibid., section entitled "The World Denies the Lordship of Christ."
[70] Ibid., section entitled "The State as a Minister of God for Good."
[71] Ibid., section entitled "The State as an Agent of the Powers."

III. Ethical principles

The investigation leads now to the ethical principles on which non-resistance is predicated. The Mennonite Church has not produced a comprehensive system of ethics which would be recognized as such in the formal sense. Just as in theological matters the source book is the Bible, so also in ethics. For this reason J. Lawrence Burkholder, in a discussion of Mennonite ethics in *The Mennonite Encyclopedia*, says:

> Methodologically Mennonite ethics must be understood first and fundamentally as Biblical ethics. The exclusive source of ethical instructions is the Bible—more precisely the New Testament. The Biblicism of the Mennonites comes through most impressively in the settling of ethical questions. Sufficient for a valid imperative is a clearly stated command of Christ to His disciples or a command by one of the apostles. . . . Generally speaking, Mennonite ethics belongs to the *imitatio Christi* tradition.[72]

Agape-love

The fundamental ethical norm or principle is directly related to the concept of the kingdom of God. Guy F. Hershberger points out that when people came to Jesus enquiring about entrance to his kingdom, he referred them to the Ten Commandments, which he then interpreted to them.[73] Jesus said to one such inquirer: "You shall love the Lord your God with all your heart, and with all your soul, and with all your mind," and "You shall love your neighbor as yourself." And then he added, "On these two commandments depend all the law and the prophets."[74] Citing these statements, Hershberger, at the outset of his exposition of nonresistance in the New Testament, says: "Christ, therefore, endorses the Ten Commandments and the law of love as the fundamental moral law, valid for all time, and it is through His grace and power that men are enabled to keep this law."[75] That is to say that the principle fundamental to the Ten Commandments is the principle of love. In Jesus' terms, this love is to govern one's attitude and behavior toward

---

[72] J. Lawrence Burkholder, "Ethics," *The Mennonite Encyclopedia*, 4:1080.

[73] Hershberger, *War, Peace, and Nonresistance*, 40.

[74] Matt. 22:37–40. (RSV).

[75] Hershberger, *War, Peace, and Nonresistance*, 40.

God and one's attitude and behavior toward one's fellow men and women. The basic principle of life for the disciple of Christ, for the citizen of his kingdom, is therefore love. "This is the central idea of the Christian ethic according to Mennonites."[76] The ground of this ethical principle is not merely the command of Christ, however important that may be, but the total life and death of Christ in its redemptive expression.

> In the cross of Christ the love of God was manifested for the world and the love which is expected of Christians ethically is a re-enactment of the drama of redemption. In other words, the emphasis is on sacrificial love even though Mennonites use the term love to cover relationships of mutuality. Mennonites have clearly perceived that the full meaning of love is known supremely in the cross and the Christian ethic therefore must start with nothing less than complete self-giving.[77]

The distinctive character of love in this usage is identified by the Greek New Testament term *agape*. Agape-love, as distinct from self-love and mutual love, is self-giving love. This is the love God has shown toward humanity. It is the love that filled the life of Jesus, and it is the love required of those who would follow Jesus. Agape begins where individuals experience the love of God in personal redemption and regeneration. This they experience by the act of yieldedness on their part. Gordon Kaufman points out that historically this was an important element in the thinking of the Anabaptists: "*Gelassenheit* [yieldedness] is the first step to true brotherhood, the overcoming of selfishness."[78] Christians may be called on to expend themselves without regard for success or reward. Such love becomes possible when they know they are sustained by the divine love which frees them from anxiety about themselves and about the rightness of their action. They are, therefore, free to love (in the agape sense) their fellow men and women, friend or foe, as God loves them. The ultimate criterion or norm is agape.

It is in this concept of the nature of love for God and love for humanity that nonresistance has its roots. According to Don E.

---

[76] Burkholder, "Ethics," *The Mennonite Encyclopedia*, 4:1081.
[77] Ibid.
[78] Kaufman, "Some Theological Emphases of the Early Swiss Anabaptists," 93.

Smucker, in his study "The Theological Basis for Christian Paci-fism," "Nonresistance is applied *agape* insofar as this comes through earthen vessels—and this is the medium through which God works—nonresistance will always need forgiveness and justification by faith, that faith which worketh by love. Insofar as the earthen vessel is a medium of God's agape it becomes wholly good."[79] Here it is recognized that Christians, however devoted to agape-love, may yet fail, but their failure may be forgiven. In the measure in which they fulfill the demand of agape, they are a medium of God's love. Failure is no justification for compromise. Reinhold Niebuhr recognizes agape as the New Testament ethic but considers it impossible of realization. It is an "impossible possibility," he says, and suggests an alternative as follows: "It is not even right to insist that every action of the Christian must conform to *agape,* rather than to the norm of relative justice and mutual love by which life is maintained and conflicting interests are arbitrated in history."[80] To this suggestion the Mennonite response is that obedience to the love ethic must be maintained at whatever cost; it may lead to the cross as it did for Jesus. "Mennonitism" says Robert Friedmann, "stands for the testimony of a concrete Christianity which reveals the essence of life in *love* and Cross."[81] There is a direct connection between the cross of Christ and the cross of the disciple, a connec-tion Jesus enjoined when he said: "If any man would come after me, let him deny himself and take up his cross and follow me."[82] This continuity as the basis of Mennonite conviction is expressed by John H. Yoder as follows:

> Christ is *Agape;* self-giving, nonresistant love. At the Cross this nonresistance, including the refusal to use political means of self-defense, found its ultimate revelation in the uncomplaining and forgiving death of the innocent at the hands of the guilty. This death reveals how God deals with evil; here is the only valid starting point for Christian paci-fism or nonresistance. The Cross is the extreme demonstra-

---

[79] Donovan E. Smucker, "The Theological Basis for Christian Pacifism," *Menno-nite Quarterly Review* 27 (July 1953): 177.

[80] Reinhold Niebuhr, *The Nature and Destiny of Man* (New York: Charles Scribner's Sons, 1943), 2:76.

[81] Robert Friedmann, *Mennonite Piety through the Centuries* (Goshen, IN.: The Men-nonite Historical Society, 1949), 268.

[82] Matt. 16:24 (RSV).

tion that agape seeks neither effectiveness nor justice, and is willing to suffer any loss or seeming defeat for the sake of obedience.[83]

The ethical principle from which nonresistance emerges is, therefore, clearly agape or self-sacrificing love.

IV. Nonresistance (An exposition)

Nonresistance is the term used in the Anabaptist-Mennonite tradition to denote the faith and life of those who believe that the will of God requires the renunciation of warfare and other coercive means for the furtherance of personal or political ends.[84] The resistance of evil by force and the meting out of punishment are held to involve necessarily an inward disposition of vengeance and hatred or lovelessness. The termination of life, as in capital punishment and warfare, which are a part of state responsibility, is ruled out for the Christian, and pacifism is endorsed. The result of this view is to limit the degree of responsibility the Christian can assume in the state government. Because of the belief that the use of violence is morally wrong, i.e., that it is a violation of God's moral law, the individual Christian who participates in warfare in any way is willfully disobedient to God. This is sin, which brings the individual under divine condemnation.[85]

Nonresistance is held as the right action for the Christian, not only because of the desire to refrain from sin, but also because it is understood to be the positive expression of love. Melvin Gingerich in an essay on "Alternative Service" says: "It needs to be remembered that Christian nonresistance rests on a much broader foundation than a revulsion to war. It is based on Christ's command to love all men and from this point of view Christian service is more than alternative service. It is a positive ministry of sacrificial service to men who are in need at all times and under all circumstances."[86] Even though the term is negative in form, it conveys a positive meaning. Nonresistance is not merely the withdrawal from a conflict situ-

---

[83] John H. Yoder, *Peace without Eschatology?* (Scottdale, PA: Mennonite Publishing House, 1954), 7.

[84] Guy F. Hershberger, "Nonresistance," *The Mennonite Encyclopedia*, 3:897.

[85] Guy F. Hershberger, "Peace and War in the New Testament," *Mennonite Quarterly Review* 17 (April 1943): 59–72.

[86] Melvin Gingerich, "Discipleship Expressed in Alternative Service," in *The Recovery of the Anabaptist Vision*, ed. Hershberger, 272.

ation but the positive expression of the way of love as portrayed in the New Testament, particularly in the example of Jesus Christ. The term derives from the statement of Jesus in the Sermon on the Mount, "Do not resist one who is evil."[87] Other terms on the subject which are used synonymously in Mennonite literature are "biblical nonresistance" and "Christian pacifism." Both seem to be more specific and more positive in connotation. Hershberger explains: "Certain forms of pacifism or nonviolence, however, being based more upon humanitarian, philosophical, or political considerations than upon New Testament ethics, are not to be confused with nonresistance."[88] The specific content of the term *nonresistance* (biblical nonresistance, Christian pacifism) is the substance of the ensuing paragraphs. As has been shown above, nonresistance is directly related to the faith of the Mennonite Christian. It is a way of life that proceeds directly from personal response to God and his will as understood in the scriptures. Nonresistance is therefore based on this foundation. In Hershberger's exposition, he notes first of all the element of the covenant; second, the example of Jesus Christ; and direct teaching in the New Testament.[89]

Nonresistance and the covenant
Hershberger affirms that in the scriptures God's relationship with humankind takes the form of a covenant.[90] God, the Creator, whose nature is love, is holy and righteous. The human creature responds with love toward God, seeking to walk in holiness and righteousness by obedience to the commands of God. In the Old Testament, the imperative for this response to God was "You shall be holy; for I the Lord your God am holy."[91] In the New Testament, Jesus said to his followers, "You shall love the Lord your God with all your heart, and with all your soul, and with all your mind. This is the great and first commandment. And a second is like it. You shall love your neighbor as yourself. On these two commandments depend

---

[87] Matt. 5:39 (RSV).
[88] Hershberger, "Nonresistance," *The Mennonite Encyclopedia*, 3:897.
[89] Hershberger, *War, Peace, and Nonresistance,* 40–45.
[90] Guy F. Hershberger, *The Way of the Cross in Human Relations* (Scottdale, PA: Herald Press, 1958), 6.
[91] Lev. 19:2 (RSV).

all the law and the prophets."[92] Hershberger asserts on the basis of a number of pertinent scripture references:

> Underlying both covenants is the fundamental moral law which is God's plan for human conduct, yesterday, today, and forever. The difference between the two is this, that whereas under the old covenant God made a concession to the hardness of men's hearts (Matthew 19:8), under the new covenant He gives His children a new heart so that they are able to accomplish that which men of a stony heart did not accomplish under the old covenant. The new covenant is better than the old because the consciences of men are now cleansed "from dead works to serve the living God."[93]

The new covenant requires a certain high standard of morality consistent with the nature of God, and also provides for the carrying out of that standard of morality. It is a two-way agreement, whereby humans are responsible to meet certain conditions of behavior appropriate to their relationship to God. The essential nature of this behavior is characterized by love. In the view of the Mennonite faith as expressed by Hershberger, this means that "to violate the command of love is to walk in rebellion against God; to bring disorder and confusion into human relationships. To obey the command of love is to identify one's self and to synchronize one's life with the divine order in all of man's affairs." [94] In this light, nonresistance shows the greatest possible relevance to the constructive purposes of society, and is the way by which God's will may be effected in society. Obedience on this plane is the true test of love for God. Love and obedience are believed to be inextricably linked together, as Hershberger says: "Throughout the Scriptures love and obedience are associated in the most intimate manner. . . . In the divine order of things there can be no love without obedience, nor obedience without love."[95] A statement of Jesus in support of this view is cited, namely: "If you keep my commandments, you will abide in my love, just as I have kept my Father's commandments and abide in his love."[96]

---

[92] Matt. 22:37–40 (RSV).
[93] Hershberger, *War, Peace, and Nonresistance*, 42.
[94] Hershberger, *The Way of the Cross in Human Relations*, 6–7.
[95] Ibid.
[96] John 15:10 (RSV).

This obedience-love relationship is thus believed to be directly related to the covenant between God and his repentant child. It is an essential ingredient of the experience of faith. In the covenant, furthermore, God's grace is promised to help the Christian to perform his will. In fact, the life of nonresistance is considered so exacting in its demands that it can be realized only with supernatural aid. "The man of the new covenant is saved by grace, and with the indwelling Spirit of God to direct his steps he is enabled to keep the moral law."[97] Continuing in biblical terms, Hershberger characterizes the life and outlook of the Christian in his relationship to God as follows: "His life has been transformed by the power of God, hence he lives peaceably with all men. He does not avenge himself; he renders to no man evil for evil. If his enemy hungers he feeds him; he overcomes evil with good."[98] In the denomination's official statement on the question of "Peace and the Christian Witness," the implication of the covenant relationship is affirmed as follows: "We believe . . . that the Christian, having been laid hold of by God through Christ, must follow his Lord in all things regardless of consequences. He must pay the price of complete discipleship, for to him the commands of Christ and the principles of the Gospel are not mere counsels to be accepted or rejected as may seem good at the moment, but rather imperatives which must be followed to the end. Once the premise is accepted that Christ speaks with authority from heaven, only one thing remains, that is to obey His command. And this the new man in Christ will desire from his heart to do."[99] The covenant relationship thus is understood to imply obligations. The obligations are found to be enunciated clearly and exemplified perfectly in Jesus Christ.

Nonresistance and the example of Jesus

God's will and nature were revealed in the person and ministry of Jesus Christ in such a way that his disciples might know and do the will of God. Truth and morality became incarnate in him. Thus humanity is left without excuse as to the meaning of "be ye holy, even as I am holy." This belief appears in the denomination's official statement as follows:

---

[97] Hershberger, War, Peace, and Nonresistance, 42.
[98] Ibid., 43.
[99] Peace and the Christian Witness, 4.

In the life and work of Him, who in His incarnation became one with man, is given the full revelation of God's will, reaching its supreme meaning at Calvary. Integral to this divine-human life of our Lord was His innocent and nonresistant endurance of the evil inflicted upon Him, His identification of Himself in His suffering with all sinners, thus bearing man's sin in His own body on the cross, and His triumphant victory over sin by the very means of His death. What He taught in the Sermon on the Mount He fulfilled in His life and practice, including the cross.[100]

In his life and work, Jesus showed love unstintingly to all people, without regard to social status or race. Hershberger cites as evidence instances in which Jesus helped different kinds of people in a variety of needs.[101] The supreme expression of his love, however, is found in his death on the cross. In this he constitutes a perfect example of nonresistance, for he did not use any of the privilege or power at his disposal to prevent or resist the working of the forces of evil that were converging in his crucifixion. Hershberger describes briefly the suffering Jesus experienced at the hands of his enemies prior to the crucifixion and summarizes by saying that "the life and death are a perfect example of love and nonresistance."[102] A statement of the Apostle Peter is cited to show the connection between this event and the spirit of Christ and the disciple, upon which Hershberger comments:

> Peter admonishes Christians who suffer wrongfully to bear it with patience. In fact, this is the Christian's very calling: "For hereunto were ye called: because Christ also suffered for you, leaving you an example, that ye should follow his steps: who did no sin, neither was guile found in his mouth: who when he was reviled, reviled not again; when he suffered, threatened not; but committed himself to him that judgeth righteously (1 Peter 2:21-24).[103]

Thus the death of Christ on the cross, while understood as more than a noble example of self-sacrifice and high morality, does nev-

---

[100] Ibid., 4.
[101] Hershberger, *War, Peace, and Nonresistance*, 44.
[102] Ibid., 45.
[103] Ibid., 45.

ertheless, in the terms of Peter, demand the same of his followers. Regard for the significance of the cross as God's redemptive atoning act for sinful humanity should not minimize its significance for Christian morality. Hershberger's affirmation represents the traditional teaching of the Mennonite Church when he says:

> This was the cross life of Christ, of which the cross death was the logical sequence and crowning achievement. The good life brought the opposition of evil men; but the way of love and nonresistance left no room for retaliation. By His assumed human limitations He declined to escape from the wrath of evil men. Thus the Son of God gave His life on the cross. By this act He endured the wrath of God and redeemed sinful men, reconciling them to God. Christ came to redeem sinners and He did it by way of the cross: the cross life of love and nonresistance, and the cross death of Calvary. This in turn becomes the way for the Christian who has been redeemed and reconciled to God.[104]

If, therefore, disciples of Christ are to live out in their lives the morality incumbent on them as Christians, they will find it to be "the way of the cross." This is suffering that is self-giving, sacrificial, and nonresistant toward the evildoer at whose hands one is required to suffer.

Nonresistance and the direct teaching of the New Testament
Under this heading it is necessary to consider the direct teachings of Jesus and of the apostles that unquestionably support the nonresistant ethic, as well as some that appear to limit its sphere.

1. Nonresistance and the direct teaching of Jesus. The official statement of the Mennonite Church assumes that the commands of Jesus, and his precepts, were given to be applied to life here and now by his disciples. As Lord of his kingdom, he has given instructions as to the rules that should obtain in this kingdom. Citizenship in this kingdom is also referred to as discipleship. In either case, the implication is that life is to be ordered after the likeness and teaching of Jesus as Lord. Thus the statement reads:

> This way of discipleship is not only a command to be obeyed; it is the way of victory and peace for the individual and

---

[104] Hershberger, *The Way of the Cross in Human Relations*, 23.

society, to be practiced in the here and now and not to be postponed to some future kingdom. With a joyful belief in the reality of God's reign, we therefore forthrightly establish our lives on the power of Christ. We are convinced that the teachings of Jesus and the power of the Gospel are the solution to the problems of sin in man and society; and that the reason society is still in its broken state is either because men reject Christ and His Gospel or because those who have taken the name of Christ will not live that Gospel and take up the cross of utter discipleship laid upon them by their Lord.[105]

Here it is asserted that the following of Christ in the context of a sinful society is an exacting vocation. It is not the negative or passive line of least resistance, as its language may suggest. Edward Yoder comments as follows: "To go a second mile with the man who asks for one mile is not negative but aggressive; it is a powerful kind of resistance. But it is not resisting evil men on their own low unregenerate level of conduct."[106] Hershberger explains that when Jesus set aside the civil law of Moses which prescribed "eye for eye and tooth for tooth," he was not speaking of mere personal retaliation or compensation. He was, rather, referring to a particular legal procedure whereby an offense was reported to the civil authorities and then to the magistrate, who in turn administered justice. What Jesus did, in effect, was forbid his followers to refer their grievances to civil authorities for revenge against their offenders. Likewise, in instructing them to "go the second mile," he was not speaking figuratively but specifically and literally. For it was the practice of the Roman government to requisition the services of its subjects as needed for road building or courier duties. To this practice Christians should not object, nor should they refuse but rather give more service than was required.[107] Thus the precept of Jesus not only negates retaliation but requires good for evil and in a "more than duty" measure. Hershberger points out that this pattern of forgiveness and of doing good for evil was not limited to personal relationships among Christian people but was to be observed in all relationships. This unqualified and unlimited application of the love

---

[105] *Peace and the Christian Witness,* 4.
[106] Edward Yoder, *Must Christians Fight?* 11.
[107] Hershberger, *War, Peace, and Nonresistance,* 47.

ethic is a distinctive one in the Anabaptist-Mennonite tradition, as shown by contrast in an appraisal by Hershberger:

> They insisted that the Christian was one individual whose ethic as a citizen of the state must be no different from his personal ethic as a Christian; and in so doing they rejected the ethic of Luther. Their strict adherence to the Sermon on the Mount and the New Testament ethic also made it impossible for them to accept the Calvinistic doctrine of the sphere of common grace which enables the Christian to serve as an agency of the divine wrath.[108]

Luther's solution to the problem had been the concept of the two kingdoms—the inward kingdom ruled by the Sermon on the Mount and the external kingdom "put under the sword." To the question, how can the Christian, who belongs to both these domains and has to live in both, contrive to practice a dual morality? the answer was: "As a Christian, in his personal life and personal relations, he must abide by the first order, the order of grace; as a Christian citizen, in his outward calling, to the second, the order of creation."[109] For Calvin there was one realm in which the law of God was the authority, and the church and state together were the instruments of his will: "Church and state were to work together in one loyal alliance for a common end. . . . For Calvin the State was not merely a means of punishment and an antidote for sin, but also, and especially, a good and holy ordinance of God, a valuable instrument for maintaining his glory in the world."[110] Thus Christians who purport to obey the commands of Christ as given in the Sermon on the Mount would resolve problems of conflicting demands in different ways. In the tradition of Luther, their action would be determined by its context, personal or nonpersonal. In the tradition of Calvin, their action would be determined by reference to the universal sovereignty of God, whom they obey in the service of the church and of the state. In the tradition of the Anabaptist-Mennonite, their action would be subjected to the love ethic of the New Testament, and if this could not be integrated into the requirements of citizen-

---

[108] Hershberger, *The Way of the Cross in Human Relations*, 155.
[109] G. J. Heering, *The Fall of Christianity*, trans. J. W. Thompson (New York: Fellowship Publications, 1943), 51.
[110] Ibid., 57.

ship of the state, they must suffer the consequences. The absolute unquestioned reference to the validity of the literal intention of Christ's commands is illustrated in the following statement in a book written to guide young Mennonite Christians in their consideration of military service: "If every person were at liberty to accommodate the teachings of Christ to his own convenience and what he considers practicable, or at the command of the State or any other secular institution then indeed there could be no way to know with certainty how to follow Christ."[111]

The application of the love ethic as enunciated by Jesus, involving nonresistance in all relationships, is considered mandatory for all disciples, in personal life, in relationships within the church brotherhood, in community relationships, and in relation to the state. Historically, the greatest conflict has arisen in applying nonresistant faith to the normal requirements of state citizenship. Refusal to use "the sword" was justified in terms of a higher responsibility, however irrelevant such aloofness may have appeared to the abstainers or to others. The church believed, as J. Lawrence Burkholder points out, that "it was a positive force for good which pointed toward a new community of love. Love did not simply demand withdrawal from some of the major functions of society. It called for the creation of a new society, where peace and brotherhood would reign."[112]

2. Nonresistance and the direct teaching of the apostles. The same love ethic is believed to be sustained by the teaching of the apostles. Hershberger cites the following statement from the writings of Paul: "Avenge not yourselves, beloved, but give place unto the wrath of God: for it is written, Vengeance belongeth unto me; I will recompense, saith the Lord. But if thine enemy hunger, feed him; if he thirst give him to drink. . . . Be not overcome of evil, but overcome evil with good.[113] Also cited is the classic exposition of love recorded in the letter to the Corinthians;[114] especially the phrase "love . . . seeketh not its own," with the observation that self-seeking, which is often at the root of strife, is ruled out by love.[115] Paul

[111] Yoder, *Must Christians Fight?* 23.
[112] J. Lawrence Burkholder, "The Anabaptist Vision of Discipleship" in *The Recovery of the Anabaptist Vision*, ed. Hershberger, 145.
[113] Rom. 12:19–21 (AV).
[114] 1 Cor. 13.
[115] Hershberger, *War, Peace, and Nonresistance,* 48.

said further: "For though we live in the world we are not carrying on a worldly war, for the weapons of our warfare are not worldly but have divine power to destroy strongholds."[116] Another Pauline statement, describing the qualifications of servants of the Lord, says they "must not be quarrelsome but kindly to every one."[117]

Peter, the apostle, is also cited in a statement where he pointed to the suffering of Jesus as the example for all Christians to follow: "For to this you have been called, because Christ also suffered for you, leaving you an example, that you should follow in His steps. He committed no sin; no guile was found on his lips. When he was reviled, he did not revile in return; when he suffered he did not threaten; but he trusted to him who judges justly."[118] Peter again speaks in the spirit of the Sermon on the Mount of Jesus in these words: "Do not return evil for evil or reviling for reviling; but on the contrary bless, for to this you have been called, that you may obtain a blessing."[119]

John, the apostle, is cited as follows: "By this we know love, that he laid down his life for us; and we ought to lay down our lives for the brethren."[120] "If anyone says 'I love God' and hates his brother, he is a liar; for he who does not love his brother whom he has seen, cannot love God whom he has not seen. And this commandment we have from him, that he who loves God should love his brother also."[121]

James, the apostle, is cited as follows: "What causes wars, and what causes fightings among you? Is it not your passions that are at war in your members?"[122]

These citations are given in the official statement of the church as supporting its commitment to the way of nonresistance.[123]

But Paul creates a problem for the Mennonite view in his letter to the Christians in Rome, when he says: "Let every person be subject to the governing authorities. For there is no authority except from God, and those that exist have been instituted by God.

---

[116] 1 Cor. 10:3–4 (RSV).
[117] 2 Tim. 2:24 (RSV).
[118] 1 Pet. 2:21–23 (RSV).
[119] 1 Pet. 3:9 (RSV).
[120] 1 John 3:16 (RSV).
[121] 1 John 4:20–21 (RSV).
[122] James 4:1 (RSV).
[123] *Peace and the Christian Witness*, 3.

Therefore he who resists the authorities resists what God has appointed, and those who resist will incur judgment."[124] In this and in subsequent statements, Paul urges Christians to fulfill their obligations to the state without any apparent reservation. Recognition of and obedience to the state are enjoined as matters of conscience. This means paying of taxes, "respect to whom respect is due, and honor to whom honor is due." The state's coercive right, even to the use of the "sword," is authorized by God.

Following immediately on these instructions, Paul reiterates that love is the fulfillment of the law, and cites "Thou shalt not kill." It would appear that Paul saw no conflict between obedience to the state and the command not to kill.

The apparent contradiction can be resolved in one of two ways: by abstaining from state service, which at certain times and in certain official capacities involves the taking of human life, or by defining the killing referred to in the Decalogue as that which is motivated by personal hatred. In the Mennonite view, the choice is made to abstain from any participation in the execution of coercion authorized by the state, or any other institution. This view is made explicit officially as follows:

> We recognize that in a world where the evil and the good exist side by side, there is a necessary place, authorized by God Himself for the use of force by the state in the restraint of evil and the protection of the good, though always under restrictions deriving from the higher laws of God. But we hold that the Christian cannot be the executor of this force, his call being to operate on the basis of love. If he abandons this way, he effectually destroys the only hope for the world, since force can never create righteousness or a Christian society, it can at best only restrain the evil in varying degrees.[125]

That the Christian may thus stand aloof from state responsibility is held justified by the comparative silence of the New Testament on political matters. Hershberger says, in discussing the relationship of the Christian to the state, that the New Testament

> has nothing to say about how the affairs of state should be conducted. It does not suggest that the Christian should play

---

[124] Rom. 13:1–2 (RSV).
[125] *Peace and the Christian Witness*, 5.

any role in the state itself, and everywhere it assumes that he is not a part of the state. It simply recognizes the state and the obligation of the Christian toward it. The Sermon on the Mount is not a piece of legislation for a secular state in a sinful society. It is a set of principles to govern the sons of the Kingdom of heaven.[126]

Thus the teaching of Paul, the apostle, on the relationship of the Christian to the state is understood not to conflict with the love ethic. By inference, it is presumed that Christians are not to serve in the state structure. Their attitude as Christian citizens is to be characterized by respectful obedience. They are to pray for rulers. They are to abide by the laws and to refrain from hindering the state in fulfilling its functions. A limitation in obedience to the state is the prior claim of God and the claims of the kingdom of God. Resistance to the state is thus authorized on the basis of the sovereignty of God. The biblical authority for such action is the record of the apostles who, on an occasion of conflict with the Jewish ecclesio-civil authorities, said: "We must obey God rather than men."[127] Hershberger's conclusion in this connection is: "This must certainly be the Christian's answer when the state requests him to violate God's moral law and the principle of nonresistance."[128] This is the position the Mennonite Church has taken in relation to the state—obedience insofar as its laws do not require the violation of the higher law of God. The priority of citizenship in the kingdom of God over citizenship in a worldly kingdom becomes especially pronounced in the time of war, when universal conscription for military service requires clear-cut decision. But to refrain from participation in the military services is regarded as the most constructive contribution to the social welfare, and as the will of God for the Christian. Anything short of this is regarded as sin and brings the Christian under judgment of God.[129]

Dynamics of nonresistance
Our inquiry into the meaning of nonresistance must include some analysis of the moral motives or dynamics involved in the accep-

---

[126] Hershberger, *War, Peace, and Nonresistance,* 49.
[127] Acts 5:29 (RV).
[128] Hershberger, *War, Peace, and Nonresistance,* 51.
[129] Supra, 152.

tance, propagation, and application of it as an ethical norm. It is not within the scope of this study to assess the power of these motives or dynamics; nor would one be so presumptuous as to suggest that they were all within the province of ethics. However, some can be identified as they appear in the literature, especially that addressed to the adherents of nonresistance to encourage them in their faith and practice. The analysis is made then from a theoretical point of view. While Mennonite preaching, writing, and piety have had a strong ethical emphasis, no one has attempted to treat the ethics systematically as a separate theological discipline.[130] A document that appears to bring together the major motivating factors in the acceptance, propagation, and application of nonresistance is "Our Heritage of Faith." This is "A Statement of Position for the guidance of workers and prospective workers under the Mennonite Central Committee." It is further described as "an expression of what we believe to be basic convictions commonly held by all bodies co-operating in the work of Relief, Peace, and Civilian Public Service conducted by the Mennonite Central Committee." The statement was drawn up in 1942 and represents the basis on which the organization and its program have functioned since the establishment of the committee in 1920. Since the Mennonite Central Committee represents nonresistance in action, it would seem that this particular document ought to embody the dynamics believed to be inherent in, and related to, the principle of nonresistance. The document, "Our Heritage of Faith"[131] is as follows:

Part I. *With all Evangelical Christians*

1. We hold steadfastly to the Gospel of Jesus Christ as the power of God unto salvation, believing that it is only by grace through faith in Christ's atoning death on the cross and His glorious resurrection that men are saved from their sins and receive eternal life.

2. We believe that all who receive the Lord Jesus by faith are born again of the Holy Spirit with power to overcome sin and live a life pleasing to God.

---

[130] J. Lawrence Burkholder, "Ethics," *The Mennonite Encyclopedia*, 4:1079.

[131] Adopted by the Mennonite Central Committee, December 29, 1942. Appears as Appendix 10 in Hershberger, *War, Peace, and Nonresistance*, 388.

3. We likewise hold that the Holy Scriptures of the Old and New Testaments are the inspired Word of God and accordingly the Word of life and the supreme and final authority in faith and practice.

Part II. *We are grateful for the noble heritage of faith from our Mennonite and Brethren in Christ forefathers which we most heartily accept and cherish, holding:*

1. That the whole of life must be brought under the lordship of Christ and that obedience to His will in all things is the ultimate test of discipleship.

2. That a way of life is taught by Christ and the Scriptures which is God's plan for the individual and for the race, and that those who espouse discipleship of Christ are bound to live in this way, thus manifesting in their personal life and social relationships the love and holiness of God. We believe that this way of life means the fullest exercise of love, scriptural nonresistance to evil, and complete avoidance of the use of violence, including warfare. We believe further that the Christian life will of necessity express itself in nonconformity to the world in life and character.

3. That the Christian Church consists only of believers who have repented from their sins, have accepted Christ by faith, are born again, are baptized on confession of faith, and sincerely endeavor by the grace of God to live the Christ life of holiness and love.

4. That the Church is a brotherhood in which all bear one anther's burdens, and in which each considers himself a steward unto God of his life and possessions, and consecrates all that he has to the kingdom of God.

5. That the Church, the Bride of Christ, has a high and holy calling, not only ministering to its own membership, but testifying to the will of God to the world at large.

6. That it is the duty and privilege of all believers to witness for Christ and His Gospel to all men everywhere, to teach all things commanded by Him, and in His name and Spirit to minister to the needs of all men both spiritually and materially.

7. That while, in this world, true believers will suffer tribulation, yet God is faithful to His own and will give the crown of life to all who are faithful unto death, and that accordingly we should always abound in the work of the Lord, for as much as we know that our labor is not in vain in the Lord.

A final paragraph of the document states: "We commend this statement to all our officers, representatives, and workers as a guide in the formulation of policies, in the direction of work, and in the choice of workers. We also commend it to all prospective candidates for service as a description of the basis of faith and life on which they will be expected to labor."

The dynamics for nonresistance which seem to dominate might be classified as follows: the dynamic of faith, the dynamic of discipleship, the dynamic of love, the dynamic of responsibility, and the dynamic of hope. An elaboration of each demonstrates its significance in and relationship to the exercise and application of nonresistance.

1. The dynamic of faith. Implied is the existential phenomenon of faith whereby the gracious transforming power of God is at work in the life of the believer. The two agencies by which faith becomes dynamic mentioned in this statement are the authoritative Word of God and the indwelling Holy Spirit. To illustrate the significance of faith as a dynamic, Hershberger quotes Kenneth Latourette, a church historian:

> Christians have found a special power which came in a peculiar way after the resurrection of Jesus and which has continued to come, and through which they have been convinced that they are in immediate fellowship with Jesus Himself and with the God who is at once the Creator, the dominant power in the universe, and the one whom through Jesus they have learned to call Father.
>
> . . . Nor can there be doubt that through that experience they themselves have been transformed. Through it they have been lifted out of moral defeat and impotence into victory and from despair to triumphant hope.[132]

---

[132] Hershberger, *The Way of the Cross in Human Relations*, 400; quoting Kenneth S. Latourette, *Anno Domini: Jesus, History, and God* (New York: Harper and Brothers, 1940), 236.

That faith is intimately related to nonresistant action is borne out by one of the conclusions in *War, Peace, and Nonresistance,* in which Hershberger says: "The keeping of the nonresistant faith requires a deep and vital Christian faith."[133] The demands of nonresistance are such that they can be met and fulfilled only insofar as the individual believer has been enlightened and transformed by the grace of God. Faith in this sense is more than an intellectual acceptance; it is a personal transformation. In the words of the above statement (Part I, Article 2), it is the working of the Holy Spirit, with power to overcome sin and to live a life pleasing to God.

   2. The dynamic of discipleship. A strong element of the Anabaptist-Mennonite tradition has been the concept of discipleship. Christian faith does not mature in pious enjoyment or intellectual rationalization but in a life disciplined according to the teachings of the Bible.[134] As a dynamic for nonresistance, its significance lies in the desire to imitate the spirit and ministry (including the sacrificial death) of Jesus Christ. In scriptural terms, this dynamic resides in the statement of Jesus, "If any man will come after me, . . . follow me."[135] Smucker sees in this condition of discipleship the ultimate truth of the Christian life, explaining that:

> The cross of Christ is the basis of our salvation. It is His cross. True Christianity will have these two crosses: His cross and our cross. We take up our cross, at His call, to follow Him.

> In this sense the imitation of Christ still remains as the ultimate truth of the Christian life. Not a code, not an ideal, not an impossible possibility, not the wholly other, not the simple teachings of Jesus, and not an ancient irrelevance. Rather the imitation of Christ is the culmination of a pilgrimage started by Calvary's cross, confirmed by the resurrection, empowered by the Holy Spirit, and inspired by a great cloud of witnesses in the Christian Church.[136]

Discipleship is understood to be complete identification with the suffering of Christ in his redemptive mission to the world. It implies

---

[133] Hershberger, *War, Peace, and Nonresistance,* 335.
[134] Robert Friedmann, "Anabaptism and Protestantism," *Mennonite Quarterly Review* 24 (January 1950): 24.
[135] Matt. 16:24–25 (RSV)
[136] Smucker, "The Theological Basis for Christian Pacifism," 178.

subjection to his lordship and the desire to honor and obey him. This spirit is expressed in the document "Our Heritage of Faith" in the words, "The whole of life must be brought under the lordship of Christ and that obedience to His will in all things is the ultimate test of discipleship."

3. The dynamic of love. Nonresistance derives from belief in love as the nature of God, who in redemptive action has revealed his modus operandi as love. Believers who have experienced the love of God in forgiveness and regeneration pray that they in turn may be emissaries of this love to others. Thus, as in the statement ("Our Heritage of Faith") above, it is said that this way of life means "the fullest exercise of love, scriptural nonresistance to evil, and complete avoidance of the use of violence, including warfare" (Part II, Article 2). The love here described is understood as agape-love which Smucker says

> rescues Christian pacifism from moralism and idealism wherein pacifism is viewed as an ethical ideal to which to aspire. In place of this we now have God's own love manifest in Christ. Thus love for neighbor is God's own love energizing the human heart. Love is not, as in Plato, an upward movement of the human soul seeking the divine but the downward movement of self-giving divine love. Love is not the love of the worthily beautiful but the unmerited love for the sinner, for the enemy. Love then is God's gift.[137]

This love motivates the acceptance, the propagation, and the practice of nonresistance. It enables the Christian to outlast, outlive, and outlove the forces of unrighteousness, in spite of suffering. If nonresistant love eventuates in a martyr's death, it is but a means of bringing glory to God and furthering the witness of his love. The example of Christ's suffering and self-giving on the cross is the extreme demonstration of love, "and the Christian must follow his Master in suffering for the sake of love."[138]

4. The dynamic of responsibility. The individual Christian, as a citizen of the kingdom of God, is understood to bear personal responsibility for helping to realize the kingdom of God on earth. This is to be fulfilled especially within the church, but ultimately

---

[137] Ibid.," 176.
[138] Yoder, *Peace without Eschatology?* 8.

in the larger frame of reference of the world. Bender points to the importance of responsibility when he says, with reference to the witness of love, that "at least the Christian brotherhood shall manifest in its own life and service uncompromisingly the way of love in order that a world grown cynical of Christian pretensions unfulfilled may not lose faith altogether in the Gospel of the Prince of Peace."[139]

The sense of responsibility goes beyond the present temporal age to the belief in eternal life and judgment. To obey the commandments and to live in the way of love is to anticipate reward in eternity. To disobey the commandments and to follow in the way of violence is to incur the judgment of God.[140] To disregard known truth is to sin and be subject to the judgment of God. A scripture reference is cited by Hershberger in this connection: "For if we sin willfully after that we have received the knowledge of the truth, there remaineth no more a sacrifice for sins, but a certain fearful expectation of judgment, and a fierceness of fire which shall devour the adversaries. . . . It is a fearful thing to fall into the hands of the living God."[141] The hope of reward is mentioned in the document "Our Heritage of Faith" (Part II, Article 7) in the sentence, "That, while in this world, true believers will suffer tribulation, yet God is faithful to His own and will give the crown of life to all who are faithful unto death."

Responsibility is significant because it is held that men and women have free will and are therefore responsible for their choices and their deeds. The positive and negative motivation inherent in responsibility becomes apparent. The effect is asserted by Kaufman as follows: "In the responsibility which it puts on the individual believer for his every act, it leads to a far greater concern and striving toward a highly moral life."[142]

5. The dynamic of eschatological hope. The eschatological hope resides in the belief that the kingdom Jesus instituted will be consummated in a glorious victory according to God's will and plan. An intimation of this hope is in this phrase ("Our Heritage of

---

[139] H. S. Bender, "Mennonite Peace Action," *Mennonite Quarterly Review* 24 (April 1950): 151.

[140] *Peace and The Christian Witness*, 2.

[141] Heb. 10:26–31; quoted in Hershberger, *War, Peace, and Nonresistance*, 54.

[142] Kaufman, "Some Theological Emphases of the Early Swiss Anabaptists," 96.

Faith," Part II, Article 7): "Forasmuch as we know that our labor is not in vain in the Lord." It is held that the consummation of history is by the design and power of God alone. This provides hope and persistence in testing experiences. The belief is expressed by Hershberger as follows:

> It is the God of history, and not the doings of evil men that determines the destiny of the world and the end of history. As God's breaking into history in the incarnation did not depend on human ingenuity (although man was involved) so His breaking through in the parousia and the consummation of the age will also be the mighty work of God and not the doings of man, although man again will be involved; indeed every knee shall bow and every tongue confess that Jesus Christ is Lord, to the glory of God the Father.[143]

This eschatological hope anticipates the vindication of God's glory in truth and righteousness; and a kingdom of peace wherein the Prince of Peace will reign. To live in conformity to the laws of God now is to participate in the glory that is to come. It is therefore a dynamic for living the nonresistant way.

Thus, in answer to the question of dynamic or moral motive for the exercise of nonresistance, it may be proposed that theoretically these are dominant: the dynamic of faith, the dynamic of discipleship, the dynamic of love, the dynamic of responsibility, and the dynamic of eschatological hope.

Application of nonresistance

There is abundant evidence in the literature of the Mennonite Church of the twentieth century, and particularly since the Second World War, that there is a serious effort to relate nonresistant faith to contemporary problems. In an official statement of August 23, 1951, the areas in which nonresistant faith is thought to be relevant are delineated. The delineation encompasses three areas as follows: (a) service and witness; (b) social, economic, and political relations; (c) war and military service. Nonresistance is not applicable in the same way in each of these areas; and area by area this inquiry will attempt to identify and classify the techniques employed in the application of nonresistance in relation to conflict situations.

---

[143] Hershberger, *The Way of the Cross in Human Relations*, 407.

1. **Nonresistance in service and witness.**
   a. *Witness.* It is considered the major task of the church as a voluntary association of believers to represent and to communicate to the whole world the gospel of Jesus Christ. This is understood to be a God-given commission and the most important contribution to the welfare of society. Witness is to take the form of the spoken word, the written word, and the living of Christ-like lives. The abstinence from military service which this is believed to imply has been interpreted by non-sympathetic fellow citizens as cowardice and indifference to the responsibilities of citizenship. Frequently there has been persecution[144]—especially in war time—which is regarded as an opportunity to witness by nonresistant acceptance of the abuse.[145]
   b. *Service.* A spirit of service in any vocation is a Christian virtue and obligation. Social welfare, relief and rehabilitation, and disaster service are not only approved but supported and promoted by the denomination. Through the mission boards and the Mennonite Central Committee, money, material aid, professional personnel, skilled and unskilled service are channeled to hundreds of needy areas around the world. The major program is that administered by the Mennonite Central Committee, which has been described by John D. Unruh in *In the Name of Christ.*[146] Service is rendered without regard for race or creed to those who are aged, orphaned, mentally ill, physically ill, crippled, blind, deaf, and to refugees, victims of disaster, and other conditions of need.
   c. *Cultural and social rehabilitation.* Particularly recognized is the responsibility to prevent tensions from growing into conflicts that may result in violence and even warfare. Attention has been directed to the problem of race relations. A conference convened for this special purpose formulated a statement that summarizes pertinent

---

[144] C. Henry Smith, *The Story of the Mennonites* (Newton, KS.: Mennonite Publication Office, 1957), 4th ed., 794–801.
[145] Hershberger, "Nonresistance," *The Mennonite Encyclopedia*, 3:903.
[146] John D. Unruh, *In the Name of Christ* (Scottdale, PA: Herald Press, 1952).

theological factors, condemns race prejudice as sin, and formulates the denomination's program of education and practice. The perspective of social responsibility is expressed by Hershberger as follows: "There are two societies in our world, the Christian order and the pagan disorder. Here is true Christian responsibility: to keep the Christian order Christian, in order that it may bear witness to the world's disorder, and if need be make a sacrifice for it."[147]

2. Nonresistance in social, economic, and political relations. It is recognized that selfishness, pride, and greed in social, economic, and political relationships engender animosities that, when extended to intergroup and international relationships, result in strife and violence. Christians have a responsibility, therefore, to prevent such strife at its source, insofar as it resides within their power to do so.[148]

Nonresistance is applied in the first instance by using it to determine business practice, employer-employee relationships, neighborly-community relationships, good stewardship of natural resources, payment of taxes, and maintenance of public facilities such as schools, hospitals, and roads.

Nonresistance requires abstention from participation in "activities, organizations, investments or systems that use methods of force and violence, compromise Christian ethics, or do not permit full exercise of Christian love and brotherhood."[149]

Nonresistance is applied in refraining from employment in industries producing armaments and other military equipment.[150]

Nonresistance is applied in refraining from the purchase of war bonds. Civilian bonds are approved.[151]

Nonresistance is applied by farmers who in wartime make excess profits from their produce, when they comply with the suggestion that "such profits should be conscientiously devoted

---

[147] Hershberger, *The Way of the Cross in Human Relations*, 196.

[148] *Peace and the Christian Witness,* 6.

[149] Ibid., 3.

[150] *Peace, War, and Military Service,* A statement adopted by the Mennonite General Conference at Turner, Oregon, August 1937 (Scottdale, PA: Mennonite Publishing House), 3. See Appendix A.

[151] Melvin Gingerich, *Service for Peace* (Akron, PA: The Mennonite Central Committee, 1949), 355–59.

to charitable purposes, such as bringing relief to the needy, or spreading the Gospel of peace and love."[152]

Nonresistance is applied in direct witness to the state under certain terms. The official statement declares the terms as follows:

> Though we recognize fully that God has set the state in its place of power and ministry, we cannot take part in those of its functions or respond to any of its demands which involve us in the use of force or frustrate Christian love; but we acknowledge our obligation to witness to the powers-that-be of the righteousness which God requires of all men, even in government, and beyond this to continue in earnest intercession to God on their behalf.[153]

The modes of the witness to the state are suggested in the same document as oral and written conversation with state officials, works of mercy (feeding and clothing the needy), ministries of reconciliation in tension areas (racial, social, political).[154] Government service is not forbidden absolutely[155] but is limited to that which does not involve the exercise of or cooperation with the use of force.[156] In a most incisive definition of the meaning of nonresistance in the twentieth century, Smucker concludes: "The political order will remain on the periphery of our Mennonite lives, though it will be dealt with frequently. The main focus must be upon non-coercive deeds of faith and works: missionary work, opposition to racial intolerance, regard for other minorities, interest in religious liberty, living a life of simplicity, creating healthy small communities, relief and social reconstruction."[157]

3. Nonresistance in war and military service. Nonresistance is most decisive at the point of military service and training for military service. Combatant service, noncombatant service,[158] and

---

[152] *Peace, War, and Military Service*, 3, see Appendix A.

[153] *Peace and the Christian Witness*, 6.

[154] Ibid., 13–14.

[155] Smucker, "The Theological Basis for Christian Pacifism," 174.

[156] Robert Kreider, "Anabaptists and the State," in *The Recovery of the Anabaptist Vision*, ed. Hershberger, 190.

[157] Donovan E. Smucker, "A Mennonite Critique of the Pacifist Movement," *Mennonite Quarterly Review* 20 (January 1946): 88.

[158] Melvin Gingerich, *What of Noncombatant Service?* 2nd ed. (Scottdale, PA: Herald Press, 1957), 7.

any indirect support (insofar as is possible) are proscribed as being inconsistent with a commitment to the nonresistant love ethic. In a discussion of noncombatant service, for the guidance of Mennonite youth, Gingerich says: "Consistency also requires that those who are opposed to aiding war should not serve in organizations temporarily allied with the military in the prosecution of war, should not purchase war bonds, or should not knowingly participate in the manufacture of munitions and weapons of war either in peacetime or wartime."[159] Abstention applies also to chaplaincies in the armed forces.[160] Nonresistance is evidenced, therefore, by complete abstention from military and related services. Nonresistance is applied by withdrawal.

The legality of such abstention or withdrawal from military participation has been established after many years of negotiations with the United States government and among representatives of the peace churches. Abstention from military service for reasons of conscience was legalized by the Selective Training and Service Act of 1940. This act of the United States government provided for absolute exemption for ministers and theological students and conditional exemption for conscientious objectors who were divided into two classes: those objecting to participation in combat service only, and those objecting to participation in all military service. The text of the act is found in Yoder and Smucker, *The Christian and Conscription*.[161]

As a result of this legislation, provision was made for alternative service of "national importance under civilian direction."[162] This program became organized as Civilian Public Service. It was a program authorized by the state and administered and largely supported by the peace churches involved. Inductees served without remuneration.[163] Gingerich's *Service for Peace* is a comprehensive historical study of the Civilian Public Service program, in which he records the development and scope of this alternative to military service. It includes a summary evaluation of the Civilian Public Service program by Smucker.[164] Gingerich reports, in his essay "Dis-

---

[159] Ibid., 13.
[160] Hershberger, *War, Peace, and Nonresistance*, 366.
[161] Yoder and Smucker, *The Christian and Conscription*, 87.
[162] Ibid., 88.
[163] Ibid., 99.
[164] Gingerich, *Service for Peace*, 410–11.

cipleship Expressed in Alternative Service," that, in the six and one-half years that men were drafted under the Selective Service law, approximately 12,000 men were assigned to Civilian Public Service, of whom 38 percent were Mennonites. Of a total of 151 camps set up under Civilian Public Service, twenty-six were operated by the Mennonite Central Committee. Services rendered in and through the camps included soil conservation, dairy testing, and other agricultural services; forestry and national park service; mental and public health services; "guinea-pig" experiments in nutrition and disease. A total of 1,500 men served in mental hospitals. Cost to the United States government for the total program was $1,333,000.00. The balance of 3,000,000.00 was contributed by the supporting churches through the Mennonite Central Committee.[165]

Since World War II, under the Universal Military Training and Service Act there is provision for alternative service for conscientious objectors in "civilian work contributing to the maintenance of the national health, safety, or interest."[166]

Thus nonresistance is applied in respect to war and military service by abstention on the one hand, and by participation in government-approved alternative service on the other, and under the provisions of the Universal Military Training and Service Act as well. A survey of like provisions for conscientious objectors in other countries appears in Hershberger's *Military Conscription and the Conscientious Objector*.[167]

In this examination of the application of nonresistance, it becomes clear that there is greater scope in pre-conflict situations—that is, the lessening or prevention of tensions prior to open conflict. When conflict is in process, nonresistance as commonly applied has conformed to two modes. The first and most pronounced is that of withdrawal. The second and most recent is that of alternative service. Also, as evidenced in certain consultations and conferences, there is emerging a recognized need to find ways and means to engage in constructive participation in conflict. Burkholder poses the problem in the following terms:

---

[165] Gingerich, "Discipleship Expressed in Alternative Service," 266–67.
[166] *Questions and Answers on the Classification and Assignment of Conscientious Objectors*, 3rd printing, rev. ed. (Washington, DC: National Service Board for Religious Objectors, 1961), 7.
[167] Guy F. Hershberger, *Military Conscription and the Conscientious Objector* (Akron, PA: Mennonite Central Committee, 1962).

A place must be made in Mennonite ethics for power. Traditionally the Mennonite position has assumed that Christians can live without the exercise of power—that is, power in the form of compulsion and force. It may be agreed that, given the ideal combination of saintliness and simplicity, a small Christian society can live with a minimum of power. But certainly business organizations, educational institutions and even highly organized mutual aid societies cannot operate by the pure principles of the "love feast." All institutions are to a certain degree political in character even though the service motive and personal piety can mitigate the political principle. For this reason Mennonites must re-examine the validity of nonresistance as a comprehensive norm for all Christian relations. It is the view of the writer that if nonresistance were actually practiced as an absolute principle, it would literally take Christians out of this world. A practical alternative would be nonviolent resistance as an approximation of the absolute ideal, which affords at the same time an opportunity to participate in the "ambiguous" struggles for justice in society.[168]

In this chapter the investigation has traced the history of nonresistance as a doctrine of the Mennonite Church as it has been formulated and transmitted from one generation to the next since 1525. The documents present in unsophisticated language the basic presuppositions, the ethical principles, the dynamics, and the practical implications for human relationships.

Nonresistance is found to be a way of life based on the belief that the Christian faith as understood from the Bible requires total commitment to Jesus Christ as Lord. The role of Christians is that of disciples whose chief objective is the worship, imitation, and service of their Lord. This implies discipline of their thought and behavior in conformity to what they understand to be the will of their Lord. The Bible is held to be the source of this knowledge. Accepting the principle of agape-love as normative for all relationships, the use of coercion directly or indirectly is excluded. Thus understood, nonresistance represents a dogmatic intuitional ethic

---

[168] J. Lawrence Burkholder, "The Problem of Social Responsibility from the Standpoint of the Mennonite Church" (ThD diss., Princeton Theological Seminary, Princeton, NJ, 1958), 350.

which is held to be absolute. It is the belief of those who accept it that it is a divine vocation to hold to this ethic as the best means of resolving conflict in human relationships at whatever cost in suffering or apparent ineffectiveness. To be consistent in observing this ethic as individual Christians, and collectively as the church, is to witness to God's perfect will.

Chapter 5

Satyagraha and nonresistance compared

A COMPARATIVE STUDY OF SATYAGRAHA and nonresistance reveals some basic similarities and differences. These appear in each stage of the structure of this examination, namely, the history, the metaphysical presuppositions, the ethical principles, the definition, the dynamics, and the application. In this design, definition, dynamics, and application have appeared as parts of the exposition of the respective doctrines.

I. History

Satyagraha evolved in the arena of political and social activity over a period of years, absorbing content and form in the dialectic of activity and reflection. Satyagraha came to be recognized as a distinctive political instrument of nonviolent character.

Nonresistance emerged as a distinct religious doctrine in the context of the Protestant Reformation. It took form as a Christian ethic which had direct political implications in the conception and practice of the separation of Church and State. The primary aim of its proponents, however, was religious reform and not political reform. Their concern was for the purity of the church and a truer representation of Christian commitment.

In satyagraha, Gandhi found himself involved in the field of political and social reform as a leader of millions of unarmed, poverty-stricken compatriots whose chief objective was self-rule. The choice of satyagraha as a nonviolent instrument seems to have been made on the basis of religious idealism along with a consideration for political realism. Gandhi counted on the high moral sensitivity of the opponent, the British Imperial Authority. There were also, between the two world wars, strong pacifist influences. And finally, the religious idealism that satyagraha represented could move the masses of India. But, taking due account of these factors, it is the view of this investigator that Gandhi was essentially religious in his approach to the political and social problems of his day. He understood satyagraha as holding onto truth through all the relativities of a political and social revolution. The soul force thus marshaled derived primarily from identification with an ultimate transcendent moral reality.

Nonresistance represented the faith and reflection of a religious community that formulated and reformulated its doctrines as absolute norms for its members. Persons who disagreed and disobeyed were formally excommunicated and at times socially ostracized; hence the continuity of the doctrine for more than four hundred years has been sustained. It was also tested in the crucible of debate and persecution. But it retained its form largely by abstinence from political and military activity. Thousands lost their lives during the Reformation period in order to hold intact this doctrine, as well as other distinctive doctrines. But nonresistance was not formulated as a technique for social or political reform. It was predicated on the assumption that a commitment to the Christian way of life was the highest contribution to the common welfare, and that this commitment precludes the employment of direct forms of coercion, and especially violent coercion.

A strong contrast emerges then in that satyagraha, as a technique of direct action, was conceived pragmatically, while nonresistance, as a technique of abstinence from direct action, was conceived dogmatically.

II. Metaphysical presuppositions

Both satyagraha and nonresistance have metaphysical presuppositions. Belief in the moral governance of the universe by a supernatural power or law is an essential ingredient of both. Belief in the ultimate realization of morality, within the power and design of ultimate reality, is a common element in both satyagraha and nonresistance.

Differences appear in the conception of the nature of ultimate reality. Gandhi equated God and truth, and crystallized his concept of God in the equation "Truth is God." This was his expression of the fact that human knowledge of ultimate reality is only partial. Gandhi, in the tradition of Hinduism, asserted that ultimate reality—which had a thousand names and many incarnations—was indefinable. But ultimate reality, or God, or truth, operated as a dependable supernatural moral principle in the universe. In the Mennonite view, ultimate reality is the God of the Judaeo-Christian conception, namely, the almighty, holy creator, sustainer, and redeemer of the universe. He has revealed himself in history and in the scriptures, as a spiritual being. God is believed to have revealed himself in the Bible, which gives this measure of certainty in Mennonite thought about the nature of God. There is, therefore, dissimilarity in identity and in the degree of certainty about the nature of ultimate reality.

Closely related to the concept of God is the identification of the source of authority. For Gandhi, satyagraha did not depend on an authoritative scripture. In postulating satyagraha, as in any other matter, Gandhi asserted the authority of reason as superior to that of any scripture. For the Mennonite, on the contrary, nonresistance finds ultimate sanction in an authoritative scripture, especially the New Testament. For this reason, nonresistant Christians find themselves in an irreconcilable confrontation with the problems of force, military necessity, and political responsibility in society. Satyagrahis determine their course of action by a rational process. The absolutism of nonresistance is rigid and final, as it purports to be the representation of an authoritative scripture. Satyagraha is fashioned to meet the demands of an immediate conflict situation; forms and degrees of action or inaction are determined by the principles of satyagraha and the requirements of the existential situation. Nonresistance has no such flexibility. It is a literal conformity to an understanding of the New Testament spirit and teaching.

Another point of difference in the metaphysical category pertains to the conception of the nature of humankind. Satyagraha in its Hindu orientation recognizes good and evil in humanity, but asserts that the human is essentially good. Therefore people may be expected to respond positively when confronted with the true and the good. Mennonite belief holds that natural humankind is essentially evil and that they become good and responsive to good only by the gracious act of God. They may be transformed by the processes identified in theological terms as regeneration and sanctification. Optimism with regard to human nature is noted in the belief that all men and women may experience this transformation; in fact it is God's will that they should.

On the question of personal free will, Gandhi believed in the law of deed or karma, which regards present existence as being in continuity with previous existence and future rebirth and existence. Thus free will is partly an agent in determining the karma and partly determined by the karma. In Mennonite belief, free will is also postulated, along with the eternal responsibility for decision and action. Reward and punishment beyond this temporal existence are contingent on one's deeds and on one's personal acceptance or rejection of Jesus Christ as redemptive Lord.

In regard to society: Gandhi assumed that satyagraha could be applied universally and that it did not depend on any sectarian dogma. It could be practiced by Hindus, Muslims, Christians; in fact, by anyone who was prepared to take the pledge. This required belief in God; but as Gandhi defined God (truth), the atheist was not excluded.

III. Ethical principles

Satyagraha and nonresistance are predicated on the assumption that there is an inextricable continuity between religion and morality. To know the truth is to do the truth, for Gandhi. To love God is to obey him, is the Mennonite credo. Therefore satyagraha and nonresistance have in common that they constitute ethical norms, each having its distinctive religious significance and framework. Nonresistance claims to have a clearer knowledge about the objectivity of the norm as defined and illustrated in the Bible. Satyagraha does not claim the same objectivity, for the test of satyagraha resides in the individual consciousness, and humans are not equipped to know the truth perfectly. Without this knowledge, the best that can be achieved is an estimate of the right and the good. The processes of self-suffering and prayer are employed to reduce self-interest and clarify insight. The Mennonite nonresistant claims dogmatic authority in the Bible, and the test of a conscience conditioned by the Bible. The Hindu satyagrahi claims insight by intuition. The term *faith* is used by both to express the relationship that extends to some object beyond the self, in which is found the sense of the right and the good. Thus both satyagraha and nonresistance are clearly ethical norms with religious determinants.

Both satyagraha and nonresistance are conceived to be an integral part of a whole way of life. The individual who expects to behave nonviolently or nonresistantly in any one area of life should observe the same kind of behavior in all relationships; in the family, in the community, in business, in politics. Nonviolence (satyagraha or nonresistance) is most apt to be sustained in face of violence where there has been a discipline of the body, of the mind, and of the spirit. Both depend for success on rigid discipline accepted and sustained by the strength of will embodied in the vow.

Close to the necessity of discipline is the concept of self-suffering. The perspective differs, however, in that for satyagraha, the element of motivation seems to predominate, while in nonresistance, suffering is regarded as the logical outworking of identification with Jesus Christ. The motivation in satyagraha is the power of self-suffering to move the opponent by appealing to justice and sympathy. There is also its self-purificatory function, whereby the will is refined and strengthened. In nonresistance, the motivation is to bring glory to God through obedience and purity. The suffering is thereby considered an end in itself; whether it moves the opponent is incidental.

Another observable difference is in the definition of violence and nonviolence. Within the definition according to satyagraha, there is greater toleration; coercion may be brought to bear on the opponent, if necessary, in the form of social, economic, and political pressure; in the form of self-suffering, it includes solicitation of supernatural power. Legitimate coercion is the minimum necessary to achieve reconciliation or justice. Within the definition of violence according to nonresistance, all forms of coercion (apart from petition—appeal to justice and conscience) are excluded. Only that which is consistent with self-sacrificing agape-love is sanctioned. It is restrictive in its requirement of discipline and nonviolence. Mennonite nonresistance, however, is held to be applicable and possible only to those who claim Jesus Christ as Lord and have realized the spiritual transformation of the new birth. It is feasible only under these conditions and therefore prescribed as a norm for Christians. Differentiating terms are "in the perfection of Christ" and "outside the perfection of Christ." The scope of nonresistance thus becomes limited to a much more rigidly defined group than that of satyagraha, a grouping that is determined by respective metaphysical presuppositions.

In the design of satyagraha, there are measures for reducing the element of hatred even where strong coercive measures are employed. Nonresistance holds that the elimination of hatred eliminates forms of coercion that satyagraha allows.

IV. Definition of satyagraha and nonresistance

According to the exposition of each above, it has been noted that satyagraha is a principle of social action informing and controlling the conduct of social conflict, in which the end and the means thereto are consistent with the requirements of truth, nonviolence, and self-suffering.

Nonresistance has been found to be the literal application to all relationships in society of the love-ethic of the New Testament. This is held as the ethic of the spiritual kingdom to which Christians owe prior loyalty. This loyalty in turn justifies their abstention from duties with which they cannot conscientiously comply; especially those that are not consistent with the divine moral law. The positive expression of the love-ethic is to "overcome evil with good."

Satyagraha and nonresistance thus defined imply a positive, dynamic approach to the mitigation of evil in society. It would appear that the term *nonresistance* is inadequate to comprehend the positive dynamic content of the command to overcome evil with good. Agape-love, the essence of nonresistance, as has been shown, is indeed positive. "Nonviolent resistance" would be more accurate. This does not equate satyagraha and nonresistance (nonviolent resistance), for satyagraha sanctions coercive means and seeks ends beyond the limits of agape-love as defined in the Mennonite view.

Dynamics

Comparing dynamics in satyagraha and nonresistance reveals one prominent contrast. The hypothesis of satyagraha is that right means applied toward right ends, in social and political reform, will ultimately be realized by virtue of the good in humanity. Nonresistance, on the other hand, asserts that the realization of the overthrow of evil resides in the will and power of God. To the extent that human society conforms to the divine design, it may be regarded as bringing about the realization of the overthrow of evil.

On the personal level, a common term is love. It is employed as descriptive of behavior and as descriptive of an emotional state. In nonresistance, however, love denotes in addition a supernatural gift which is believed to refine and energize individuals in such a way that their perspective, motivation, and endurance are characterized by divine love. In fact, they become, in this view, an instrument of divine love, their power to act in this way coming from beyond themselves. Satyagraha purports to reduce and refine emotional states of love and hatred on the human plane, so that the conduct of conflict is consistent with the requirements of truth, nonviolence, and self-suffering. The process may be described in psychological terms as sublimation. Satyagraha purports to transform the destructive power of violence into the constructive power of nonviolence. This is believed to be accomplished through the discipline of the will.

The dynamic of responsibility, while differing in content, is present in both. The moral governance of the universe and the implications of eternal judgment for the Mennonite Christian, and the implications of karma (the law of the deed) for the Hindu satyagrahi, accent personal responsibility, for right action.

Application
In the respective discussions of application of satyagraha and nonresistance above, the forms or modes have been described. As comparison is made between the two schemes, it becomes clear that satyagraha and nonresistance overlap in a limited measure only. Nonresistance, as conceived by the Mennonite Church, is primarily applicable in the prevention of conflict by constructive action which reduces tension or removes causes of tension. It is applicable furthermore in reducing tension and clarifying witness against violence by withdrawal. It functions in that it cultivates the mental and spiritual resources that enable persons to suffer injustice and abuse. In relation to power organizations, such as labor organizations and the state government, nonresistance has witnessed against violence by withdrawal. Beyond these measures, nonresistance provides no technique for the conduct of conflict.

Satyagraha as conceived by Gandhi is also concerned with the prevention of conflict by removing some of the social and economic causes through the program of Sarvodaya (welfare of all), but in addition, it proposes a technique for the conduct of conflict.

This comparison reveals also the respective roles of nonresistance and satyagraha in the field of pacifism. The role of nonresistance is primarily that of witness to an ideal and the prevention of tension and conflict, while that of satyagraha comprises both of these, and a technique for conducting conflict. The limitation of nonresistance derives from its metaphysical presuppositions. It is asserted that the observance of this limitation is in itself a legitimate expression of social and political responsibility. Satyagraha, having a broader definition of nonviolence and a more flexible metaphysics, has greater scope for experimentation in the debated continuum between violence and nonviolence.

V. Conclusion

In considering the techniques employed by satyagraha for direct action in conducting social and political conflict, representatives of nonresistance will realize that there are basic and significant differences in metaphysical presuppositions, and that there are differences in ethical principles and dynamics. This does not, of necessity, obviate cooperative participation in peace action. Nor does it prevent the assimilation of a mode of action if it is deemed consistent with its own metaphysical and ethical framework. In fact, it is a conclusion of this study that an implication of nonresistant love is involvement in some kinds of conflict situations. Love does not avoid responsibility because of fear of failure. Some of the forms of satyagraha that could conceivably be conducted in a manner consistent with the love-ethic are negotiations, arbitration, agitation, demonstration, strike, economic boycott, nonpayment of taxes, and noncooperation. Violence may enter into any one of these, but violence may enter into complete withdrawal in the form of hate. These modes of social action would represent love, insofar as they retained emotional and physical discipline and were performed in the interest of a suffering minority (other than the one conducting the action), or in the interest of a principle of justice.

As historically demonstrated under Gandhi's leadership, nonviolent action can become violent and destructive. The course he took by way of corrective was the self-purificatory fast and the cessation of satyagraha action. Inherent in satyagraha action and in such action performed under the motivation of agape-love is a self-regulating principle that tests the rightness of the cause and the action.

If nonresistance were to incorporate peace action in the forms mentioned or in others which might be indicated under other social or political situations, a more appropriate term would be nonviolent resistance. It is the opinion of this investigator that in the development of a systematized agape-love ethic, a major consideration must be the discovery of the meaning of agape-love in responsible citizenship.

Selected bibliography

A. Books

Aman, T. A. *What Does Gandhi Want?* New York, London: Oxford University Press, 1942.

The Amsterdam Assembly Series, *Man's Disorder and God's Design,* Report of Section IV, "The Church and International Disorder." New York: Harper and Brothers, 1948.

Andrews, Charles Freer, ed. *Mahatma Gandhi at Work.* New York: The Macmillan Company, 1931.

———. *Mahatma Gandhi's Ideas.* New York: The Macmillan Company, 1930.

———. *Mahatma Gandhi, His Own Story.* New York: The MacmillanCompany, 1930.

Arnold, Edwin. *The Song Celestial* (Bhagavad Gita). Bombay: Jaico Publishing House, 1957.

Bainton, Roland H. *Christian Attitudes toward War and Peace.* New York: Abingdon Press, 1960.

———. *The Reformation of the Sixteenth Century.* Boston: Beacon Press, 1952.

Barzun, Jacques, and Henry F. Graff. *The Modern Researcher.* New York: Harcourt, Brace and Company, 1957.

Bender, Harold S. *Conrad Grebel, ca. 1498–1526; The Founder of the Swiss Brethren Sometimes Called Anabaptists.* Goshen, IN: Mennonite Historical Society, 1950.

Bernard, Theos. *Hindu Philosophy.* New York: The Philosophical Library, 1947.

Bernays, Robert. *"Naked Faquir."* New York: Henry Holt, 1932.

Birla, Ghanshyam Dass. *In the Shadow of the Mahatma.* Bombay: Orient Longmans, 1953.

Bondurant, Joan Valerie. *Conquest of Violence; The Gandhian Philosophy of Conflict.* Princeton, NJ: Princeton University Press, 1958.

Bouquet, A. C. *Hinduism.* London, New York: Hutchinson University Library, 1948.

Bonhoeffer, Dietrich. *The Cost of Discipleship*. New York: The Macmillan Company, 1949.

Bose, Nirmal Kumar. *Studies in Gandhism*. 2nd ed. Calcutta: India Associated Publishing Company, 1947.

Bowles, Chester. *The New Dimensions of Peace*. New York: Harper and Brothers, 1956.

Brittain, Vera. *Humiliation with Honor*. New York: Fellowship Publications, 1943.

Cadoux, C. John. *The Early Christian Attitude to War*. London: George Allen and Unwin Ltd., 1919.

———. *The Early Church and the World*. Edinburgh: T. and T. Clark, 1952.

Case, Clarence Marsh. *Non-Violent Coercion*. New York, London: The Century Company, 1923.

Castell, Alburey. *An Elementary Ethics*. New York: Prentice Hall Inc., 1954.

Catlin, George Edward Gordon. *In the Path of Mahatma Gandhi*. Chicago: H. Regnery Company, 1950.

Chander, Jag Parvesh. *Teachings of Mahatma Gandhi*. Lahore: The Indian Printing Works, 1945.

Charles, Howard. *Before You Decide*. Akron, PA: Mennonite Central Committee, 1948.

Churchill, Winston S. *India: Speeches and an Introduction*. London: Thornton Butterworth, 1951.

Church Polity Committee of the Mennonite General Conference. *Mennonite Church Polity*. Scottdale, PA: Mennonite Publishing House, 1952.

Coatman, John. *Years of Destiny: India 1926-32*. London: Jonathan Cape, 1932.

The Continuation Committee of the Historic Peace Churches and the Fellowship of Reconciliation. *Peace Is the Will of God*. Amsterdam, Holland: J. H. Debussy, 1953.

———. *The Christian and War*. Amsterdam: J. H. Debussy, 1958.

Cormack, Margaret L. *She Who Rides a Peacock*. Bombay: Asia Publishing House, 1961.

Curti, Merle Eugene. *Peace or War: The American Struggle 1636-1936*. New York: W. W. Norton and Company, Inc., 1936.

Das Gupta, Arun Chandra. *Non-Violence; the Invincible Power, Its Primordiality, Practicability and Precedents.* 2nd ed. Calcutta: Khadi Pratisthan, 1946.

Dasgupta, Surendranath. *Indian Idealism.* London: Cambridge University Press, 1933.

Datta, Dhirendra Mohan. *The Philosophy of the Mahatma.* Madison, WI: University of Wisconsin Press, 1953.

de Ligt, Barthelemy. *The Conquest of Violence.* London: George Allen and Unwin Ltd., 1937.

Desai, Mahadev Haribhai. *A Righteous Struggle: A Chronicle of the Ahmedabad Textile Labourers' Fight for Justice.* Edited by Bharatan Kumarappa. Translated by Somnoth P. Dave. Ahmedabad: Navajivan Publishing House, 1951.

———. *The Story of Bardoli: Being a History of the Bardoli Satyagraha of 1928 and Its Sequel.* Ahmedabad: Navajivan Publishing House, 1929.

De Vries, Egbert. *Man in Rapid Social Change.* Garden City, NJ: Doubleday, 1961.

Dhawan, G. N. *The Political Philosophy of Mahatma Gandhi.* Ahmedabad: Navajivan Publishing House, 1946.

Diwakar, R. R. *Satyagraha.* Chicago: H. Regnery Company, 1948.

Encyclopedia of Religion and Ethics. New York: Charles Scribner's Sons, 1926.

Fay, Sidney B. *The Origins of the World War.* New York: The Macmillan Company, 1930.

Ferré, Nels F. S. *Christ and the Christian.* New York: Harper and Brothers, 1958.

Fischer, Louis. *A Week with Gandhi.* New York: Duell, Sloan and Pearce, Inc., 1942.

———. *Gandhi and Stalin; Two Signs at the Cross-Roads.* New York: Harper and Brothers, 1947.

———. *The Life of Mahatma Gandhi.* New York: Harper and Brothers, Inc., 1950.

———. *The Life of Mahatma Gandhi.* London: Jonathan Cape, 1951.

Fox, George. *Journal.* New York: E. P. Dutton and Company, 1924.

Friedmann, Robert. *Mennonite Piety through the Centuries.* Goshen, IN: The Mennonite Historical Society, 1949.

Fromm, Erich. *The Art of Loving.* New York: Harper and Brothers, 1957.

————. *The Sane Society.* New York: Rinehart and Company, Inc., 1955.

Fülöp-Miller, René, Rene. *Lenin and Gandhi.* Translated by F. S. Flint and D. F. Tait. London: G. P. Putnam's Sons, 1927.

Gandhi, M. K. *All Men Are Brothers.* Paris: UNESCO; New York: Columbia University Press, 1958.

————. *An Appeal to Eve Briton in South Africa.* Durban: Natal Indian Congress, 1894.

————. *Autobiography: The Story of My Experiments with Truth.* Boston: Beacon Press, Inc., 1947.

————. *Bapu's Letters to Mira.* Edited by Mira. Ahmedabad: Navajivan Publishing House, 1949.

————. *Christian Missions: Their Place in India.* Ahmedabad: Navajivan Publishing House, 1941.

————. *Communal Unity.* Ahmedabad: Navajivan Publishing House, 1949.

————. *Conquest of Self: Being Gleanings from His Writings and Speeches.* Compiled by R. K. Prabhu and U. R. Rao. Bombay: Thacker, 1946.

————. *Constructive Programme: Its Meaning and Place.* 2nd ed. Ahmedabad: Navajivan Publishing House, 1944.

————. *Correspondence with Mr. Gandhi: August 1942–April 1944.* Delhi: Government of India, 1944.

————. *Delhi Diary.* Ahmedabad: Navajivan Publishing House, 1948.

————. *Ethics of Fasting.* Edited by Jag Pravesh Chander. Lahore: Indian Printing Works, 1944.

————. *For Pacifists.* Ahmedabad: Navajivan Publishing House, 1949.

————. *From Yeravda Mandir.* Ahmedabad: Navajivan Publishing House, 1930.

————. *Gandhi-Jinnah Talks.* New Delhi: Hindustan Times, 1944.

————. *Gandhiji's Correspondence with the Government 1942-44.* 2nd ed. Ahmedabad: Navajivan Publishing House, 1945.

————. *Gandhi's Autobiography: The Story of My Experiments with Truth.* Washington: Public Affairs Press, 1948.

————. *Gandhi's Letters to a Disciple.* New York: Harper and Brothers, 1950.

————. *The Gandhi Sutras; the Basic Teachings of Mahatma Gandhi Arranged with Introduction and Biographical Sketch by D. S. Sarma.* New York: Devon-Adair, 1949.

————. *Gokhale: My Political Guru.* Ahmedabad: Navajivan Publishing House, 1955.

———. *The Gospel of Selfless Action or the Gita according to Gandhi.* Translated by Mahadov H. Desai. Ahmedabad: Navajivan Publishing House, 1946.

———. *The Grievance of the British Indians in South Africa: An Appeal to the Indian Public.* 2nd ed. Madras: Price Current Press, 1896.

———. *Hind Swaraj or Indian Home Rule.* Ahmedabad: Navajivan Publishing House, 1938.

———. *Hindu Dharma.* Edited by Bharatan Kumarappa. Ahmedabad: Navajivan Publishing House, 1950.

———. *Hindu Dharma.* Edited by Bharatan Kumarappa. Ahmedabad: Navajivan Publishing House, 1958.

———. *The Indian Franchise: An Appeal.* Durban: Natal Indian Congress, 1894.

———. *The Indian States' Problem.* Ahmedabad: Navajivan Publishing House, 1941.

———. *India of My Dreams.* Compiled by R. K. Prabhu. Bombay: Hind Kitabs, 1947.

———. *My Appeal to the British.* Edited by Arand T. Hingorani. New York: The John Day Company, 1942.

———. *My Religion.* Ahmedabad: Navajivan Publishing House, 1958.

———. *Non-Violence in Peace and War.* 2 vols. Ahmedabad: Navajivan Publishing House, 1944.

———. *Ramanama.* Ahmedabad: Navajivan Publishing House, 1949.

———. *Sarvodaya.* Ahmedabad: Navajivan Publishing House, 1958.

———. *Satyagraha.* Edited by Bharatan Kumarappa. Ahmedabad: Navajivan Publishing House, 1951.

———. *Satyagraha in South Africa.* Translated by Valji G. Desai. Rev. ed. Ahmedabad: Navajivan Publishing House, 1950.

———. *Selected Writings of Mahatma Gandhi.* Compiled by Ronald Duncan. Boston: Beacon Press, 1951.

———. *Self-Restraint vs. Self-Indulgence.* One-volume ed. Ahmedabad: Navajivan Publishing House, 1947.

———. *Songs from Prison.* Adapted by John Hovland. London: George Allen and Unwin Ltd.; New York: The Macmillan Company, 1934.

———. *Speeches and Writings.* Madras: Natesan, 1917.

———. *The Story of My Experiments with Truth.* Ahmedabad: Navajivan Publishing House, 1940.

———. *To the Students.* Ahmedabad: Navajivan Publishing House, 1949.

———. *Towards Non-Violent Socialism.* Ahmedabad: Navajivan Publishing House, 1951.

———. *Truth is God.* Ahmedabad: Navajivan Publishing House, 1959.

———. *Women and Social Injustice.* Vol. 1, 3rd ed. Ahmedabad: Navajivan Publishing House, 1947.

———. *Young India (1919-1922).* Madras: Ganesan Press, 1923.

———. *Young India (1924-1926).* New York: The Viking Press Inc., 1927.

———. *Young India (1927-1928).* Madras: Ganesan Press, 1935.

George, S. K. *Gandhi's Challenge to Christianity.* London: George Allen and Unwin Ltd., 1939.

Ghoshal, U. N. A *History of Hindu Political Theories: From the Earliest Times to the End of the 17th Century A.D.* London: Oxford University Press; Bombay: Humphrey Milford, 1927.

Government of India. *The Collected Works of Mahatma Gandhi.* 4 vols. Delhi: Ministry of Information and Broadcasting, 1958.

Gingerich, Melvin. *Service for Peace: A History of Mennonite Civilian Public Service.* Akron, PA: Mennonite Central Committee, 1949.

Gottschalk, Louis. *Understanding History: A Primer of Historical Method.* New York: Alfred A. Knopf, 1958.

Gray, Harold S. *Character "Bad": The Story of a Conscientious Objector.* New York: Harper and Brothers, 1934.

Gregg, Richard Bartlett. *The Power of Nonviolence.* Philadelphia: J. B. Lippincott Company, 1934.

Griffiths, Percival Joseph. *Modern India.* New York: Frederick A. Praeger, Inc., 1957.

Halidah, Edib. *Inside India.* London: George Allen and Unwin Ltd., 1938.

Hamlin, C. H. *The War Myth in United States History.* New York: Vanguard Press, 1927.

Hartzler, J. S. *Mennonites in the World War.* Scottdale, PA: Mennonite Publishing House, 1921.

Hassler, Alfred. *Diary of a Self-Made Convict.* Nyack, NY: Fellowship Publications, 1958.

Heard, Gerald. *The Code of Christ.* New York: Harper and Brothers, 1941.

Heering, G. J. *The Fall of Christianity.* Translated by J. W. Thompson. New York: Fellowship Publications, 1943.

Henry, Carl F. H. *Christian Personal Ethics.* Grand Rapids, MI: Wm. B. Eerdmans Publishing Co., 1957.

Hershberger, Guy F. *The Mennonite Church in the Second World War.* Scottdale, PA: Mennonite Publishing House, 1951.

———. *Military Conscription and the Conscientious Objector.* Akron, PA: Mennonite Central Committee, 1962.

———. *Nonresistance and the State: The Pennsylvania Quaker Experiment in Politics, 1682-1756.* Scottdale, PA: Mennonite Publishing House, 1936.

———. ed. *The Recovery of the Anabaptist Vision.* Scottdale, PA: Herald Press, 1957.

———. *War, Peace, and Nonresistance.* 2nd ed. Scottdale, PA: The Herald Press, 1953.

———. *The Way of the Cross in Human Relations.* Scottdale, PA: Herald Press, 1958.

Hiebert, P. C., and Orie O. Miller. *Feeding the Hungry: Russia Famine, 1919-1925.* Scottdale, PA: Mennonite Central Committee, 1928.

Hinshaw, Cecil E. *Nonviolent Resistance.* Pendle Hill Pamphlet no. 88. Wallingford, PA: Pendle Hill, 1956.

Holmes, John Hayes. *My Gandhi.* New York: Harper and Brothers, 1953.

Horsch, John. *Mennonites in Europe.* Rev. ed. Scottdale, PA: Mennonite Publishing House, 1950.

Horst, Irvin B. *A Ministry of Goodwill: A Short Account of Mennonite Relief, 1939-40.* Akron, PA: Mennonite Central Committee, 1950.

Hunter, Allen A. *Christians in the Arena.* Nyack, NY: Fellowship Publications, 1958.

———. *Courage in Both Hands.* New York: Fellowship Publications, 1951.

———. *Three Trumpets Sound: Kagawa, Gandhi, Schweitzer.* New York: Association Press, 1939.

———. *White Corpuscles in Europe.* New York: Willett and Clark, 1939.

Hutheesing, Krishna (Nehru). *The Story of Gandhi.* New York: Didier Publishers, 1950.

Huxley, Aldous. *An Encyclopedia of Pacifism.* New York: Harper and Brothers, 1937.

———. *Ends and Means.* New York: Harper and Brothers, 1937.

Iyenger, A. *All Through the Gandhian Era.* Bombay: Hind Kitabs, 1950.

Jack, Homer A., ed. *The Gandhi Reader.* Bloomington, IN: Indiana University Press, 1956.

James, William. "The Moral Equivalent of War." In *Memories and Studies*. New York: Longmans, Green, 1911.

Jones, Eli Stanley. *Mahatma Gandhi: An Interpretation*. New York: Abingdon-Cokesbury Press, 1948.

Jones, Rufus M. *The Church, the Gospel and War*. New York: Harper and Brothers, 1948.

Kabir, Humayun. *Education in India*. New York: Harper and Brothers, 1957.

Kagawa, Toyohiko. *Love, the Law of Life*. Philadelphia: The John C. Winston Company, 1929.

Kelly, Thomas R. *A Testament of Devotion*. New York: Harper and Brothers, 1941.

King, Martin Luther, Jr. *Stride toward Freedom*. New York: Harper and Brothers, 1958.

King-Hall, Stephen. *Defense in the Nuclear Age*. Nyack, NY: Fellowship Publications, 1959.

Koestler, Arthur. *The Lotus and the Robot*. New York: The Macmillan Company, 1960.

Krishna Murthy, Nadig. *Mahatma Gandhi and Other Martyrs of India*. Columbia, MO: Journal Press, 1948.

Krishnayya, Pasupuleti Gupta, ed. *Mahatma Gandhi and the U.S.A.* New York: Orient and World Press, 1949.

Kuper, Leo. *Passive Resistance in South Africa*. New Haven, CT: Yale University Press, 1957.

Lehman, M. C. *The History and Principles of Mennonite Relief Work*. Akron, PA: Mennonite Central Committee, 1945.

Littell, Franklin H. *The Anabaptist View of the Church*. Boston: Starr King Press, 1958.

Lonsdale, Kathleen. *Is Peace Possible?* Harmondsworth, England: Penguin. 1957.

Macgregor, G. H. C. *The New Testament Basis of Pacifism*. Nyack, NY: Fellowship Publications, 1960.

Maitra, Sushil Kumar. *The Ethics of the Hindus*. Calcutta: University Press, 1925.

Manshardt, Clifford. *The Terrible Meek*. Chicago: H. Regnery Company, 1948.

Markovitch, Milan I. *Tolstoi et Gandhi*. Paris: H. Champion, 1928.

Maurer, Herrymon. *Great Soul: The Growth of Gandhi.* Garden City, NY: Doubleday and Company, Inc., 1948.

Menninger, Karl, and Jeanetta L. Menninger. *Love against Hate.* New York: Harcourt, Brace and Company, Inc., 1959.

The Mennonite Encyclopedia. 4 vols. Scottdale, PA: The Mennonite Publishing House, 1955–59.

Millis, Walter. *The Martial Spirit.* New York: Houghton Mifflin Company, 1931.

Mills, C. Wright. *The Causes of World War II.* New York: Simon and Schuster, 1959.

Mukerji, Dhan Gopal. *My Brother's Face.* New York: E. P. Dutton and Company, 1924.

Mumford, Lewis. *In the Name of Sanity.* New York: Harcourt, Brace and Company, Inc., 1954.

Muste, A. J. *Nonviolence in an Aggressive World.* New York: Harper and Brothers, 1940.

———. *Not by Might.* New York: Harper and Brothers, 1947.

Muzumdar, Haridas T. *Gandhi the Apostle: His Trial and His Message.* Chicago: Universal Publishing Company, 1923.

———. *Gandhi Triumphant: The Inside Story of the Historic Fast.* New York: Universal Publishing Company, 1939.

———. *Mahatma Gandhi, Peaceful Revolutionary.* New York: Charles Scribner's Sons, 1952.

Myrdal, Gunnar. *An American Dilemma.* New York: Harper and Brothers, 1944.

Nair, Pyarelal. *The Epic Fast.* Ahmedabad: M. M. Bhatt, 1932.

———. *Mahatma Gandhi: The Last Phase.* 2 vols. Ahmedabad: Navajivan Publishing House, 1956.

Nanda, Bal Ram. *Mahatma Gandhi.* Boston: Beacon Press, 1958.

Nef, John U. *War and Human Progress.* Cambridge: Harvard University Press, 1950.

Nehru, Jawaharlal. *The Discovery of India.* New York: John Day and Company, Inc., 1946.

———. *Jawaharlal Nehru, An Autobiography.* London: The Bodley Head, 1955.

———. *Nehru on Gandhi.* New York: John Day and Company, Inc., 1948.

————. *Towards a New Revolution.* New Delhi: Indian National Congress, 1956.

Neil, Alexander. *Gita & Gospel.* Calcutta: Thacker, Spink & Co., 1903.

Niebuhr, Reinhold. *Moral Man and Immoral Society.* New York: Charles Scribner's Sons, 1932.

————.*The Nature and Destiny of Man.* New York: Charles Scribner's Sons, 1943.

Niebuhr, H. Richard. *Christ and Culture.* New York: Harper and Brothers, 1951.

Nuttall, Geoffrey F. *Christian Pacifism in History.* Oxford, England: Basil, Blackwell, 1958.

Oxnam, Garfield Bromley. *Personalities in Social Reform.* New York: Abingdon-Cokesbury Press, 1950.

Park, Richard L., and Irene Tenker, eds. *Leadership and Political Institutions in India.* Princeton, NJ: Princeton University Press, 1959.

Paton, Alan. *Cry, the Beloved Country.* New York: Charles Scribner's Sons, 1948.

Payne, Ernest A. *The Anabaptists of the 16th Century and Their Influence in the Modern World.* London: C. Kingsgate Press, 1949.

Pickett, Clarence E. *For More than Bread.* Boston: Little, Brown, and Company, 1953.

Polak, Henry Solomon Leon. *Mahatma Gandhi.* London: Oldhams Press Ltd., 1949.

Power, Paul F. *Gandhi on World Affairs.* Washington, DC: Public Affairs Press, 1961.

Prabhu, R. K., ed. *Truth is God.* Ahmedabad: Navajivan Publishing House, 1959.

Prasad, Babu Rajendra. *Satyagraha in Champaran.* Madras: S. Ganesan, 1928.

Pyarelal. *A Pilgrimage for Peace: Gandhi and Frontier Gandhi among N.W.F. Pathans.* Ahmedabad: Navajivan Publishing House, 1950.

Radhakrishnan, S. *Eastern Religions and Western Thought.* New York: Oxford University Press, 1940.

————. *The Heart of Hindusthan.* 5th ed. Madras: Natesan, 1945.

————. *Indian Philosophy.* 2 vols. London: George Allen and Unwin Ltd., 1940.

————. *Mahatma Gandhi: Essays and Reflections on His Life and Work.* London: George Allen and Unwin Ltd., 1939.

————. (ed.). *The Principal Upanishads.* London: George Allen and Unwin Ltd., 1953.

Radhakrishnan, S., and J. J. Muirhead, eds. *Contemporary Indian Philosophy.* New York: The Macmillan Company, 1936.

Rasmussen, A. T. *Christian Social Ethics.* New York: Prentice Hall, 1958.

Raven, Charles E. *The Theological Basis of Christian Pacifism.* New York: Fellowship Publications, 1951.

Ray, Benay Gopal. *Gandhian Ethics.* Ahmedabad: Navajivan Publishing House, 1958.

Reynolds, Reginald. *A Quest for Gandhi.* Garden City, NY: Doubleday and Company, Inc., 1952.

Richards, Leyton. *Christian Pacifism after Two World Wars.* London: Independent, 1948.

Rolland, Romain. *Mahatma Gandhi.* London: George Allen and Unwin Ltd., 1924.

Roucek, Joseph S. *Contemporary Political Ideologies.* New York: The Philosophical Library, 1960.

Rutenber, Culbert G. *The Dagger and the Cross.* Nyack, NY: Fellowship Publications, 1951.

Sahgal, Nayantara. *Prison and Chocolate Cake.* New York: Alfred A. Knopf, 1954.

Schweitzer, Albert. *Indian Thought and Its Development.* Translated by Mrs. Charles E. B. Russell. London: Hodder and Stoughton, 1936.

Scott, Roland W. *Social Ethics in Modern Hinduism.* Calcutta: Y.M.C.A. Publishing House, 1953.

Sharma, Jagdish S. *Mahatma Gandhi: A Descriptive Bibliography.* Delhi: S. Chand and Company, 1955.

Sharp, Gene. *Gandhi Wields the Weapon of Moral Power.* Ahmedabad: Navajivan Publishing House, 1961.

Sheean, Vincent. *Lead, Kindly Light.* New York: Random House, 1949.

Shridharani, Krishnalal J. *The Mahatma and the World.* New York: Duell, Sloan and Pearce, Inc., 1946.

————. *My India, My America.* New York: Duell, Sloan and Pearce, Inc., 1941.

———. *War without Violence.* New York: Harcourt, Brace and Company, Inc., 1939.

Sibley, Mulford A., and Philip E. Jacob. *Conscription of Conscience.* Ithaca: Cornell University Press, 1952.

Simons, Menno. *The Complete Writings.* Scottdale, PA: Herald Press, 1956.

Smith, C. Henry. *The Story of the Mennonites.* Rev. ed. Newton, KS: Mennonite Publication Office, 1957.

Smith, Edward C. *New Dictionary of American Politics.* New York: Barnes and Noble, 1949.

Smyth, Newman. *Christian Ethics.* New York: Charles Scribner's Sons, 1927.

Sorokin, Pitirim A. *Altruistic Love.* Boston: Beacon Press, 1950.

———. *The Ways and Power of Love.* Boston: Beacon Press, 1954.

Tendulkar, D. G. *Mahatma.* 8 vols. Bombay: Jhoneri and Tendulkar, 1952.

Thoreau, Henry David. *Walden.* New York: The New American Library, 1960.

Tolstoi, Leo. *The Kingdom of God is Within You.* Boston: L. C. Page and Company, 1905.

———. *The Law of Love and the Law of Violence.* New York: Rudolph Field, 1948.

Toynbee, Arnold J. *War and Civilization.* New York: Oxford University Press, 1950.

Trocmé, André. *Stages of Non-Violence.* Nyack, NY: Fellowship Publications, 1953.

Troeltsch, Ernst. *The Social Teaching of the Christian Churches.* 2 vols. Translated by Olive Wyon. New York: Harper and Brothers, 1960.

Unruh, John D. *In the Name of Christ: A History of the Mennonite Central Committee and Its Service, 1920–1951.* Scottdale, PA: Herald Press, 1952.

Varma, V. P. *The Political Philosophy of Mahatma Gandhi and Sarvodaya.* Agra: Lakshmi Narain Agarwal Publishers, 1959.

Wenger, John C. *The Doctrines of the Mennonites.* Scottdale, PA: Mennonite Publishing House, 1952.

———. *Even unto Death.* Richmond, VA: John Knox Press, 1961.

———. *Glimpses of Mennonite History and Doctrine.* Scottdale, PA: Herald Press, 1949.

———. *Introduction to Theology.* Scottdale, PA: Herald Press, 1954.

———. *Separated unto God.* Scottdale, PA: Mennonite Publishing House, 1952.

Williams, George H., and Angel M. Mergal. *Spiritual and Anabaptist Writers.* Philadelphia: Westminster Press, 1957.

Woolman, John. *Journal and Other Writings.* New York: E. P. Dutton and Company, Inc., 1952.

Yoder, Edward. *Must Christians Fight?* 2nd ed. Akron, PA: Mennonite Central Committee, 1943.

Yoder, Edward, and Donovan E. Smucker. *The Christian and Conscription.* Akron, PA: Mennonite Central Committee, 1945.

Yoder, John H. *Peace without Eschatology?* Scottdale, PA: Mennonite Publishing House, 1954.

———. *Reinhold Niebuhr and Christian Pacifism.* Scottdale, PA: Herald Press, n.d.

Yoder, Sanford C. *For Conscience Sake: A Study of Mennonite Migrations Resulting from the World War.* Scottdale, PA: Mennonite Publishing; House, 1940.

B. Periodical literature

Albrecht, P. "Civilian Public Service Evaluated by Civilian Public Service Men." *Mennonite Quarterly Review* 22 (January 1948): 5–18.

Baehr, Karl. "Secularization among the Mennonites of Elkhart County, Indiana." *Mennonite Quarterly Review* 16 (July 1942): 131–60.

Baker, Oliver Edwin. "The Effects of Urbanization on American Life and on the Church." *Mennonite Quarterly Review* 19 (April 1945): 117–42.

Bender, Harold Stauffer. "Anabaptist Theology of Discipleship." *Mennonite Quarterly Review* 24 (January 1950): 25–32.

———. "The Anabaptist Vision." *Mennonite Quarterly Review* 18 (April 1944): 67–88.

———. "Church and State in Mennonite History." *Mennonite Quarterly Review* 13 (April 1939): 83–103.

———. "Conrad Grebel, the First Leader of the Swiss Brethren." *Mennonite Quarterly Review* 10 (January 1936): 5–45; (April 1936): 91–137; (July 1936): 151–60.

———. "The Founding of the Mennonite Church in America at Germantown 1683–1708." *Mennonite Quarterly Review* 7 (October 1933): 227–50.

———. "Mennonite Peace Action." *Mennonite Quarterly Review* 24 (April 1950): 149–55.

———. "The Pacifism of the Sixteenth Century Anabaptist." *Mennonite Quarterly Review* 30 (January 1956): 5–18.

Bender, Wilbur Joseph. "Pacifism among the Mennonites, Amish Mennonites and Schwenkfelders of Pennsylvania to 1783." *Mennonite Quarterly Review* 1, no. 3 (July 1927): 23–40; 1, no. 4 (October 1927): 21–48.

Correll, E. "Research on the Relations between Friends and Mennonites in Europe in the Seventeenth Century." *Mennonite Quarterly Review* 1, no. 3 (July 1927): 73–74.

Correll, E. H., and H. S. Bender, trans. and ed. "Conrad Grebel's Petition of Protest and Defense to the Zurich Council in 1523." *Mennonite Quarterly Review (The [Goshen] College Record Review Supplement)* 27, no. 4 (January 1926): 23–32.

Erb, Paul. "Nonresistance and Litigation." *Mennonite Quarterly Review* 13 (April 1939): 75–82.

Ewert, Wilhelm. "A Defense of the Ancient Mennonite Principle of Non-resistance by a Leading Prussian Mennonite Elder in 1873." *Mennonite Quarterly Review* 11 (October 1937): 284–90.

Friedmann, Robert. "Anabaptism and Pietism." *Mennonite Quarterly Review* 14 (April 1940): 90–128; (July 1940): 149–69.

———. "Anabaptism and Protestantism." *Mennonite Quarterly Review* 24 (January 1950): 12–24.

———. "An Anabaptist Ordinance of 1633 on Nonresistance." *Mennonite Quarterly Review* 25 (April 1951): 116–27.

———. "Concerning the True Soldier of Christ." *Mennonite Quarterly Review* 5 (April 1931): 87–99.

———. "The Schleitheim Confession (1527) and Other Doctrinal Writings of the Swiss Brethren in a Hitherto Unknown Edition." *Mennonite Quarterly Review* 16 (April 1942): 82–98.

Gandhi, M. K. "Nonviolence the Greatest Force." *The World Tomorrow* 9, no. 5 (October 1926), 3.

Geiser, Samuel. "An Ancient Anabaptist Witness for Nonresistance." *Mennonite Quarterly Review* 25 (January 1951): 66–69.

Gerber, Samuel. "The Mennonites of Switzerland and France, 1936–1948 and the Present Outlook." *Mennonite Quarterly Review* 24 (April 1950): 118–23.

Gingerich, Melvin. "Mennonite Church in World War II: A Review and Evaluation." *Mennonite Quarterly Review* 25 (July 1951): 183–200.

Hartman, Peter S. "Civil War Reminiscences." *Mennonite Quarterly Review* 3 (July 1929): 202–9.

Hershberger, Guy Franklin. "Biblical Nonresistance and Modern Pacifism." *Mennonite Quarterly Review* 17 (July 1943): 115–35.

———. "Christian Nonresistance: Its Foundation and Its Outreach." *Mennonite Quarterly Review* 24 (April 1950): 156–62.

———. "False Patriotism." *Mennonite Quarterly Review* 1, no. 1 (January 1927): 9–27; 1, no. 2 (April 1927): 29–45.

———. "Is Alternative Service Desirable and Possible?" *Mennonite Quarterly Review* 9 (January 1935): 20–36.

———. "John Horsch, a Proponent of Biblical Nonresistance." *Mennonite Quarterly Review* 21 (July 1947): 136–59.

———. "The Mennonite Attitude and the Modern Peace Movement as Illustrated by the St. Louis Meeting of the World Alliance." *Mennonite Quarterly Review* 2 (April 1928): 111–18.

———. "Mennonites in the Civil War." *Mennonite Quarterly Review* 18 (July 1944): 131–44.

———. "The Modern Social Gospel and the Way of the Cross." *Mennonite Quarterly Review* 30 (April 1956): 83–103.

———. "Nonresistance and Industrial Conflict." *Mennonite Quarterly Review* 13 (April 1939): 135–54.

———. "Peace and War in the New Testament." *Mennonite Quarterly Review* 17 (April 1943): 59–72.

———. "Peace and War in the Old Testament." *Mennonite Quarterly Review* 17 (January 1943): 5–22.

———. "Some Religious Pacifists of the Nineteenth Century." *Mennonite Quarterly Review* 10 (January 1936): 73–86.

———. "What about the Outlawry of War?" *Mennonite Quarterly Review* 2 (July 1928): 159–75.

Horsch, John. "The Character of the Evangelical Anabaptists as Reported by Contemporary Reformation Writers." *Mennonite Quarterly Review* 8 (July 1934): 123–35.

———. "An Historical Survey of the Position of the Mennonite Church on Nonresistance." *Mennonite Quarterly Review* 1, no. 3 (July 1927): 5–21; 1, no. 4 (October 1927): 3–20.

Kaufman, G. D. "Some Theological Emphases of the Early Swiss Anabaptists." *Mennonite Quarterly Review* 25 (April 1951): 75–99.

Klassen, C. F. "The Mennonites of Russia, 1917–1928." *Mennonite Quarterly Review* 6 (April 1932): 69–80.

Krahn, Cornelius. "Menno Simons' Fundament-Boek of 1539–1540." *Mennonite Quarterly Review* 13 (October 1939): 221–32.

Kreider, Robert S. "Environmental Influences Affecting the Decisions of Mennonite Boys of Draft Age." *Mennonite Quarterly Review* 16 (October 1942): 247–59.

King, Martin Luther, Jr. "Nonviolence and Racial Justice." *Christian Century* 74 (February 6, 1957), 165–67.

Miller, Orie O. "Our Peace Message." *Mennonite Quarterly Review (The [Goshen] College Record Review Supplement)* 27, no. 10 (September 1926): 23–28.

———. "Our Peace Policy." *Mennonite Quarterly Review* 3 (January 1929): 26–32.

———, and H. S. Bender, "A Brief Account of the Third Mennonite World Conference Held at Amsterdam, Elspeet and Witmarsum, Netherlands, June 29 to July 3, 1936." *Mennonite Quarterly Review* 11 (January 1937): 3–13.

Miller, William Robert. "A Select Bibliography of Notable Books for Pacifists." *Fellowship* 28 (March 1960), 21.

Mininger, Paul E. "Culture for Service." *Mennonite Quarterly Review* 29 (January 1955): 3–15.

———. "The Religious, Educational and Social Program of the Mennonite Community of Tomorrow." *Mennonite Quarterly Review* 19 (April 1945): 156–70.

Moraes, Frank R. "Gandhi Ten Years After." *Foreign Affairs* 56 (January 1958), 253–56.

Natesan, B. "Gandhi and Thoreau." *Gandhi Marg* 2 (July 1958), 218–22.

Newman, A. H. "The Significance of the Anabaptist Movement in the History of the Christian Church." *Mennonite Quarterly Review (The [Goshen] College Record Review Supplement)* 27, no. 4 (January 1926): 15–22.

Nelson, John Oliver, "The New Testament Power for Social Change." *Journal of Religious Thought* 15 (Autumn-Winter 1957–1958): 5–14.

Nelson, William Stuart. "The Tradition of Non-Violence and Its Underlying Forces." *Journal of Religious Thought* 16 (Summer-Autumn 1959): 121–36.

Sharp, Gene. "A Study of the Meanings of Non-Violence," part 3. *Gandhi Marg* 4, no. 2 (April 1960).

Smucker, Donovan E., "Anabaptist Historiography in the Scholarship of Today." *Mennonite Quarterly Review* 22 (April 1948): 116–27.

———. "A Mennonite Critique of the Pacifist Movement." *Mennonite Quarterly Review* 20 (January 1946): 81–90.

———. "The Theological Basis for Christian Pacifism." *Mennonite Quarterly Review* 27 (July 1953): 163–68.

———. "The Theological Triumph of the Early Anabaptist-Mennonites." *Mennonite Quarterly Review* 19 (January 1945): 5–26.

———. "Whither Christian Pacifism?" *Mennonite Quarterly Review* 23 (October 1949): 257–68.

———. "The Wisdom of Christ and the Culture of Man: The Theology of War and Its Cultural Relationships." *Mennonite Quarterly Review* 26 (July 1952): 192–209.

Snow, Charles P. "The Moral Un-neutrality of Science." *Science* 133, no. 3448 (January 27, 1961), 256–59.

Stauffer, Ethelbert. "The Anabaptist Theology of Martyrdom." *Mennonite Quarterly Review* 19 (July 1945): 179–214.

Sudermann, Jacob. "The Origin of Mennonite State Service in Russia, 1870–1860." *Mennonite Quarterly Review* 17 (January 1943): 23–46.

Swartzentruber, A. Orley. "The Piety and Theology of the Anabaptist Martyrs in van Braght's 'Martyrs' Mirror.'" *Mennonite Quarterly Review* 28 (January 1954): 5–26; (April 1954): 128–42.

Unruh, Benjamin H. "The Background and Causes of the Flight of the Mennonites from Russia in 1929." *Mennonite Quarterly Review* 4 (October 1930): 267–81; 5 (January 1931): 28–41.

Verduin, Leonard. "Menno Simons' Theology Reviewed." *Mennonite Quarterly Review* 24 (January 1950): 53–64.

Wenger, J. C. "Franconia Mennonites and Military Service, 1683–1923." *Mennonite Quarterly Review* 10 (October 1936): 222–45.

———. "The Schleitheim Confession of Faith." *Mennonite Quarterly Review* 19 (October 1945): 243–53.

———, trans. and ed. "Three Swiss Brethren Tracts." *Mennonite Quarterly Review* 21 (October 1947): 275–84.

Widmer, Pierre. "From Military Service to Christian Nonresistance." *Mennonite Quarterly Review* 23 (October 1949): 246–56.

Yoder, Edward. "Christianity and the State." *Mennonite Quarterly Review* 11 (July 1937): 171–95.

———. "The Christian's Attitude toward Participation in War Activities." *Mennonite Quarterly Review* 9 (January 1935): 5–19.

———. "Conrad Grebel as a Humanist." *Mennonite Quarterly Review* 3 (April 1929): 132–46.

———. "The Conscientious Objector: Review and Discussion." *Mennonite Quarterly Review* 7 (July 1933): 191–99.

———. "The Obligation of the Christian to the State and Community: 'Render to Caesar.'" *Mennonite Quarterly Review* 13 (April 1939): 104–22.

Yoder, John Howard. "Caesar and the Meidung." *Mennonite Quarterly Review* 23 (April 1949): 78–98.

———. "Reinhold Niebuhr and Christian Pacifism." *Mennonite Quarterly Review* 29 (April 1955): 101–17.

Young, Warren C. "The Christian Hope and the Social Order." *Mennonite Quarterly Review* 28 (April 1954): 83–101.

C. Doctoral dissertations

Burkholder, John Lawrence. "The Problem of Social Responsibility from the Perspective of The Mennonite Church." ThD diss., Princeton Theological Seminary, Princeton, NJ, 1958.

Lind, Ivan R. "The Problem of War in the Old Testament." ThD diss., Southwestern Baptist Theological Seminary, Dallas, TX, 1956.

Mathews, James K. "The Techniques of M. K. Gandhi as Religious." PhD diss., Columbia University, New York, NY, 1957.

Nickel, Jacob W. "An Analytical Approach to Mennonite Ethics." ThD diss., Iliff School of Theology, Denver, CO, 1959.

Toews, Abraham P. "The Problem of Mennonite Ethics." ThD diss., Concordia Theological Seminary, St. Louis, MO, 1959.

Waltner, Erland W. "An Analysis of the Mennonite Views on the Christian's Relation to the State in the Light of the New Testament." ThD diss., Eastern Baptist Theological Seminary, Philadelphia, PA, 1948.

D. Pamphlets

A Declaration of Christian Faith and Commitment. Akron, PA: Mennonite Central Committee, Peace Section, 1950.

Peace and the Christian Witness. Scottdale, PA: Herald Press, Mennonite General Conference, n.d.

Peace, War, and Military Service (Mennonite General Conference, Turner, Oregon). Scottdale, PA: Mennonite Publishing House, 1937.

Questions and Answers on the Classification and Assignment of Conscientious Objectors. Rev. ed. Washington, DC: National Service Board for Religious Objectors, 1961.

E. Newspapers

Gandhi, M. K. *Harijan,* April 15, 1933.

———. *Harijan,* March 28, 1936.

———. *Harijan,* June 18, 1938.

———. *Harijan,* April 13, 1940.

———. *Harijan,* October 13, 1940.

———. *Harijan,* July 20, 1947.

———. *Young India,* June 16, 1920.

———. *Young India,* August 11, 1920.

———. *Young India,* March 3, 1921.

Appendix A
Peace, war, and military service

A Statement of the position of The Mennonite Church

Resolutions adopted by the Mennonite General Conference at Turner, Oregon, August 1937

Introduction

IN VIEW OF THE PRESENT troubled state of world affairs, with wars and rumors of wars threatening the peace of the world, we, the representatives of The Mennonite Church, assembled in General Conference near Turner, Oregon, on August 25 and 26, 1937, and representing sixteen conferences in the United States and Canada, one in India and one in Argentina, S. A., do desire to set forth in the following statement our faith and convictions in the matter of peace and nonresistance as opposed to participation in war and military service, earnestly admonishing our membership to order their lives as becometh Christians in accord with these principles.

In doing so we do not establish a new doctrine among us, but rather give fresh expression to the age-old faith of the Church which has been held precious by our forefathers from the time that the Church was founded in Reformation times in Switzerland (1525) and in Holland (1533), at times even at the cost of despoiling of goods and exile from native land, and in some cases torture and death. On a number of former occasions since our settlement in America we have set forth our nonresistant, peaceful faith in memorials to officers of state, such as the petition of 1775 to the colonial assembly of Pennsylvania, and in addresses to the President of the United States and to the Governor General of Canada during and after the World War in 1915, 1917, and 1919, and at other times, thus testifying to our rulers and to our fellow citizens of our convictions. Since our position has been fully and authoritatively expressed in our confession of faith, known as "The Eighteen Articles," adopted in Dortrecht, Holland, in 1632 and confirmed at the first Mennonite Conference held in America in Germantown in 1725, reaffirmed in the declaration of the 1917 General Conference at Goshen, Indiana, and in the statement of faith adopted by the General Conference at Garden City, Missouri, in 1921, we do not consider it necessary at this time to set forth our position in detail, but rather merely to affirm in clear and unmistakable terms the main tenets of our peaceful and nonresistant faith as they apply to present conditions.

Our position on peace and war

1. Our peace principles are rooted in Christ and His Word, and in His strength alone do we hope to live a life of peace and love toward all men.

2. As followers of Christ the Prince of Peace, we believe His Gospel to be a Gospel of Peace, requiring us as His disciples to be at peace with all men, to live a life of love and good will, even toward our enemies, and to renounce the use of force and violence in all forms as contrary to the Spirit of our Master. These principles we derive from such Scripture teachings as: "Love your enemies"; "Do good to them that hate you"; "Resist not evil"; "My kingdom is not of this world: if my kingdom were of this world, then would my servants fight"; "put up thy sword into its place; for all they that take the sword shall perish with the sword"; "Dearly beloved, avenge not yourselves"; "If thine enemy hunger, feed him; if he thirst, give him drink; for in so doing thou shalt heap coals of fire on his head"; "Be not overcome of evil, but overcome evil with good"; "The servant of the Lord must not strive; but be gentle to all men"; "The weapons of our warfare are not carnal"; "Christ also suffered for us, leaving us an example, that ye should follow his steps, who did no sin, neither was guile found in his mouth; who . . . when he was reviled, reviled not again; when he suffered, he threatened not"; "Not rendering evil for evil, or railing for railing; but contrariwise blessing"; "If a man say I love God and hateth his brother, he is a liar . . . and this commandment have we from him, that he who loveth God loveth his brother also"; and other similar passages, as well as from the whole tenor of the Gospel.

3. Peace within the heart as well as toward others is a fruit of the Gospel. Therefore he who professes peace must at all times and in all relations with his fellow men live a life that is in harmony with the Gospel.

4. We believe that war is altogether contrary to the teaching and spirit of Christ and the Gospel, that therefore war is sin, as is

all manner of carnal strife; that it is wrong in spirit and method as well as in purpose, and destructive in its results. Therefore, if we profess the principles of peace and nevertheless engage in warfare and strife we as Christians become guilty of sin and fall under the condemnation of Christ, the righteous Judge.

Our position on military service
In the light of the above principles of Scripture we are constrained as followers of Christ to abstain from all forms of military service and all means of support of war, and must consider members who violate these principles as transgressors and out of fellowship with the Church. Specifically our position entails the following commitments:

1. We can have no part in carnal warfare or conflict between nations, nor in strife between classes, groups, or individuals. We believe that this means that we cannot bear arms personally nor aid in any way those who do so, and that as a consequence we cannot accept service under the military arm of the government, whether direct or indirect, combatant or noncombatant, which ultimately involves participation in any operation aiding or abetting war and thus causes us to be responsible for the destruction of the life, health, and property of our fellow men.

2. On the same grounds consistency requires that we do not serve during war time under civil organizations temporarily allied with the military in the prosecution of the war, such as the Y.M.C.A., the Red Cross, and similar organizations which, under military orders, become a part of the war system in effect, if not in method and spirit, however beneficial their peace-time activities may be.

3. We can have no part in the financing of war operations through the purchase of war bonds in any form or through voluntary contributions to any of the organizations or activities falling under the category described immediately above, unless such contributions are used for civilian relief or similar purposes.

4. We cannot knowingly participate in the manufacture of munitions and weapons of war either in peace time or in war time.

5. We can have no part in military training in schools and colleges, or in any other form of peace-time preparation for service as part of the war system.

6. We ought carefully to abstain from any agitation, propaganda, or activity that tends to promote ill-will or hatred among

nations which leads to war, but rather endeavor to foster good will and respect for all nations, peoples, and races, being careful to observe a spirit of sincere neutrality when cases of war and conflict arise.

7. We ought not to seek to make a profit out of war and wartime inflation, which would mean profiting from the shedding of the blood of our fellow men. If, however, during war time, excess profits do come into our hands, such profits should be conscientiously devoted to charitable purposes, such as the bringing of relief to the needy, or the spreading of the Gospel of peace and love, and should not be applied to our own material benefit.

Our willingness to relieve distress

According to the teaching and spirit of Christ and the Gospel we are to do good to all men. Hence we are willing at all times to aid in the relief of those who are in need, distress, or suffering, regardless of the danger in which we may be placed in bringing such relief, or of the cost which may be involved in the same. We are ready to render such service in time of war as well as in time of peace.

Our attitude during war time

If our country becomes involved in war, we shall endeavor to continue to live a quiet and peaceable life in all godliness and honesty; avoid joining in the wartime hysteria of hatred, revenge, and retaliation; manifest a meek and submissive spirit, being obedient unto the laws and regulations of the government in all things, except in such cases where obedience to the government would cause us to violate the teachings of the Scriptures so that we could not maintain a clear conscience before God (Acts 5:29). We confess that our supreme allegiance is to God, and that we cannot violate this allegiance by any lesser loyalty, but rather must follow Christ in all things, no matter what it cost. We love and honor our country and desire to work constructively for its highest welfare as loyal and obedient citizens; at the same time we are constrained by the love of Christ to love the people of all lands and races and to do them good as opportunity affords rather than evil, and we believe that this duty is not abrogated by war. We realize that to take this position may mean misunderstanding and even contempt from our fellow men, as well as possible suffering, but we hope by the grace of God that we may be able to assume, as our forefathers did, the sacrifices and suffering which may attend the sincere practice of this way of life, without malice or ill-will toward those who may differ with us.

If once again conscription should be established, we venture to express the hope that if service be required of us it may not be under the military arm of the government, and may be such that we can perform it without violating our conscience, and that we may thus be permitted to continue to enjoy that full liberty of religious faith and conscience which has been our privilege hitherto.

Resolution of appreciation

We desire to express our appreciation for the endeavors of our governments, both in the United States and Canada, to promote peace and good will among nations, and to keep from war. In particular, do we desire to endorse the policy of neutrality and non-participation in disputes between other nations. We invoke the blessings of God upon the President of the United States and the Prime Minister of Canada as well as upon the heads of state in the various lands in which our missionaries are serving, in their difficult and arduous duties as chief executives, and pray that their endeavors toward peace may be crowned with success.

We cherish our native lands, the United States of America, and the Dominion of Canada, as homelands to which our forefathers fled for refuge in times of persecution in Europe, and we are deeply grateful for the full freedom of conscience and liberty of worship which has been our happy privilege ever since the days of William Penn and which is vouchsafed to us as well as to all our fellow-citizens by the national constitutions and the constitutions of the several states and provinces. We pray that the blessings and guidance of a beneficent God may continue to rest upon our nations, their institutions, and their peoples.

Adopting resolution

We hereby adopt the above statement as representing our position on peace, war, and military service, and we instruct the Peace Problems Committee to bring this statement to the attention of the proper governmental authorities of the United States and Canada and other lands in which our missionaries are laboring. We would likewise suggest to each of our district conferences that they endorse this statement of position and bring it to the attention of every congregation and of all the members individually, in order that our people may be fully informed of our position and may be strengthened in conviction, that we may all continue in the simple, peaceful, nonresistant faith of the Scripture as handed down to us by our forefathers of former times.

As a matter of practical application, we request our Peace Problems Committee, as representing the Church in these problems, to carefully and prayerfully consider the problems which may arise in case our members become involved in conscription, giving particular attention to the proposed legislation on this matter which is now before Congress or its committees.

WEYBURN W. GROFF, PhD, is an ordained minister of the Mennonite Church and a retired educator who taught at Union Biblical Seminary (Yavatmal, India) and Associated Mennonite Biblical Seminary (Elkhart, Indiana). His articles on Hinduism and Mahatma Gandhi appear in *The Mennonite Encyclopedia,* vol. 5. He did graduate work at Princeton Theological Seminary, New York Theological Seminary, Vancouver School of Theology, and the Faculty of Theology of Cambridge University in England. Dr. Groff lives in Goshen, Indiana. He is a lover of the natural world; watercolors, oils, pen and ink, and papers of many kinds have tantalized him and released his artistic energy.

CPSIA information can be obtained at www.ICGtesting.com
Printed in the USA
LVOW01s1139100913

351728LV00001B/33/P